Blockchain

A Practical Guide to Developing Business, Law, and Technology Solutions

Joseph J. Bambara
Paul R. Allen

McGraw Hill Education

New York   Chicago   San Francisco
Athens   London   Madrid   Mexico City
Milan   New Delhi   Singapore   Sydney   Toronto

Library of Congress Cataloging-in-Publication Data

Names: Bambara, Joseph J., author. | Allen, Paul R., 1964- author.
Title: Blockchain : a practical guide to developing business, law, and
  technology solutions / Joseph J. Bambara and Paul R. Allen.
Description: New York : McGraw-Hill Education, [2018] | Includes index.
Identifiers: LCCN 2017059425 | ISBN 9781260115871 (alk. paper)
Subjects: LCSH: Blockchains (Databases) | Electronic commerce.
Classification: LCC QA76.9.D32 B34 2018 | DDC 005.74—dc23 LC record available at
https://lccn.loc.gov/2017059425

McGraw-Hill Education books are available at special quantity discounts to use as premiums and sales promotions, or for use in corporate training programs. To contact a representative, please visit the Contact Us pages at www.mhprofessional.com.

Blockchain: A Practical Guide to Developing Business, Law, and Technology Solutions

1 2 3 4 5 6 7 8 9   LCR   21 20 19 18

ISBN   978-1-260-11587-1
MHID   1-260-11587-9

Sponsoring Editor Lisa McClain	**Acquisitions Coordinator** Claire Yee	**Production Supervisor** James Kussow
Editorial Supervisor Jody McKenzie	**Technical Editor** Sean McKeough	**Composition** Cenveo Publisher Services
Project Editor Emilia Thiuri, Fortuitous Publishing	**Copy Editor** Lunaea Weatherstone	**Illustration** Cenveo Publisher Services
Project Manager Radhika Jolly, Cenveo® Publisher Services	**Proofreader** Paul Tyler **Indexer** Jack Lewis	**Art Director, Cover** Jeff Weeks

About the Contributors

Kedar Iyer is a software engineer who has worked with satellite systems, autonomous robotics, and blockchain technologies. He was the co-founder of LetsChai, an India-based dating site. His most recent focus has been on blockchain technologies. He is the creator of PeerBet, a peer-to-peer sports betting platform on the Ethereum blockchain. He has a degree in mechanical engineering from UCLA and currently lives in Brooklyn, New York.

Solomon Lederer, PhD, is a founder of blockmatics.tech, a blockchain training and consulting firm, and the founder of Coinspace, a blockchain-focused co-working space. He is also partner and head of technology at Iterative Instinct, a private investment fund focused on crypto-assets. He has a doctorate in distributed and ad hoc sensor networks, where he developed novel ways for networks to self-organize. Before blockchain, he worked as a software engineer in the defense and finance industries. He has been working with/teaching blockchain technology and Ethereum since 2014.

René Madsen is an enterprise solution architect at Progressive A/S, specializing in blockchain development and big data for many enterprise organizations across western Europe. He is also an adjunct lecturer at Copenhagen Business School in Denmark. He has a master's degree in computer science from Copenhagen University and an MBA from Edinburgh Business School, Heriot-Watt University.

Michael Wuehler is a founder of Ethereum and INFURA. He is a blockchain evangelist at ConsenSys, a leading blockchain venture production studio. He leads a global team in building an ecosystem of consumer-centric products and enterprise solutions using blockchain technologies, primarily Ethereum. He is a business and information systems leader with 25 years of experience and a broad-based background that spans technical and business infrastructure, transformation, and operations. He attended the University of Chicago Booth School of Business. He lives in New York City.

About the Technical Editor

Sean T. McKeough is the co-founder of Blockmatics, a leader in the blockchain education space. He regularly meets with leaders from a variety of industries to help them understand this transformative technology and how they might apply it to their business or passion. Sean is a community organizer at heart and is a regular in the New York and Colorado blockchain event scene. You can get in touch with Sean at 21.co/mckeough.

Contents at a Glance

Contents

Acknowledgments

We would like to acknowledge all the incredibly hard-working folks at McGraw-Hill Education, especially Lisa McClain and Claire Yee. We would also like to thank Sean McKeough for his help in editing the technical material in this book and providing valuable and timely response to our work.

—Joseph J. Bambara and Paul R. Allen

A very special thanks to my lady, Hillary Brower, and my co-author, Paul R. Allen, especially for his friendship and for being a great partner no matter what we try. Thanks to my family, who are always there when I need them.

—Joseph J. Bambara
Port Washington, New York

As always, a very special thank you to my family for being a source of strength, support, and ideas. Evelyn, thank you for encouraging me to write "the latest last book." I won't be writing another . . . at least for a couple of years! A very special thank you to my co-author, Joseph J. Bambara, who first introduced me to blockchain and then correctly predicted that we would write about it one day!

—Paul R. Allen
New York, New York

Introduction

Blockchain technology is robust like the Internet, but unlike the web2 Internet of today, it stores identical blocks of information across its network. For this reason, a blockchain cannot be controlled by any single entity nor does it have a single point of failure. By storing data across its network, the blockchain eliminates the risks that come with data being held centrally. Blockchain networks lack centralized points of vulnerability that computer hackers can exploit easily.

Today's Internet has security problems that are familiar to everyone. We all rely on username and password credentials to access our assets online. Blockchain uses encryption technology to improve security. By allowing data and information to be widely distributed, blockchain technology has created the backbone of the new Internet, web3. Though it was originally devised for the digital currency Bitcoin, the business and technology communities are finding many uses for blockchain. Knowledge of this new technology will be required by not only programmers but by all businesses. In the next five to ten years, blockchain will change the business models in all types of industries—and perhaps change the way people work and live.

We have been involved in computing technology since its first practical use on Wall Street circa 1974. We have used and written about the evolving technology tools starting with IBM Assembler, Fortran, COBOL, and data access methods like QSAM, BDAM, and VSAM, all the way to present-day REST web services, Java, and SQL and everything in between (including client/server tools like PowerBuilder). We have been fortunate in that our passions for learning and becoming proficient in each new and emerging technology have served us well in the business community. We recognized blockchain technology as an ingenious invention, as it combines the best of what came before it in database design, cryptography, and virtual machine containers with the very capable distributed computing environment of today. Our passion for the technology was based on love at first sight. We have brought together a robust network of blockchain entrepreneurs, fellow blockchain technologists, and others who have made critical contributions to the coverage and text of this book.

Target Audience

The target audience for this book includes anyone interested in blockchain technology as well as its use cases. It is also for anyone developing a blockchain application—what is required to build solutions in this space. Additionally, web and application developers of all levels as well as tech-savvy businesspeople and even attorneys who want to stay current with technology in general and blockchain specifically would find the discussions in this book of interest.

What This Book Covers

The book covers blockchain definition, use cases, distributed technology, and especially blockchain development, with a good deal of code snippets and best practices. It targets the Ethereum blockchain, introducing Solidity and other aspects of the Ethereum framework. Additionally, there are two chapters devoted to setup, coding, validation, and deployment of a complete and comprehensive blockchain betting application.

How to Use This Book

Each chapter in the book can stand alone, describing a particular aspect of blockchain technology and its use cases. That said, there is a sequence whereby each chapter builds on the previous chapters to provide a solid conceptual understanding of blockchain. This is coupled with a comprehensive treatment for getting started as a designer and developer of blockchain applications. This includes the Ethereum technology stack and code, and deployment techniques and examples, including an entire application from code start to deployment finish.

How This Book Is Organized

In **Chapter 1**, we provide an overview of everything blockchain. We introduce it as a distributed database technology with the capability to execute smart contracts. The expanding universe of blockchain application is covered. The efficiencies and cost savings provided by blockchain technologies—especially the private blockchains adopted by the financial community—are also briefly examined. In parallel, the use of blockchain is shown to affect global transactions, and this will push it forward toward maturity. Blockchain and its timing are critical to maintaining global transactions and providing trust in the integrity of those transactions. For these reasons and more, we argue that blockchain is here to stay, and the chapters herein will provide you with a comprehensive map and toolset with what you need as a designer or developer to successfully make the trip.

While blockchain technology is at the heart of cryptocurrencies like Bitcoin and Ethereum, it clearly is a technology with widespread applicability in many sectors of business. **Chapter 2** gives some depth to real-world use cases in the financial services industry, including sections on cryptocurrency and digital tokens. We then show how common business use cases ultimately lead to faster throughput, reduced costs, improved accuracy, greater transparency, and quality, reliability, simplicity, and traceability.

The chapter also discusses smart property and smart contracts and how they can be used in conjunction in the not-too-distant future of blockchain technology. Chapter 2 closes with how blockchain and the Internet of Things (IoT) will have a consortium of startups and companies to help define and refine security and interoperability, management, and coordination between connected devices. While IoT is still in its early stages of evolution and currently comprises mostly technologies that either collect data or allow remote monitoring and control, this will change as devices become smarter and artificial intelligence is added. This network of things will transition toward becoming a network of autonomous devices that talk to each other and (hopefully) make smart decisions without the need for human intervention or interpretation. In short, we live in exciting times for blockchain technology.

Chapter 3 introduces some of the components of the Web 3.0 architecture. Distributed networking and storage are happening now and promise solutions that could save the global economy trillions annually. The Web today needs a new security model and an architecture designed around contemporary use cases. The technology stack is just beginning to emerge. It includes Swarm, IPFS, Storj, Golem, and Whisper, just to mention a few of a growing number of components that represent the most ambitious solutions to this problem.

As the global infrastructure adapts to the new demands we are putting on it, unforeseen opportunities will open before us. New tools will change not only the way we work and use web conveniences but also the way we organize ourselves in groups. We are living in an interesting time in history, where the Web begins to bring more knowledge and action capacity for its users, resulting in considerable changes in several aspects of daily life. This new Web is moving fast toward a more dynamic environment, where the democratization of the capacity of action and knowledge can speed up business in almost all areas. Imagine a future with hundreds of real decentralized applications—for example, one in charge of registering land titles and mortgages and handling local taxes, and a more general application in charge of managing the supply chain of registered tenants, their monthly lease payments, as well as mortgage and expense payments. One could easily link information from properties registered in the first application with the tenants and their use of the properties registered in the second application. All this in an easy way using the whole stack of semantic web technology and—something that is not possible to date—ensuring that all data is 100 percent true, guaranteed by the smart contracts. The real questions we must ask are: How will the world of Web 3.0 differ from the world of Web 2.0? How will this technology penetrate beyond the cultures that created it? One thing is for sure: blockchain will be at the center of this new world.

Chapter 4 is primarily about blockchain and the law. We show that smart contracts may be the most transformative current blockchain component, especially for lawyers. We explore why Professors Marco Iansiti and Karim R. Lakhani of the Harvard Business School said:

> "The implications are fascinating. . . . If contracts are automated, then what will happen to traditional firm structures, processes, and intermediaries like lawyers and accountants? . . . Their roles would all radically change. . . . [W]e are decades away from the widespread adoption of smart contracts. . . . A tremendous degree of coordination and clarity on how smart contracts are designed, verified, implemented, and enforced will be required. We believe the institutions responsible for those daunting tasks will take a long time to evolve. And the technology challenges—especially security—are daunting. . . . [L]aw firms will have to change to make smart contracts viable. They'll need to develop new expertise in software and blockchain programming."

The chapter also explores how blockchain provides new possibilities for the way we interact and exchange information, and as such brings forth challenging and complex legal issues and pushes the boundaries of existing laws. We see that blockchain technology is something that our laws will have to adapt to, just as they adapted to the Internet, medical technology, e-discovery, and social media. There is a huge change before us as lawyers and as developers to embrace it and be part of its evolution.

We show how regulation around blockchain is still up in the air, not only globally but also in each state here in the United States. Businesses operating in regulated industries should seek guidance from their regulators before integrating critical, customer-facing, or data-handling processes with platforms like Ethereum. We examine the large strides made in the financial services arena with private and consortium varieties of blockchain. We see clearly that this is an indication that financial institutions are playing in and watching this space very closely.

Chapter 5 covers terminology (including block attributes) and concepts as well as the technology stack, blockchain development platforms, and APIs. It also covers the Ethereum Virtual Machine and Ethereum dapps, DAOs, and autonomous smart contracts.

In **Chapter 6**, we introduce the Solidity smart contract programming language and the tools that make it simple and easy to fast-track deploy a smart contract to the Ethereum blockchain. In this chapter, you get to create your first simple smart contract.

In **Chapter 7**, we introduce tools and techniques that are a little more complicated and support a workflow to handle the development of more complex solutions.

In **Chapter 8**, we look into use cases for private and consortium blockchain solutions. We review private blockchain technology such as Hyperledger, Monax, Ethereum, Hyperledger Fabric, Quorum, and the Hyperledger tools Cello, Composer, and Explorer. We explore the many options for permissioned private blockchains and show why the list is likely to grow. In many cases, government/industry regulation dictates that private control will be needed. That being said, the freedom, neutrality, and openness that started Bitcoin on the public blockchain are important to keep in mind. The focus of decentralizing control and consensus on the public platform is clearly something to think about. There is a great deal of chatter and concern around privacy, identity, speed, and cost of the public blockchain solutions. It is important to note that by creating privately administered smart contracts on public blockchains, or cross-chain exchange layers that sit in between public and private blockchains, it is possible to deliver some degree of the properties of private blockchains on the public platforms. Time will tell if these types of capabilities and properties ever get built into the public blockchain.

While blockchains are heralded as a technological breakthrough that will solve many problems, it's clear that they face a large number of unique challenges. **Chapter 9** reviews these challenges and why they are not insurmountable, though they require a lot of work to develop infrastructure and safety mechanisms to overcome them.

In **Chapter 10**, we introduce the development life cycle of a fully functioning betting application built on Ethereum. While the focus was primarily on coding with Solidity, we made sure to provide the reader with an entire application and explain each line of code and every setup move required to build the application.

In **Chapter 11**, we show the reader how to deploy the application built in Chapter 10. We also step through the development of a simple front end to run the application. If you have read, understood, and tried some of the code in this chapter, you can now write new scripts to deploy and test your own smart contracts. You can create a contract, and you can create a front end to interact with it. In short, once you get through this whole book, you will be ready to design, code, test, and deploy an Ethereum blockchain application.

1

Introduction to Blockchain

For the world of technology users, blockchain represents a dramatic improvement to the landscape of information collection, distribution, and governance. That point has been espoused these past few years in the books and presentations that hype and imagine this new world. This book is one of the first to address the development of blockchain applications. As such, we will present a development road map to the emerging options and trends. That said, this is the first edition of what will be a series following the blockchain development evolution. This book is aimed at all levels of developers, software engineers, and anyone interested in the basics of blockchain technology, as well as the languages and tools required to build decentralized applications. We will introduce everything needed to understand the technology, write "smart contracts," build applications that interact with them, and deploy and maintain these applications on a host of emerging platforms.

So, let's begin. Simply put, a blockchain is a database encompassing a physical chain of fixed-length blocks that include 1 to N transactions, where each transaction added to a new block is validated and then inserted into the block. When the block is completed, it is added to the end of the existing chain of blocks. Moreover, the only two operations—as opposed to the classic CRUD—are add transaction and view transaction. So the basic blockchain processing consists of the following steps, which are numbered 3, 4, and 5 in Figure 1-1:

1. Add new and undeletable transactions and organize them into blocks.
2. Cryptographically verify each transaction in the block.
3. Append the new block to the end of the existing immutable blockchain.

More comprehensively, a blockchain is also a distributed database that maintains a doubly linked list of ordered blocks. Each block averages 1 megabyte (see https://blockchain.info/charts/avg-block-size) and contains control data of approximately 200 bytes, such as a timestamp, a link to a previous block, some other fields (as depicted in Figure 1-2, to be discussed later), and 1 to N transactions as can fit in the remaining space.

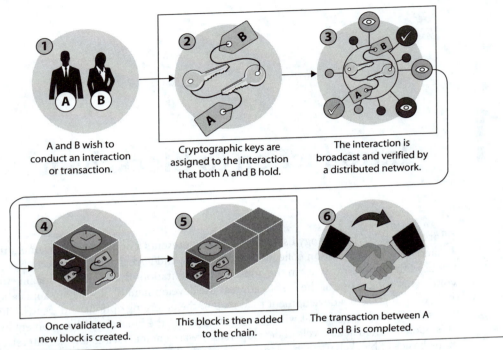

FIGURE 1-1   Public blockchain transaction flow

The blocks once recorded are designed to be resistant to modification; the data in a block cannot be altered retroactively. Through the use of a peer-to-peer network and a distributed timestamping server, a public blockchain database is managed autonomously. Blockchains are an open, distributed ledger that can record transactions between two parties efficiently and in a verifiable and permanent way as depicted in Figure 1-1.

The ledger itself can also be programmed to trigger transactions automatically. Blockchains are secure by design and an example of a distributed computing system with high byzantine fault tolerance. Decentralized consensus can therefore be achieved with a public blockchain. As we shall discuss in detail later, these features make blockchains ideal for recording events, medical records and other records management activities, identity management, transaction processing, and a host of emerging applications. Moreover, blockchain technologies allow us to achieve large-scale and systematic cooperation in an entirely distributed and decentralized manner. This can be considered and implemented as a global governance tool, capable of managing social interactions on a large scale and dismissing traditional central authorities. For example, in 2015, libertarian political activist Vit Jedlička declared Gornja Siga—a seven-square-kilometer patch of uninhabited forest between Croatia and Serbia—to be the "Free Republic of Liberland." He used the Bitcoin blockchain as a provisional government and released a constitutional document setting out how this new country would be governed: voluntary taxation, an almost nonexistent government, and zero restrictions whatsoever on speech and information.

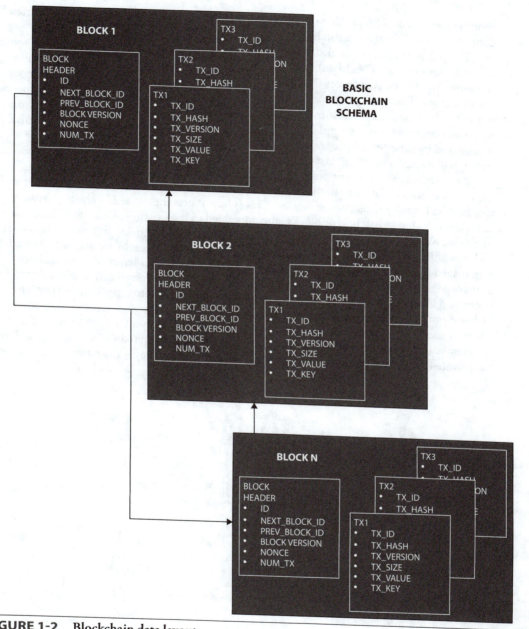

FIGURE 1-2   Blockchain data layout

Let's look at some analogies that illustrate what is different about the public blockchain. It's both a database and the software that envelops it. As software, it is like BitTorrent, a program that allows you to upload and download files directly with others also running the BitTorrent software. So instead of uploading a file to a file-sharing service, such as Dropbox, and then sending your friend a link to download the file, you just upload the file directly to your friend's computer. This is what we mean by a peer-to-peer (p2p) program (see Figure 1-3).

The public blockchain is also a peer-to-peer program with one very important difference: not only does it move files (data) from peer to peer, it also ensures that all the peers have the same exact data. It enforces this. If the data changes on one machine, it changes on all the machines. There are rules specifying exactly how a change can be made, and if someone doesn't follow them and modifies their copy illegally, they're ignored. It's no different from an email program trying to send an email without the proper SMTP headers—it won't be recognized by other email programs. By the same token, if your version gets deleted or corrupted, it's not a problem, just re-sync with your peers and you get a fresh valid copy.

As noted, the way current public blockchains like Bitcoin and Ethereum work is that instead of changing data within the dataset, new data is just appended onto the old. In other words, data is only written, never deleted. This is how it gets the name *blockchain*, because new data is added in batches, or blocks, and appended to the existing blocks, forming a chain of blocks. Not only does everyone have the same database (blockchain), but everyone gets a locker within the blockchain that only they can access. Normally, exclusive access to something is managed with usernames and passwords. The public blockchain has no central authority to manage usernames and passwords, so instead it uses cryptography. Each user is able to generate a locker address and a private key code that allows them to unlock the locker. The locker is only an analogy, of course. In reality it's just an ID number (referred to as an address), which is tagged to a user's data. The private key is a code that allows the user to prove they're the creator (or owner) of that *address*. Only the person who generated the address would have the private key, and no one can ever determine what the private key is from the address alone.

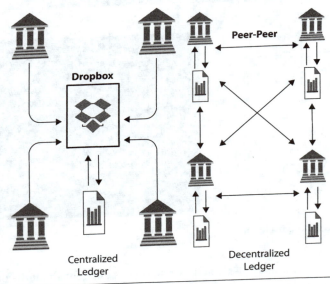

Centralized
Ledger

Decentralized
Ledger

FIGURE 1-3 **Decentralized versus centralized data stores**

So while everyone can see the data tagged with your address in the blockchain, no one is allowed to modify it. It can only be modified by the person who can prove they're the owner via the private key. For example, if bitcoins are tagged with your address, they cannot be moved (i.e., tagged with another address) unless the private key is used.

What's also amazing about this system is that anyone can generate an address by themselves, in isolation, without concern that it will clash with anyone else's address. The reason for this is that there are so many possible addresses, it is essentially impossible to clash with another address, even if you tried.

It gets better. Not only is static data stored in the dataset, but you can store executable code in it too. Say you have a piece of code written in JavaScript-type language, such as Ethereum Solidity, sitting there on everyone's machine waiting to be executed. Remember that data is only written to the blockchain, never erased, so you now have a piece of code no one can change. Everyone can be certain the way it's written is the way it will always run.

This code is also tagged with someone's address. The owner of that address gets to decide what operations are open to the public and what only they can execute. They only get to make this decision at the time the code is written. Once written, it cannot be changed. Everyone will still be able to see the code and what it's doing, but can only interact with it in the ways specified by the owner.

Let's start with the original motivation to create a blockchain: money. Our current monetary system is based on records of how much money is out there and who has how much of it. We rely on our governments and banks to maintain these records. But a blockchain allows us to keep these records ourselves, since it guarantees that the record is the same for everyone. We each keep this dataset—that is, the blockchain that contains a record of every single transaction that happens in the particular monetary system. Since everyone's copy is synchronized with everyone else's, no one has to worry about fraudulent or conflicting entries. There's now no need for a bank to manage our records. The blockchain does it instead. As far as how money gets created and distributed in the first place, that is another story, but the Bitcoin network as well as other cryptocurrencies handle that as well.

That is just on the data, or ledger, side of things. It gets far more interesting when computer code is managed in that way too. Let's imagine a legal contract: Certain actions are taken under certain conditions. Even after the parties sign, they must still rely on the good faith of the other or our justice system to carry out their side of the agreement. Let's take an example. Donald hates flight delays. AIGore Insurance tells him if he pays them $5 and his flight is delayed by more than an hour, AIGore will return his $5 and pay him an additional $20. A simple insurance scheme, or perhaps it's a bet. In any case, when Donald gives AIGore $5 he has to trust them that they will carry out their end of the bargain. However, by using a blockchain he can eliminate this risk. Collectively, they write the conditions of their agreement in computer code, and initialize the contract with enough funds to make good on either side: Donald sends $5 worth of cryptocurrency, and AIGore Insurance sends $20. Then an hour after Donald's flight is scheduled to arrive, the computer code contract will do the following:

1. Look up Donald's flight on www.flightstats.com.
2. If it was delayed more than an hour, send Donald $25.
3. Otherwise, send AIGore Insurance $25.

This code, once it's written to the blockchain, cannot be removed or altered. Neither party can unilaterally remove the money. Donald and AIGore are guaranteed that the terms of the contract will be executed. In the Ethereum blockchain, this is termed a *smart contract*; much more on that as we proceed. We will examine the code for an application that does just that. See http://fdd.etherisc.com/ for details on how this type of insurance is implemented using the blockchain.

Blockchain: An Information Technology

As mentioned, a blockchain is a distributed ledger of transactions implemented as data batched into blocks that use cryptographic validation to link the blocks together. Each block references and identifies the previous block using a hashing function which forms an unbroken chain (i.e., blockchain).

A public blockchain is not stored in one central computer. Nor is it managed by any central entity. Instead, it is distributed and maintained by multiple computers or nodes that compete to validate the newest block entries before the other nodes to gain a reward for doing so.

The block validation system is designed to be immutable. That is to say, all transactions old and new are preserved forever with no ability to delete. Anyone on the network can browse via a designated website and see the ledger. This provides a way for all participants to have an up-to-date ledger that reflects the most recent transactions or changes. In this way, blockchain establishes trust, which as we shall see facilitates transactions and brings many cost-saving efficiencies to all types of transactional interactions.

A Distributed Trusted Information Technology

From a technical point of view, the blockchain is a distributed, transparent, immutable, validated, secured, and pseudo-anonymous database existing as multiple nodes such that if 51 percent of the nodes agree then trust of the chain is guaranteed. The blockchain is distributed because a complete copy lives on as many nodes as there are in the system. The blockchain is immutable because none of the transactions can be changed. The blockchain is validated (e.g., in the Bitcoin space) by the miners who are compensated for building the next secure block. The blockchain is pseudo-anonymous because the identity of those involved in the transaction is represented by an address key in the form of a random string.

That said, this is an evolving space and, like the cloud computing paradigm, there are public, private, and even hybrid blockchains, which we will explore in detail later in this chapter. These blockchain variations on the basic theme are the result of enterprise architects looking to implement blockchain applications to save time and fees. Enterprise requirements around scaling, performance, the need to know the identity of those involved in the transaction, and other things provide its emerging variations. Blockchain evangelists reckon distributed ledger technology has the potential to upend centralized database practices in institutional finance and most other transaction-based technology. In 2017, the technology shifted from hype to commercial reality. For blockchain to succeed, the application development life cycle, which facilitated large web applications using tools like HTML, CSS, JavaScript, REST web services, Java, SQL, and NOSQL data stores, will have to be amended to integrate the blockchain onto that stack. We will need integrated development environments (IDEs) and continuous integration and testing procedures to move applications and their attendant code from development to QA and ultimately reliable production implementations. Additionally, because blockchains cannot access data outside their network on their own, third-party services (known as oracles, agents, or data feeds) will also need to be integrated. These oracles or agents typically access and verify real-world occurrences and submit this information to a blockchain to be used by smart contracts. They provide external data when needed and push it onto the blockchain. Such conditions could be anything, such as the flight delay information we saw in the insurance example. The blockchain will have to operate efficiently, scale well, handle the know-your-client (KYC) process, create the aforementioned oracles or APIs that produce and consume off-chain services to verify events and data and handle/convert real-world money to and from cryptocurrencies, and integrate well with different chains. This is all in progress, and we will explore some of these IDEs and development processes in detail as we proceed.

Implementation Trends

A lot has changed since blockchain first emerged as the technology underpinning the cryptocurrency Bitcoin as a distributed ledger of transactions and asset ownership that is maintained by a network of computers over the Internet. More proof of its ability to reduce costs and speed up post-trade processes has emerged in the past year. We will explore this in detail.

A key factor to its rapid growth is the backdrop against which it has launched. Financial institutions and infrastructures are under pressure both to comply with regulation and to reduce cost. That pressure coincided with this technology coming into existence. It's the intersection of requirement and opportunity that's causing the rapid growth. The technology will make moves from "proof-of-concept" technology into production, especially in cross-border payments and trade finance. In this book, we will examine the development life cycle that is emerging with the blockchain. Having been developers for over 30 years, we have witnessed lots of changes in technology starting from the IBM Assembler/COBOL days. We like to kid our colleagues with the fact that we may have worked on the first blockchain.

Back in 1974, no Wall Street firm had its own computer. All processing was done by the famous payroll firm Automatic Data Processing (ADP), located a few blocks away from the heart of Wall Street. The licensed securities exchange firms would drop their stack of punch cards containing the transactions into a designated dropbox. They also dropped off one of their master data magnetic tapes containing the sort of "blockchain"—that is, all transactions to date for that particular organization in sequential order stored in IBM's QSAM format. The programs written in Fortran, COBOL, or IBM assembler could only read data sequentially front to back. The cards representing the transactions would be added to the end of the existing chain of QSAM records, creating/writing a new tape file and hence a new state of the database or simple blockchain. Next came the emergence of early database technology like IBM IMS, IDMS, and ADABAS, followed by the dawn of the ever-enduring SQL in the mid-1980s. Then the open source revolution led to the Linux/Python/Java/SQL/NOSQL/HTML/JavaScript technology stack where web development and database development have matured to create the big data/web-enabled world we live in. Blockchain will further disrupt this evolution to bring trust firmly back into the picture. That said, it will have to be integrated into this existing development paradigm. These changes are emerging. Early adopters of blockchain used first-generation IDEs to develop applications and, as we shall see, JavaScript-type languages for things like smart contracts, to be discussed in a later chapter. Moreover, integrating blockchain with existing applications will also present challenges that we will examine.

As further impetus to the rise of blockchain, we expect 2018 will be dominated by last-minute preparations for the incoming revised European Union Revised Payment Services Directive (PSD2) effective in May of that year. As PSD2 becomes implemented, banks' monopoly on their customers' account information and payment services will disappear. PSD2 enables bank customers—both consumers and businesses—to use third-party providers to manage their finances. That means you may be using Google to pay your bills, make transfers, and analyze your spending. Banks will provide these third parties access to their customers' accounts through open APIs (application program interfaces). The EU directive opens the door to any interested company, with provisions that will make it easier for startups to access data from banks. This will allow the startups to use blockchain to better penetrate some functions currently performed by banks. With the creation of open banking platforms, there will be opportunities for financial technology (fintech) firms to partner with banks to create new wave customer experiences and provide increased transparency on performance and fee structures. We believe that 2018 is the year that fintech catches up with the hype: validating blockchain-based technologies with promise, scale, customers, and adoption. We are all seeing signs that are consistent with a technology going mainstream in the next five years and changing the transactional landscape for many more years to follow.

Trust: The Byzantine Generals Problem

Back in early days of business computing, circa 1980, computer scientists began to examine reliability and computers. It was determined that a reliable computer system must be able to cope with the failure of one or more of its components. A failed component may exhibit a type of behavior that is overlooked and problematic, namely, sending conflicting information to different parts of the system. The problem of coping with this type of failure is expressed abstractly as the *Byzantine Generals Problem*, from the 1982 scholarly paper by Leslie Lamport, Robert Shostak, and Marshall Pease (www-inst.eecs.berkeley.edu/~cs162/fa12/hand-outs/ Original_Byzantine.pdf). This abstract problem and the solutions thereof are used in developing highly reliable and trusted blockchain implementations.

The Byzantine Generals Problem Explained: Why Trust Is So Important

The Byzantine Generals Problem (BGP) is one of many in the field of agreement protocols. Lamport framed his paper around a story problem. This was the style of the day as evidenced by the attention received by another computer scientist, Edsger Dijkstra and his dining philosophers problem, based on a classic operating system synchronization problem.

To set the table for this problem—and as the musical *Hamilton* will be on Broadway long after this book is out of print—we see that the BGP problem was relevant in the American Revolution. At the start of the conflict, the Continental Congress ordered an oath of allegiance to be administered to all army officers. George Washington, the commander-in-chief, administered it to the general officers. When Washington began to read the oath to Major General Charles Lee, Lee withdrew his hand from the Bible. When Washington demanded a reason for the strange conduct, according to *The Writings of George Washington*, Lee replied, "As to King George, I am ready enough to absolve myself from all allegiance to him; but I have some scruples about the Prince of Wales." This odd reply elicited much laughter. Lee was then playing a desperate game of treason, and probably had some problems with his conscience about taking such an oath which he (and later Major General Benedict Arnold) would violate.

The BGP is built around a similar story line: the commanding general who makes a decision to attack or retreat, and must communicate the decision to his lieutenant generals. A given number of these actors are traitors (possibly including the general). Traitors cannot be relied upon to properly communicate orders; worse yet, they may actively alter messages in an attempt to subvert the process.

In the analogy, the generals are collectively known as processes, the general who initiates the order is the source process, and the orders sent to the other processes are messages. Traitorous generals and lieutenant generals are faulty processes, and loyal generals and lieutenant generals are correct processes. The order to retreat or attack is a message with a single bit of information: a one or a zero.

A solution to an agreement problem must pass three tests: termination, agreement, and validity. As applied to the Byzantine Generals Problem, these three tests are:

1. A solution has to guarantee that all correct processes eventually reach a decision regarding the value of the order they have been given.
2. All correct processes have to decide on the same value of the order they have been given.
3. If the source process is a correct process, all processes must decide on the value that was original given by the source process.

The best way we know to implement a reliable trustworthy computer system (e.g., blockchain) is to use many different processors to compute the same result, and then to perform a majority vote on their outputs to obtain a single value. See Figure 1-4, which views the BGP and blockchain issues in a side-by-side analogy.

GENERALS		BLOCKCHAIN
Agree on a Strategy	Objective	Agree on Valid Transactions
Separated Camps	Spacial Distribution	Distributed Nodes in the Network
Loyal Troop and Generals	The Good Ones	Truthful Nodes
Traitors	The Bad Ones	Evil Nodes
Corrupt a Message	The Attack	Add an Invalid Transaction to the Blockchain
How to know which Message is True	The Problem	How to know which Transaction is Valid
Don't have	A Solution	Proof-of-Work
Don't have	Consensus	Blockchain with More Difficulty

FIGURE 1-4   BGP and blockchain compared

This is true whether one is implementing a blockchain using distributed nodes to protect against the failure of reaching a consensus on the next block, or a missile defense system using redundant computing sites to protect against the destruction of individual sites by a nuclear attack. The only difference is in the size of the replicated processor. The use of majority voting to achieve reliability is based upon the assumption that all the nonfaulty processors will produce the same output. This is true so long as they all use the same input. However, any single input message comes from a single physical component, and a malfunctioning component can give different values to different processors. Moreover, different processors can get different values even from a nonfaulty input unit if they read the value while it is changing. The solution is a trust mechanism of value verification and acceptance for each input/transaction recorded by a majority of processors and synchronization of the input transaction across the distributed processors. The quality of trust is a foundational element of business. Trust, particularly in the global economy where every link in the transaction requires a separate ledger, is expensive, time-consuming, and inefficient. The application of blockchain as it matures will provide a viable alternative to the current procedural, organizational, and technological infrastructure required to create institutionalized trust.

Byzantine Fault Tolerance in Use Today: Why Airplanes Are Safe

Byzantine fault tolerance (BFT) refers to the aforementioned BGP. One example of BFT in use is Bitcoin. The Bitcoin network works in parallel to generate a chain of hashcash-style proof-of-work. The proof-of-work chain is the key to overcoming Byzantine failures and reaching a coherent global view of the system state.

Some aircraft systems, such as the Boeing 777 Aircraft Information Management System (via its ARINC 659 SAFEbus® network), the Boeing 777 flight control system, and the Boeing 787 flight control systems, use Byzantine fault tolerance (see Figure 1-5). Because these are real-time systems, their Byzantine fault tolerance solutions must have very low latency. For example, SAFEbus can achieve Byzantine fault tolerance on the order of a microsecond of added latency.

Some spacecraft, such as the SpaceX Dragon flight system, consider Byzantine fault tolerance in their design. Byzantine fault tolerance mechanisms use components that repeat an incoming message (or just its signature) to other recipients of that incoming message. All these mechanisms make the assumption that the act of repeating a message blocks the propagation of Byzantine symptoms. For systems that have a high degree of safety or security criticality, these assumptions must be proven to be true to an acceptable level of fault coverage. When providing proof through testing, one difficulty is creating a sufficiently wide range of signals with Byzantine symptoms. Such testing likely will require specialized fault injectors.

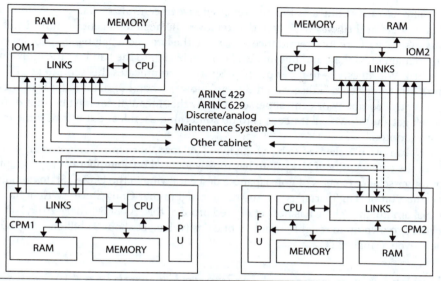

FIGURE 1-5   BFT and airplane safety ARINC 659 SAFEbus

Satoshi Nakamoto's Blockchain Breakthrough

Satoshi Nakamoto is the name used by the unknown person or persons who designed Bitcoin and created its original reference implementation, Bitcoin Core. As a part of the implementation, they also devised the first blockchain database and solved the double-spending problem for digital currency. They were active in the development of Bitcoin up until December 2010.

Satoshi Nakamoto: The Man, the Myth, the Mystery

If the mystery is of interest, we suggest you view the film *Banking on Bitcoin*. The film reviews the life stories and public misconceptions surrounding the cryptocurrency's rise. The movie is well paced and informative, using interviews with financial columnists from the *Wall Street Journal* and the *New York Times*, early adopting Bitcoin entrepreneurs like Charlie Shrem and Erik Voorhees, and establishment figures such as the Winklevoss brothers and former New York State Superintendent of Financial Services Benjamin Lawsky. It is a pretty good tour of the history of cryptographic technology. Like lots of new technology, blockchain and Bitcoin are the work of a small group of coders known as cypherpunks. They contributed to the ideas that became the building blocks of Bitcoin. In the mid-1990s, just a handful of people had the knowledge necessary to develop a blockchain currency. The movie explores theories that Satoshi Nakamoto, the unknown creator of Bitcoin, may well have been one the original cypherpunks as he is rumored to have lived within a few city blocks of other cypherpunks, such as cryptographer Hal Finney.

The narrative contrasts the differences between centralized banking systems and the public ledger at the heart of Bitcoin that removes the need for a central authority. It highlights Bitcoin's power to reduce remittance fees, serve the two and a half billion people on the planet who remain unbanked, and put financial control back into the hands of the individual.

Erik Voorhees, the founder of ShapeShift, communicates this sentiment in one of the film's first interviews: "I discovered Bitcoin's power when I understood it was not controlled by a central company or central person. I knew that meant it couldn't be shut down. And if it can't get shut down, all it needs is to do something useful, and it will become more and more adopted."

Nakamoto has claimed to be a man living in Japan, born in 1975. However, speculation about the true identity of Nakamoto has mostly focused on a number of cryptography and computer science experts of non-Japanese descent, living in the United States and Europe. It became a bit of "I'm Spartacus" as Australian programmer Craig Steven Wright has claimed to be Nakamoto, though he has not yet offered proof of this. As of February 2017, Nakamoto is believed to own up to roughly 1 million bitcoins (valued at about $4 billion USD) but has never spent even a single BTC.

Satoshi Nakamoto: Timing Is Everything

Curiously, Bitcoin's emergence was around the same time as the financial crisis of 2008. According to https://bitcoin.org, a purely peer-to-peer version of electronic cash allows online payments to be sent directly from one party to another without going through a central financial institution. Digital signatures provide part of the solution, but the main benefits are lost if a trusted third party is still required to prevent double-spending. Bitcoin is a solution to the double-spending problem using a peer-to-peer network. The network timestamps transactions by hashing them into an ongoing chain of hash-based proof-of-work, forming a record that cannot be changed without redoing the proof-of-work. The longest chain not only serves as proof of the sequence of events witnessed, but proof that it came from the largest pool of CPU power. As long as the majority of CPU power is controlled by nodes that are not cooperating to attack the network, they'll generate the longest chain and outpace attackers. The network itself requires minimal structure. Messages are broadcast on a best-effort basis, and nodes can leave and rejoin the network at will, accepting the longest proof-of-work chain as proof of what happened while they were gone. If people lose faith in a currency, the typical reaction is to start using another one.

Traditionally, money has moved to the most stable currency, which has typically been the US dollar. But Bitcoin has a couple of advantages. The first advantage is that it is not controlled by any central authority. In countries where people are distrustful of how central banks and governments manage the economy, Bitcoin may seem like a more sensible alternative.

The second is that bitcoins may be easier to obtain than other fiat currencies. It can be bought and sold via Bitcoin exchanges online but also in direct transactions via websites. Evidence suggests that during times of crisis, people are looking to Bitcoin as an alternative to their own problematic currencies. As the Greek debt crisis unfolded, Bitcoin exchanges reported an increase in volume as people traded the cryptocurrency around the world. The price of bitcoins also rose significantly as the Greece crisis deepened, lending further credence to the idea of Bitcoin as a "panic" currency.

Blockchain: Underpinning of Cryptocurrency

As we all know by now, blockchain provides the technology underpinnings of Bitcoin, which has been the subject of much interest and speculation within the technical, business, and law enforcement communities. It got a bad rap when Bitcoin became the exchange currency for dark-web sites like Silk Road. According to Coinmap (http://coinmap.org), a crowdsourced website that tracks businesses that accept Bitcoin as a method of payment, the number of such businesses is on a constant and growing rise. While the revenues from Bitcoin are still a fraction of overall revenue, wider adoption of Bitcoin and other cryptocurrencies is pretty much a given, especially as the financials see the savings of time and money gained in global transactions. For example, Rand Merchant Bank research (https://news.bitcoin.com/south-africa-bank-blockchain-40-revenue/) found that cryptocurrencies could make up to 40 percent of banks' revenue if they become a global standard. Both IBM and Microsoft offer their own versions of Blockchain-as-a-Service (BaaS) as part of their cloud platforms, and Donald Tapscott in his book *BlockChain Revolution* says that "blockchains, the technology underpinning the cryptocurrency, have the potential to revolutionize the world economy."

Types of Blockchain

As people began to understand how blockchain works, they started using it for other purposes: as data storage for things of value, identities, agreements, property rights, and a host of other things. Ethereum, which will be one of the main focuses of this book, is to date the most comprehensive blockchain innovation after Bitcoin. Like cloud computing implementations, different types or categories of blockchain have emerged. Analogous to the cloud, you have public blockchains that everyone can access and update, you have private blockchains for just a limited group within an organization to be able to access and update, and you have a third kind, a consortium of blockchains that are used in collaboration with others. While working on Wall Street, we saw this consortium type of arrangement as very common between five of the larger investment banking firms. The consortium facilitated trades at an institutional level among the members, so it makes sense that blockchain as a financial technology tool would emerge in this way. The following sections are a quick exploration of each blockchain type.

Public Blockchains

A public blockchain is one that initial creators envisioned as: a blockchain for all to be able to access and transact with; a blockchain where transactions are included if and only if they are valid; a blockchain where everyone can contribute to the consensus process. As discussed, the consensus process determines what blocks get added to the chain and what the current state is. On the public blockchain, instead of using a central server the blockchain is secured by cryptographic verification supported by incentives for the miners. Anyone can be a miner to aggregate and publish those transactions. In the public blockchain, because no user is implicitly trusted to verify transactions, all users follow an algorithm that verifies transactions by committing software and hardware resources to solving a problem by brute force (i.e., by solving the cryptographic puzzle). The miner who reaches the solution first is rewarded, and each new solution, along with the transactions that were used to verify it, forms the basis for the next problem to be solved. The verification concepts are proof-of-work or proof-of-stake.

Consortium Blockchains

A consortium blockchain such as R3 (www.r3cev.com) is a distributed ledger where the consensus process is controlled by a preselected set of nodes—for example, a consortium of nine financial institutions, each of which operates a node, and of which five (like the US Supreme Court) must sign every block in order for the block to be valid. The right to read the blockchain may be public or restricted to the participants, and there are also hybrid routes such as the root hashes of the blocks being public together with an API that allows members of the public to make a limited number of queries and get back cryptographic proofs of some parts of the blockchain state. These sort of blockchains are distributed ledgers that may be considered "partially decentralized."

Private Blockchains

A fully private blockchain is a blockchain where write permissions are kept centralized to one organization. Read permissions may be public or restricted to an arbitrary extent. Likely applications include database management and auditing internal to a single company, so public readability may not be necessary in many cases at all, though in other cases public auditability is desired. Private blockchains could provide solutions to financial enterprise problems, including compliance agents for regulations such as the Health Insurance Portability and Accountability Act (HIPAA), anti–money laundering (AML), and know-your-customer (KYC) laws. The Hyperledger project from the Linux Foundation and the Gem Health network are private blockchain projects under development. See Chapter 8 for a detailed description of Hyperledger and other private and consortium blockchain technology.

Comparing Blockchains

The distinction between public, consortium, and private blockchains is important. Even for "old school" distributed ledger adopters who prefer a traditional centralized system, they still get the addition of cryptographic auditability attached. As compared to public blockchains, private blockchains have a number of advantages. The private blockchain operator can change the rules of a blockchain. If it is a blockchain among financial partners, then where errors are discovered they will be able to change transactions. Likewise, they will be able to modify balances and generally undo anything. That said, there is a trail. In some cases, this functionality is necessary, as with property registry if a mistaken transaction is issued or some nefarious type has gained access and made themselves the new owner. This is also true on a public blockchain if the government has backdoor access keys like they did in the Clinton era. On the private blockchain, transactions are less expensive, since they only need to be verified by a few nodes that can be trusted to have very high processing power. Public blockchains tend to have more expensive transaction fees, but this will change as scaling technologies emerge and bring public-blockchain costs down to create an efficient blockchain system.

Nodes can be trusted to be very well connected, and faults can quickly be fixed by manual intervention, allowing the use of consensus algorithms that offer finality after much shorter block times. Improvements in public blockchain technology, such as Ethereum's proof-of-stake, can bring public blockchains much closer to the "instant confirmation" ideal, but private blockchains will always be faster, and the latency difference will never disappear as unfortunately the speed of light does not increase by 2x every two years like Moore's law. If read permissions are restricted, private blockchains can provide a greater level of privacy.

Given all of this, it may seem like private blockchains are unquestionably a better choice for institutions. However, even in an institutional context, public blockchains still have a lot of value. In fact, this value lies to a substantial degree in the philosophical virtues that advocates of public blockchains have been promoting all along, among the chief of which are freedom, neutrality, and openness. The advantages of public blockchains generally fall into two major categories:

- Public blockchains provide a way to protect the users of an application from the developers, establishing that there are certain things that even the developers of an application have no authority to do.
- Public blockchains are open, and therefore used by many entities, This provides some networking effects. If we have asset-holding systems on a blockchain, and a currency on the same blockchain, then we can cut costs to near-zero with a smart contract: Party A can send the asset to a program which immediately sends it to Party B which sends the program money, and the program is trusted because it runs on a public blockchain. Note that in order for this to work efficiently, two completely heterogeneous asset classes from completely different industries must be on the same database. This can also be used by other asset holders such as land registries and title insurance.

Blockchain Implementations

The concept of decentralized digital currency, as well as alternative applications like property registries, has been around for decades, but none has produced viable production implementations until now. The anonymous e-cash protocols of the 1980s and 1990s were mostly reliant on a cryptographic primitive known as Chaumian blinding (after its developer, David Chaum). Chaumian blinding provided these new currencies with high degrees of privacy, but their underlying protocols largely failed to gain traction because of their reliance on a centralized intermediary. In 1998, Wei Dai's b-money became the first proposal to introduce the idea of creating money through solving computational puzzles as well as decentralized consensus, but the proposal was scant on details as to how decentralized consensus could actually be implemented. In 2005, Hal Finney introduced a concept of "reusable proofs of work," a system that uses ideas from b-money together with Adam Back's computationally difficult Hashcash (http://hashcash.org) puzzles to create a concept for a cryptocurrency, but this once again fell short of the ideal by relying on trusted computing as a backend. As we all know, the blockchain concept was implemented as a core component of the digital currency Bitcoin. This critical and perhaps first production implementation of the blockchain made it the first digital currency to solve the double-spending problem, without the use of a trusted authority or central server. The Bitcoin design, which we examine briefly in the next section, has been the inspiration for other implementations we will explore in the chapters to come.

Bitcoin

As we mentioned, when the financial crisis of 2008 was in full throttle, Bitcoin (BTC), a decentralized currency, was implemented for the first time in practice by Satoshi Nakamoto. Bitcoin combines established primitives for managing ownership through public key cryptography with a consensus algorithm for keeping track of who owns coins, known as proof-of-work. The mechanism behind proof-of-work simultaneously solves two problems. First, it provides an effective consensus algorithm, allowing nodes in the network to collectively agree on a set of updates to the state of the Bitcoin ledger. Second, it provides a mechanism for allowing free entry into the consensus process, solving the political problem of deciding who gets to influence the consensus, while simultaneously preventing Sybil attacks—that is, attacks where a reputation system is subverted by forging identities in peer-to-peer networks. It is named after a case study of a woman diagnosed with dissociative identity disorder. It works by substituting a formal barrier to participation, such as the requirement to be registered as a unique entity on a particular list, with an economic barrier—the weight of a single node in the consensus voting process is directly proportional to the computing power that the node brings. More recently, an alternative approach has been proposed called proof-of-stake, calculating the weight of a node as being proportional to its currency holdings and not its computational resources. The discussion concerning the relative merits of the two approaches will be examined in the chapters that address the Ethereum-based blockchain and derivatives thereof. At this junction in 2018, all blockchain platforms are still evolving and will continue to do so for the foreseeable futures. As Bitcoin is the most widely used, we will explore it in some detail in the next sections. For in-depth details for developers, see https://bitcoin.org/en/developer-documentation.

Bitcoin State Transition

From a technical standpoint, the ledger of a cryptocurrency such as Bitcoin can be thought of as a state transition system, where there is a state S consisting of the ownership status of all existing bitcoins (or any asset for that matter) and a state transition function—that is, the API: EXECTX, which takes a state S and a transaction TX and outputs a new state S' which is the result. In a standard banking system, for example, the state is a balance sheet, a transaction is a request to move $cash money from A to B, and the state transition function reduces the value of A's account by X amount of $cash money and increases the value of B's account by X amount of $cash money. If A's account has less than X amount of $cash money in the first place, the state transition function returns an error. We define an API:

```
EXECTX(S,TX) results in S' (new state) or ERROR and S (no change to state)
```

If A has enough $cash money:

```
EXECTX({ A:$1000, B:$500},"send $500 :A to B") results in { A:$500, B:$1000 }
```

But if A does not have enough $cash money:

```
EXECTX({ A:$1000, B:$500 },"send $1001 from A to B") results in ERROR
```

The state in a blockchain is the "consensus view" of all transactions at any given moment borne out by the existing authenticated ledger distributed among all nodes. In the world of Bitcoin, it is the collection of all unspent transaction outputs (UTXOs) that have been minted and not yet spent, with each UTXO having a denomination and an owner (defined by a 20-byte address which is essentially a cryptographic public key). With respect to UTXOs, because each output of a particular transaction can only be spent once, the outputs of all transactions included in the blockchain can be categorized as either unspent transaction outputs (see https://bitcoin.org/en/glossary/unspent-transaction-output) or spent transaction outputs. For a payment to be valid, it must only use UTXOs as inputs.

If the value of a transaction's outputs exceed its inputs, the transaction will be rejected. But if the inputs exceed the value of the outputs, any difference in value may be claimed as a transaction fee by the Bitcoin miner who creates the block containing that transaction.

A transaction contains one or more inputs, with each input containing a reference to an existing UTXO and a cryptographic signature produced by the private key associated with the owner's address, and one or more outputs, with each output containing a new UTXO for addition to the state.

The state transition function EXECTX(S,TX) -> S' can be defined as follows:
For each input in TX:

1. If the referenced UTXO is not in S, return an error; this prevents transaction senders from spending coins that do not exist.
2. If the provided signature does not match the owner of the UTXO, return an error; this prevents transaction senders from spending other people's coins.
3. If the sum of the denominations of all input UTXO is less than the sum of the denominations of all output UTXO, return an error.
4. Return S' with all input UTXO removed and all output UTXO added.

That is a simple view of the transaction flow for Bitcoin.

Bitcoin Mining

Bitcoin combines the state transition system with a consensus system in order to ensure that everyone agrees on the order of transactions. Bitcoin's decentralized consensus process requires nodes in the network to continuously attempt to produce blocks, i.e., 1 to N transactions. The Bitcoin network is intended to create one block approximately every 10 minutes, with each block containing a timestamp, a nonce, a reference to (i.e., hash of) the previous block, and a list of all transactions that have taken place since the previous block. Every block in the Bitcoin network has the exact same structure as shown in Figure 1-6.

Each newly created block is "chained" to the last added block of the blockchain and stores its digital fingerprint. Let us examine the fields of a block, with byte sizes subject to change:

- Block identifier (4 bytes): This is an identifier for the Blockchain network. It has a constant magic number value of 0xD9B4BEF9. The magic number is not something specific to Bitcoin. It identifies the type of the file or data structure you are consuming. The consumer can check the magic number and immediately know the supposed type of that file or data structure. In this case, it indicates the start of the block, and the data is from a production network.
- Next block identifier (4 bytes).
- Block size (4 bytes): Indicates how large the block is. Since the very beginning, each block has been fixed to 1 MB. This will be increased to 2 MB. The maximum capacity is 2 GB, so the scalability factor has already been taken care of.

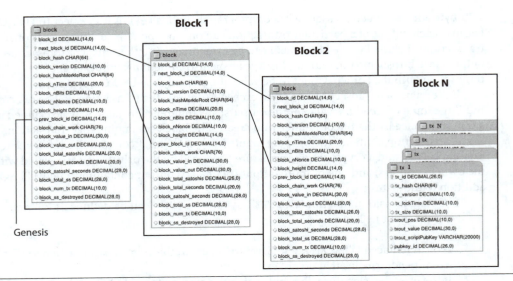

FIGURE 1-6 Bitcoin blockchain schema

- Block version (4 bytes): Each node running the Bitcoin protocol has to implement the same version and it is mentioned in this field.
- Previous block hash (32 bytes): This is a digital fingerprint (hash) of the block header of the previous (last added) block of the blockchain. It is calculated by taking all the fields of the header (version, nonce, etc.) together and applying a cryptographic function (SHA-256) twice by rearranging the bytes of the individual fields (little-endian format).
- Block Merkle root (64 bytes).
- Block timestamp (8 bytes).
- Nonce (4 bytes).

The block header is composed of the fields from Version to Nonce.

- Transaction counter (variable: 4 bytes): This is the count of transactions that are included with the block.
- Transaction list (variable: total blocksize is 1 MB): Stores the digital fingerprint of all the transactions in that block. Each individual transaction has its own structure.

You can also see the height of the block (aka the count of blocks) since the first block was created, and genesis block, the first block that was mined.

Bitcoin Blocksize and Segregated Witness

So a block has a maximum file size of 1 MB. When this block's space capacity is full, another block is created and added up in the blockchain. As the number of Bitcoin transactions is increasing, more blocks are created. This is stressing the Blockchain network and causing delays in transactions confirmation. Additionally, more mining means higher transaction. To address this the Segregated Witness ("SegWit") was proposed. So let's review—each Bitcoin transaction contains three elements:

1. Input (sender details)
2. Output (recipient details)
3. Digital Signature: this signature is called the witness, one who verifies that the sender has the right amount of balance to make the transaction

All of these elements are needed to add the transaction to a block. Of the three elements, the file size of Digital Signature is the largest, making the transactions heavy in terms of size. As the maximum capacity of each block at present is 1 MB, therefore more heavy transactions equals less transactions getting added to the block for confirmation. SegWit proposes to remove the Digital Signature Element from the transaction and add it to another new block called Extended Block. This means that any transaction that gets added in the Block for confirmation will only contain Input and Output and not the Digital Signature. This will make transactions lighter. As a result more space is available in the block, which means more transactions can be added into the block. As more transactions will get verified in the same amount of time, the Bitcoin network will be faster. Thus, we are removing the Witness—the Digital Signature—segregating it to another block (hence the name "Segregated Witness"). So, the advantages of SegWit are:

- it will reduce the file size of transactions,
- there will be faster confirmation of transactions, and
- transaction fees will be lower.

Thus, SegWit will improve the Bitcoin network scaling ability. Moreover, consensus is not required to make SegWit work. SegWit even works where users do not upgrade their software versions to the newest version. That said, we will make numerous blockchain software improvements as it gains traction in the application development world.

Bitcoin and Merkle Root

Each block contains a list of all transactions. Once the block is part of the blockchain it is an immutable record, i.e., the transaction entry in it is permanent. It also means that if a transaction is present in one block it will not be present in any other block of the blockchain. The transactions are listed as Merkle tree or a binary hash tree. It is a very popular data structure used in programming languages.

The *root* of the tree is the topmost node. The nodes at the bottom are called *leaf* nodes. Each node is simply a cryptographic hash of a transaction. The Merkle tree does not contain a list of all the transactions, but rather a hash (digital fingerprint) of all transactions as a tree structure (see Figure 1-7).

Hash of Transaction 0 = Hash[Tx(0)] = SHA256 (SHA 256 (Transaction A))
Each hash is calculated by applying the SHA-256 algorithm twice.

Similarly, to construct a parent node Hash(01), the 32-byte Hash[Tx(0)] and 32-byte Hash[Tx(1)] is concatenated as a 64-byte hash string and then SHA-256 is applied twice to give a 32-byte Hash(01).

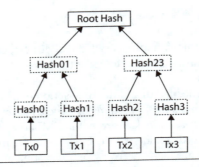

FIGURE 1-7   Merkle tree

This concept can be further expanded to any size. The biggest advantage is that it is very easy and highly efficient to determine whether a particular transaction has been included within a block (since the block contains the Merkle root—which is a digital fingerprint of all transactions contained in it).

Bitcoin and Secure Hashing

SHA stands for *secure hash algorithm*. It is used to prove data integrity. The same input(s) will always produce the exact same output. This output is always 256 bits or 32 bytes in length regardless of the length of the input (even if input is millions of bytes). Any change in the input(s) will result in a change of output. The same output can never be derived from different input(s). However, from the output we can never determine the inputs, which is why this is highly secure. You can test it yourself at a few online SHA-256 tools (such as www.xorbin.com/tools/sha256-hash-calculator). The input can be any string, even concatenating many strings. Regardless of the input the output remains 256 bits.

Over time, this creates a persistent, ever-growing blockchain that continually updates to represent the latest state of the Bitcoin ledger.

The algorithm for checking if a block is valid, expressed in this paradigm, is as follows:

1. Check if the previous block referenced by the block exists and is valid.
2. Check that the timestamp of the block is greater than that of the previous block.
3. Check that the proof-of-work on the block is valid.

Let $S[0]$ be the state at the end of the previous block.
Suppose TX is the block's transaction list with n transactions.

For all i in 0...n-1, set $S[i+1] = EXECTX(\{ (S[i],TX[i]) \}$.
If any application returns an error, exit and return false.
Return true, and register $S[n]$ as the state at the end of this block.

Essentially, each transaction in the block must provide a valid state transition from what was the canonical state before the transaction was executed to some new state. Note that the state is not encoded in the block in any way; it is purely an abstraction to be remembered by the validating node and can only be computed for any block by starting from the genesis state and sequentially applying every transaction in every block. Additionally, note that the order in which the miner includes transactions into the block matters; if there are two transactions A and B in a block such that B spends a UTXO created by A, then the block will be valid if A comes before B but not otherwise.

The one validity condition present is the requirement for proof-of-work. The precise condition is that the double SHA-256 hash of every block, treated as a 256-bit number, must be less than a dynamically adjusted target. The purpose of this is to make block creation computationally hard, thereby preventing Sybil attackers from remaking the entire blockchain in their favor. Because SHA-256 is designed to be a completely unpredictable pseudorandom function, the only way to create a valid block is simply trial and error, repeatedly incrementing the nonce and seeing if the new hash matches.

In order to better understand the purpose of mining, let us examine what happens in the event of a malicious attack. Since Bitcoin's underlying cryptography is known to be secure, the attacker will target the one part of the Bitcoin system that is not protected by cryptography directly: the order of transactions. The attacker's strategy is a simple double-spend:

1. Send 1,000 BTC to a merchant in exchange for some product (preferably a rapid-delivery digital good).
2. Wait for delivery of the product.
3. Produce another transaction sending the same 1,000 BTC to himself.
4. Convince the network that his transaction to himself was the one that came first.

Once step 1 has taken place, after a few minutes some miner will include the transaction in a block. After about an hour, five more blocks will have been added to the chain after that block, with each of those blocks indirectly pointing to the transaction and thus "confirming" it. At this point, the merchant will accept the payment as finalized and deliver the product; since we are assuming this is a digital good, delivery is instant. Now the attacker creates another transaction sending the 1,000 BTC to himself. If the attacker simply releases it into the wild, the transaction will not be processed; miners will attempt to run EXECTX({ (S, TX) }) and notice that TX consumes a UTXO that is no longer in the state. So instead the attacker creates a "fork" of the blockchain, starting by mining another version of the block pointing to the same block as a parent but with the new transaction in place of the old one. Because the block data is different, this requires redoing the proof-of-work. Furthermore, the attacker's new version of the block has a different hash, so the original blocks do not point to it; thus, the original chain and the attacker's new chain are completely separate. The rule is that in a fork the longest blockchain is taken to be the truth. In order for the attacker to make his blockchain the longest, he would need to have more computational power than the rest of the network combined to catch up and effect the so-called "51% attack."

Merkle Trees

An important scalability feature of Bitcoin is that the block is stored in a multilevel data structure. The "hash" of a block is actually only the hash of the block header, a roughly 200-byte piece of data that contains the timestamp, nonce, previous block hash, and the root hash of a data structure called the Merkle tree storing all transactions in the block. A Merkle tree is a type of binary tree, composed of a set of nodes with a large number of leaf nodes at the bottom of the tree containing the underlying data, a set of intermediate nodes where each node is the hash of its two children, and finally a single root node, also formed from the hash of its two children, representing the "top" of the tree. The purpose of the Merkle tree is to allow the data in a block to be delivered piecemeal: a node can download the header of a block from one source, the small part of the tree relevant to them from another source, and still be assured that all of the data is correct. The reason why this works is that hashes propagate upward. If a malicious user attempts to swap in a fake transaction to the bottom of a Merkle tree, this change will cause a change in the node above, and then a change in the node above that, finally changing the root of the tree and therefore the hash of the block, causing the protocol to register it as a completely different block and almost certainly with an invalid proof-of-work. The Merkle tree protocol is arguably essential to long-term sustainability.

Bitcoin Scripting

Even without any extensions, the Bitcoin protocol provides a less than robust version of the concept of smart contracts. UTXO in Bitcoin can be owned not just by a public key but also by a more complicated script expressed in a simple stack-based programming language. In this paradigm, a transaction spending that UTXO must provide data that satisfies the script. Indeed, even the basic public key ownership mechanism is implemented via a script: the script takes an elliptic curve signature as input, verifies it against the transaction and the address that owns the UTXO, and returns 1 if the verification is successful and 0 otherwise. Other, more complicated scripts exist for various additional use cases. For example, one can construct a script that requires signatures from two out of a given three private keys to validate (multisig), a setup useful for corporate accounts, secure savings accounts, and some merchant escrow situations. Scripts can also be used to pay bounties for solutions to computational problems, and one can even construct a script that says something like "this Bitcoin UTXO is yours if you can provide an SPV proof that you sent a Dogecoin transaction of this denomination to me," essentially allowing decentralized cross-cryptocurrency exchange.

Namecoin

Created in 2010, Namecoin (http://namecoin.org) is a decentralized name registration database. In decentralized protocols like Tor, Bitcoin, and Bitmessage, there needs to be some way of identifying accounts so that other people can interact with them. Namecoin is the oldest and most successful implementation of a name registration system using such an idea. It is open-source technology which improves decentralization, security, censorship resistance, privacy, and speed of certain components of the Internet infrastructure such as DNS and identities. Namecoin is a key/value pair registration and transfer system based on the Bitcoin technology.

Ripple

Ripple (www.ripple.com) is seen as one of the most advanced distributed ledger technology (DLT) companies in the industry. It focuses on the using of blockchain-like technology for payments. The Ripple protocol has been adopted by an increasing number of financial institutions to offer alternative remittance options to consumers. Ripple even has obtained a virtual currency license from the New York State Department of Financial Services, making it one of the few companies with a BitLicense. As of 2017, Ripple is the third-largest cryptocurrency by market capitalization, after bitcoin and ether. Ripple is a financial real-time gross settlement solution, currency exchange, and remittance network using distributed ledger technology. Ripple is built upon a distributed open-source Internet protocol, consensus ledger, and native currency called XRP (ripples) enabling (cross-border) payments for retail customers, corporations, and other banks. The Ripple protocol, described as "basic (settlement) infrastructure technology for interbank transactions," enables the interoperation of different ledgers and payment networks and brings together three aspects of modern payment solutions: messaging, settlement, and FX management. It allows banks and non-bank financial services companies to incorporate the Ripple protocol into their own systems and thereby allow their customers to use the service.

The protocol enables the instant and direct transfer of money between two parties. As such the protocol can circumvent the fees and wait times of the traditional correspondent banking system. Any type of currency can be exchanged, including USD, euros, RMB, yen, gold, airline miles, and rupees. Ripple has its own form of digital currency (dubbed XRP) in a manner similar to Bitcoin, using the currency to allow financial institutions to transfer money with negligible fees and wait time. One of the specific functions of XRP is as a bridge currency, which can be necessary if no direct exchange is available between two currencies at a specific time, for example, when transacting between two rarely traded currency pairs. Within the network's currency exchange, XRP are traded freely against other currencies, and their market price fluctuates against dollars, euros, yen, bitcoins, etc.

Many financial companies have subsequently announced experimenting and integrations with Ripple. A host of major banks have adopted Ripple to improve their cross-border payments, and many have completed trial blockchain projects. These banking institutions—including Santander, UniCredit, UBS, Royal Bank of Canada, Westpac Banking Corporation, CIBC, and National Bank of Abu Dhabi, among others—view Ripple's payment protocol and exchange network as a valid mechanism for offering real-time affordable money transfers.

Ethereum

Ethereum (https://ethereum.org) is a decentralized platform that runs smart contracts: applications that run exactly as programmed without any possibility of downtime, censorship, fraud, or third-party interference. If Bitcoin was blockchain 1.0, then Ethereum is blockchain 2.0 and beyond. See Figure 1-8.

Ethereum applications run on a custom-built blockchain, a shared global infrastructure that can move value around and represent the ownership of property. This enables developers to create markets, store registries of debts or promises, and move funds in accordance with instructions given long in the past (such as a will) or a futures contract without a middleman or counterparty risk. The project was bootstrapped via an ether presale in August 2014 by fans all around the world. It is developed by the Ethereum Foundation, a Swiss nonprofit, with contributions from great minds across the globe. We will explore Ethereum in great detail as it will be the focus and implementation of most of the development code we will present. From a developer's point of view, Ethereum is the platform that's most likely to succeed. In March 2017, the Ethereum Enterprise Alliance was formed. The list of participating organizations includes Microsoft, Intel, J.P. Morgan, BNY Mellon, and a host of others. Some startups have used derivatives of the Ethereum platform to produce collaborative and private blockchains that are not even concerned with cryptocurrency. The assets they transact with will be securities, insurance, title registrations, and so on.

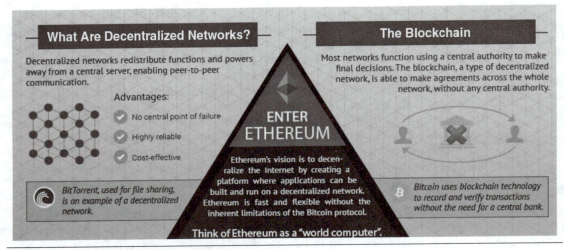

FIGURE 1-8 Ethereum blockchain platform

Blockchain Collaborative Implementations

As large enterprises have started to take notice of how the blockchain technology could save them time and money, their interest in creating enterprise versions of the blockchain has led to the creation of some collaborative implementations. These collaborative implementations are growing in number. We will examine a few of the current ones. We believe these collaborations, although the subject of some widespread criticism, will lead to a mature blockchain technology equipped with interactive development environments (IDE), debugging techniques, deployment techniques, and all the trappings required for enterprise implementations.

Hyperledger

Hyperledger (https://www.hyperledger.org) is an open-source collaborative effort created to advance cross-industry blockchain technologies. It is a consortium of companies working together to develop standardized blockchain protocols. The project aims to develop open protocols and standards by providing a modular framework that supports different components for different uses. This would include a variety of blockchains with their own consensus and storage models, and services for identity, access control, and contracts. It is a global collaboration hosted by the Linux Foundation (see Figure 1-9).

Hyperledger Fabric is the IBM contribution, a distributed ledger technology (DLT) implementation for the enterprise, with capabilities including network security, scalability, confidentiality, and performance, in a modular blockchain architecture.

Hyperledger Burrow codebase is a contribution by Monax and is an Ethereum Virtual Machine–compatible blockchain. Hyperledger Sawtooth Lake codebase is a contribution by Intel. They have targeted some applications integrating Internet of Things (IoT) sensors to

HYPERLEDGER

Business Blockchain Frameworks Hosted with Hyperledger

Hyperledger Burrow

Hyperledger Burrow (formerly known as eris-db) is a permissionable smart contract machine built in part to the specification of the Ethereum Virtual Machine (EVM).

Hyperledger Fabric

Hyperledger Fabric is an implementation of blockchain technology that is intended as a foundation for developing blockchain applications or solutions.

Hyperledger Iroha

Hyperledger Iroha is a distributed ledger project that was designed to be simple and easy to incorporate into infrastructural projects requiring distributed ledger technology.

Hyperledger Sawtooth

Hyperledger Sawtooth is a modular blockchain suite designed for versatility and scalability.

FIGURE 1-9 Hyperledger project branches

track data on a blockchain, recording data including ownership, position, location, temperature, humidity, motion, shock, and tilt. We will examine each of these branches in the "use case" chapters to follow.

Hyperledger's reference architecture is depicted in Figure 1-10. These categories are a logical structure, not a physical depiction of partitioning of components into separate processes, address spaces, or (virtual) machines. Some of these components will be built from the ground up, some will use existing open-source code, and some will interface with existing services to fulfill the required functions.

Corda

Corda (www.corda.net) is a distributed ledger platform designed to record, manage, and automate legal agreements between business partners. It is a collaborative effort by R3, a group of more than 100 financial companies. The development team is made up of financial industry veterans, technologists, new tech entrepreneurs, and subject matter experts, bringing together expertise to reengineer the financial markets ecosystem. Corda is a distributed ledger made

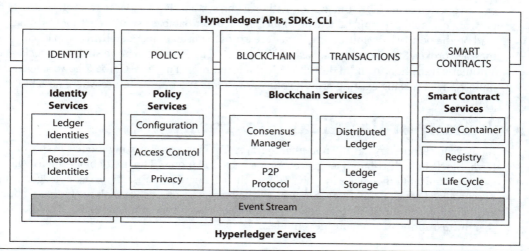

FIGURE 1-10 Hyperledger's reference architecture

up of mutually distrusting nodes that would allow for a single global database that records the state of deals and obligations between institutions and people. This would eliminate much of the time-consuming manual effort currently required to keep disparate ledgers synchronized with each other. It would also allow for greater levels of code sharing than presently used in the financial industry, reducing the cost of financial services for everyone.

From the technical point of view, Corda is a decentralized database platform with the following novel features: New transaction types can be defined using JVM bytecode. Transactions may execute in parallel, on different nodes, without either node being aware of the other's transactions. Nodes are arranged in an authenticated peer-to-peer network. All communication is direct. There is no blockchain. More likely, Corda could accurately be described as a messaging protocol. Transaction races are deconflicted using pluggable notaries. A single Corda network may contain multiple notaries that provide their guarantees using a variety of different algorithms. Thus, Corda is not tied to any particular consensus algorithm.

Data is shared on a need-to-know basis. Nodes provide the dependency graph of a transaction they are sending to another node on demand, but there is no global broadcast of all transactions. Bytecode-to-bytecode transpilation is used to allow complex, multistep transaction building protocols, called flows, to be modeled as blocking code. The code is transformed into an asynchronous state machine, with checkpoints written to the node's backing database when messages are sent and received. A node may potentially have millions of flows active at once, and they may last days, across node restarts and even upgrades. Flows expose progress information to node administrators and users and may interact with people as well as other nodes. A flow library is provided to enable developers to reuse common flow types such as notarization, membership broadcast, and so on.

The data model allows for arbitrary object graphs to be stored in the ledger. These graphs are called states and are the atomic unit of data. Nodes are backed by a relational database. Data placed in the ledger can be queried using SQL as well as joined with private tables, thanks to slots in the state definitions that are reserved for join keys. The platform provides a rich type system for the representation of things like dates, currencies, legal entities, and financial entities such as cash, issuance, deals, and so on. States can declare a relational mapping and can be queried using SQL. Integration with existing systems is considered from the start. The network can support rapid bulk data imports from other database systems without placing load on the network. Events on the ledger are exposed via an embedded JMS compatible message broker. States can declare scheduled events. For example, a bond state may declare an automatic transition to an "in default" state if it is not repaid in time. Corda follows a general philosophy of reusing existing proven software systems and infrastructure where possible.

Blockchain in Practical Use Today

Blockchain technology has the potential to transform business operating models in the long term. Blockchain distributed ledger technology is foundational. The use of blockchains will garner significant efficiencies in global supply chains, financial transactions, asset ledgers, and decentralized social networking. Some blockchain applications, as we shall see in this section, are a disruptive innovation; they enable substantially lower-cost solutions to be created, thereby disrupting existing business models.

Blockchain in the Financial Technology Space

Having been in the financial technology ("fintech") space before it was known as "fintech," the growth of global transactions has required more and more advanced technology applications to speed up and reduce transaction costs for securities such as equities. Traditional trade processes within asset management can be slow, manual, cumbersome, and filled with risk when reconciling and matching—and they're getting more complex with cross-border transactions and for nonstandard investment products, such as loans. Each party in the trade life cycle (e.g., broker dealers, intermediaries, custodians, clearing and settlement teams) currently keeps their own copy of the same record of a transaction, creating significant inefficiencies and room for error.

Unfortunately, a fair amount of trades have errors, requiring manual intervention and extending the time required to settle trades. Because it does not require an exchange to verify, clear, and settle security transactions (such as equities, repo, and leveraged loans), blockchain will save a large amount in fees and capital charges globally by moving to a shorter, and potentially customized, settlement window. Blockchain will eliminate significant fees across FX, commodities, and OTC derivatives. Blockchain technology could simplify and streamline this entire process, providing an automated trade life cycle where all parties in the transaction would have access to the exact same data about a trade. This would lead to substantial infrastructural cost savings, effective data management and transparency, faster processing cycles, minimal reconciliation, and the potential removal of brokers and intermediaries altogether.

Financial derivatives are the most common application of a smart contract, and one of the simplest to implement in code. The main challenge in implementing financial contracts is that the majority of them require reference to an external price ticker. For example, a very desirable application is a smart contract that hedges against the volatility of ether (or another cryptocurrency) with respect to the US dollar, but doing this requires the contract to know the value of ETH/USD or BTC/USD at any particular moment. They would have to leave the zone of trust. In practice, information issuers are not always trustworthy, and in some cases the banking infrastructure is too weak, or too hostile, for such services to exist. This approach is not fully decentralized, because a trusted source is still needed to provide the price ticker, although arguably this still is a massive improvement in terms of reducing infrastructure requirements (unlike being an issuer, issuing a price feed requires no licenses and can likely be categorized as free speech) and reducing the potential for fraud. The current industry trailblazers working to enable a smarter and more connected financial system by digitizing the world's assets are Digital Asset Holdings (www.digitalasset.com), Chain.com, and the aforementioned Ripple.

Blockchain in the Sharing Economy

One thing we have noticed is that large organizations rely on information provided by users to generate value within their own platform. The problem with this platform is that the value produced by the crowd is not equally distributed among those who have contributed. Most of the profits are captured by the large intermediaries who operate the block. Uber and Airbnb could be obviated in a world where we store people's online identities on the blockchain. Uber has disrupted the entire transportation industry. Some governments, however, have been quick to limit its reach in order to protect existing taxi companies. La`Zooz (http://lazooz.org) is an open-source and decentralized collaborative transportation system. More importantly,

La`Zooz is a blockchain-based ride-sharing solution that rewards its users, developers, and drivers with tokens called zooz. Unlike Uber, La`Zooz has no central authority and cannot be blocked or shut down by governments. Your identity (as anonymous as you want it to be) could be linked to reviews in the "sharing economy" on the marketplace. People can check out your review as a trusted individual by checking your ID number. It would actually promote good behavior because if you get a bad reputation you cannot delete accounts and re-register. As we have mentioned, the blockchain can't be tampered with or duplicated. Your identity and what you choose to expose can be valuable. Onename is a New York–based startup that has created an ID system using the Bitcoin blockchain. Its first service allows users to create blockchain IDs, which will soon be used to log in to websites without the need for a password.

P2P lodging sites have already begun to transform the lodging industry by making a public market in private housing. The blockchain would enable a secure, tamper-proof system for managing digital credentials and reputation; it could accelerate the adoption of P2P lodging.

Instead of central power providers, a distributed network built on blockchain technology lets people generate their own electricity to sell on the network, using their blockchain's identity to perform the transaction. With solar and high-capacity battery technology, individuals can potentially act as distributed power providers. Blockchain could be used to facilitate secure transactions of power between individuals on a distributed network who do not have an existing relationship. The fact that all transactions are verified by a consensus network means you are protected from customers who claim the transaction did not happen. The blockchain records are a more reliable truth than the central database of the existing providers. The current applications are Sun Exchange, TransActive Grid, and Grid Singularity.

Blockchain and Real Estate

The real estate market will change for sure. Homeowners buying or refinancing property are subject to significant transaction costs, including title insurance, where the title search process can be labor intensive. An individual can put a property on the blockchain so that prospective buyers can review and verify the owner of a property. Currently, this process of title searching is done manually at a steep price. This specific-use case in the US could result in quickly obtained and less expensive title insurance. Such insurance is usually required by lenders issuing a mortgage to protect their interests. Transacting real estate is a cloudy and expensive process because of middlemen. Brokers, government property databases, title companies, insurance and property databases, escrow companies, inspectors and appraisers, and notary publics are all currently needed to complete a transaction. We wait and depend on them. They exist because they hold information that we cannot access or do not have the skills needed to operate in the existing property transaction ecosystem. Public blockchains will eliminate most if not all of these roadblocks and facilitate speedy and less expensive transaction fees. Current applications providers include Bitfury (www.bitfury.com), which registers land titles via a private blockchain, and Factom/Epigraph (www.factom.com).

Blockchain and Identity

Banking regulation requires that banks know their customers (KYC). Identity data stored on a blockchain facilitates the bank's verification of the identity of new customers. Storing account and payment information in a blockchain could standardize the data required for an account, thereby improving data quality and reducing the number of falsely identified "suspicious" transactions. A tamper-proof record could also ease the process of getting to know a client and demonstrating compliance with AML regulations. Current users include the global financial messenger for payments and fund transfers, i.e., the Society for Worldwide Interbank Financial Telecommunication (SWIFT).

The blockchain can be used to keep track of digital assets. Today when we purchase a used car the seller must physically deliver the car, title, and key. In the future, car titles may be public on the blockchain and the key may be digital. All data could be verified through a blockchain. To sell a car, the seller would simply send the digital key to the new owner, who would use it to turn on and start the car. Exchanges like ShapeShift.io already demonstrate how simple the exchange of stocks, bonds, and other digital assets will be should blockchain technology take hold. How about the concept of "proof of existence" (POE) and transparency utilizing the blockchain? Provenance (https://www.provenance.org) is a real-time data platform that empowers brands to take steps toward greater transparency by tracing the origins and histories of products. With their technology, luxury brands could mitigate and potentially eliminate the sale of counterfeit goods. Outside of this area, one can only imagine what their technology could mean for the art world as well.

Blockchain and the Practice of Law

As an attorney, the concept of a smart contract immediately hooked me, Joseph, to my current obsession with blockchain. Some say blockchain will eliminate lawyers; I disagree. Lawyers will just have to be able to code or at least write a syllogistic specification describing the intent of the contract. The lawyer in the blockchain world must be a technologist as well. Creating smart contracts requires a new team, consisting of:

- Attorneys who can design the code and who have legal knowledge of contract structure and enforcement
- Technologists who provide the software engineering to implement legal constructs into smart self-executing transactional structures using blockchain

The law and smart contracts not only represent a new practice model but also a change in the global business model. A smart contract may start from a series of clauses drafted according to traditional contract doctrine, but as these clauses move onto a blockchain platform and become self-executing, doctrine becomes obscured. Don Tapscott, co-author of *Blockchain Revolution*, came up with the phrase "smart contract mediator" (SCM). Due to the self-enforcing nature of smart contracts, the nexus of disputes in transactions potentially will shift to the stage of dynamic execution. Lawyers with blockchain knowledge will act as mediators in this process, helping parties to navigate the smart contract process.

A smart contract looks and acts very different from a static contract. Understanding blockchain and DLT is critical to managing this process for clients. Many of the industries and practice areas discussed so far apply primarily to those working with large firms and representing enterprises. Hopefully for practitioners, blockchain is yet another technology that provides new opportunities for agile individual attorneys and small firms to compete for business. Smart contracts enable trustless financial services like loans, automatic execution of trade agreements, micropayments, and more. Smart contracts on the blockchain can also build on top of digital assets and stocks. The firm Steptoe and Johnson (www.steptoe.com) serves as counsel to the Blockchain Alliance (www.blockchainalliance.org), a coalition of more than 25 companies and 25 law enforcement and regulatory agencies around the world.

Blockchain Decentralized File Storage

Over the past few years, there have emerged a number of online file storage startups, the most prominent being Dropbox, seeking to allow users to upload a backup of their hard drive and have the service store the backup and allow the user to access it in exchange for a monthly fee. However, at this point the file storage market is at times relatively inefficient; a cursory look at various existing solutions shows that, particularly at the "uncanny valley" 20 to 200 GB level at which neither free quotas nor enterprise-level discounts kick in, monthly prices for mainstream file storage are such that you are paying for more than the cost of the entire hard drive in a single month.

IPFS is short for Interplanetary File System, and it does just what the name entails. Think of it as rewiring and rerouting the entire Internet so that trains run and stop on time and go where they need to go, all while greatly reducing redundancy. Designed by the technologist Juan Benet, IPFS is a peer-to-peer distributed file system that seeks to connect all computing devices with the same system of files. In some ways, IPFS is similar to the Web, but IPFS could be seen as a single BitTorrent swarm, exchanging objects within one Git repository. In other words, IPFS provides a high throughput content-addressed block storage model, with content-addressed hyperlinks. Projects like Storj intend to use blockchain technology to share files in a decentralized network. Users with extra disk space will automatically be able to rent out unused storage space. Users in need of cloud storage space can pay to store files on computers across the network. Storj estimates that this system will cut costs of data storage by about 80 percent.

Decentralized Autonomous Organizations

The general concept of a decentralized autonomous organization (DAO) is that of a virtual entity that has a certain set of members or shareholders which, perhaps with a 67 percent majority, have the right to spend the entity's funds and modify its code. The members would collectively decide how the organization should allocate its funds. Methods for allocating a DAO's funds could range from bounties and salaries to even more exotic mechanisms such as an internal currency to reward work. This essentially replicates the legal trappings of a traditional company or nonprofit but uses only cryptographic blockchain technology for enforcement. So far much of the talk around DAOs has been around the "capitalist" model of a decentralized autonomous corporation (DAC) with dividend-receiving shareholders and tradable shares. An alternative, perhaps described as a "decentralized autonomous community," would have all members have an equal share in the decision making and require 67 percent of existing members to agree to add or remove a member. The requirement that one person can only have one membership would then need to be enforced collectively by the group. Backfeed (backfeed.cc) develops resilient technology and new economic models to support free, large-scale, systematic collaboration. Based on a distributed governance model, Backfeed protocols make it possible for people to easily deploy and maintain decentralized applications and DAOs that rely on the spontaneous and voluntary contribution of hundreds, thousands, or millions of people.

Blockchain and Cloud Computing

Enigma is a decentralized cloud platform that guarantees privacy (https://www.media.mit.edu/projects/enigma/overview/). Private data is stored, shared, and analyzed without ever being fully revealed to any party. Enigma provides secure multiparty computation, empowered by the blockchain. This is as futuristic and radical as blockchain gets and will be an important innovation as it solves some of the most difficult problems in technology today: privacy and security. These core functions, layered on top of distributed cloud technology, are a dynamic combination that transforms how data is stored and retrieved, providing industries like finance, health, and civil services the underlying trust and security to truly unlock the potential of next-generation mobile applications.

Blockchain Gambling and Betting

Gambling is a multi-billion-dollar industry and was revolutionized by the Internet. Online gambling accounts for a significant proportion of all betting. Mostly, the Internet just saw the same big gaming players move their infrastructure online. However, blockchain technology changes all that. It is the missing piece that protected the established gambling industry. Now there is a host of exciting new startups reimagining the gambling industry. They are decentralizing the entire structure and are building something truly new. VDice (vdice.io) is one example of such a startup. It is billed as the world's first fully decentralized gambling platform and is wildly popular among blockchain geeks. Using the Ethereum blockchain, they have leveraged smart contract technology and have created game codes that exist without a server. These games live on the Ethereum P2P network. We will examine Ethereum and betting with a sample application developed by one of the authors, PeerBet, in detail in a later chapter that will provide a "start to finish" examination of the Ethereum blockchain development life cycle.

Summary

In summary, blockchain—the distributed database technology with the capability to execute smart contracts—is more than a platform for cryptography. The universe of "use cases," which we briefly covered, is expanding exponentially. The efficiencies and cost savings provided by blockchain technologies, especially the private blockchains adopted by the financial community, will result in widespread adoption. This will cause the technology to mature at a rapid rate. In parallel, the use of blockchain to affect global transactions will also push it forward toward maturity. Blockchain and its timing are critical to maintaining global transactions and providing trust in the integrity of those transactions. For these reasons and more, blockchain is here to stay. We will provide you with a comprehensive journey through what you need as a developer to successfully make the trip.

2 Business Use Cases

Currency and Tokens

When a conversation starts up on blockchain, it invariably turns to the subject of cryptocurrencies and just as quickly to the first and most widely known one, Bitcoin. Let's take a deeper look at cryptocurrencies and how they relate to blockchain. But first, let's review the essence of blockchain and why it works for cryptocurrencies and tokens:

- It contains proof of all transactions on the network.
- The truth/facts are permanent; they cannot be changed after they are committed.
- It can be likened to a linked list; this helps to prove integrity as each verified block points back to a prior block.
- The mining process (for Bitcoin) validates, verifies, and commits the block.
- Automatic replication and therefore high availability and resiliency help to overcome failure of any participating node.
- It is simple to reconstruct local copy if it becomes corrupt or lost.

Cryptocurrency

What is a cryptocurrency? A browser search will yield results that state something like the following:

> "...digital asset in which encryption techniques are used to regulate the generation of units of currency and verify the transfer of funds, operating independently of a central bank."

> "...encrypted decentralized digital currency transferred between peers and confirmed in a public ledger via a process known as mining."

So, what does this mean? A cryptocurrency is essentially a digital (electronic) form of currency recorded in a ledger of accounts and transactions (transfers) between peers using a method of encryption and verification. Unlike fiat currency, which is currency whose value is backed by the government that issues it, there is no central governing body. When Bitcoin—the first and most well-known digital currency—was created, it was built with a supply capped at 21 million coins. However, not all of these were put into circulation from day 1; they are gradually brought into circulation via a complex process known as mining. Mining is essentially a validation, verification, and committing process. Once all of the Bitcoins have been mined, there will be no more coins added to the circulation. It is predicted that 80 percent (or 16.8 million) will have been mined and in circulation by early 2018.

Cryptocurrency Explosion

A search on Bitcoin will reveal that it became the first decentralized cryptocurrency in 2009. Since that time, numerous cryptocurrencies have been created. In fact, at the time of writing there are more than 700 cryptocurrencies available, and a few dozen of those have even reached a market capitalization of above $10 million (see Table 2-1). While these cryptocurrencies are still very small in market share compared to fiat currencies, they continue to evolve and become more widespread.

The Future of "Real" Cash

There is little doubt in our minds that cash as we know it will cease to exist, and on the way to eradication its use will be increasingly limited and driven down to the point where it is effectively not used. The timeframe is probably over a decade, but it could be sooner. Think about it: what do you use cash for today? With our smartphones we can use applications to pay for everyday items that used to be bought only with cash, such as the breakfast or coffee that you grab on your way to work. The most common items that I (Paul) use cash for now are for a mixture of tipping and buying gum or breath mints from the newsstand (it sounds so funny to me to write newsstand, because I haven't bought a real newspaper in years, but they are still there whenever I visit).

TABLE 2-1   Top 10 Cryptocurrencies (by Market Cap)

#	Name	Market Cap (USD)	Price (USD)	Circulating Supply
1	Bitcoin	$36,203,662,674	$2,213.09	16,358,875 BTC
2	Ethereum	$16,856,972,986	$183.16	92,032,632 ETH
3	Ripple	$9,034,799,016	$0.236208	38,249,335,400 XRP
4	NEM	$1,869,255,000	$0.207695	8,999,999,999 XEM
5	Ethereum Classic	$1,537,182,848	$16.69	92,092,096 ETC
6	Litecoin	$1,252,969,571	$24.42	51,319,032 LTC
7	Dash	$826,722,501	$112.86	7,325,334 DASH
8	Monero	$603,347,476	$41.49	14,541,297 XMR
9	Bytecoin	$459,404,438	$0.002511	182,953,122,444 BCN
10	Stellar Lumens	$361,596,835	$0.037418	9,663,661,946 XLM

Now think about this: Instead of cash we have bought into using a variety of payment methods that have become more and more convenient in our digital age. We either use credit or debit cards, or mobile applications, as mentioned earlier. All of these noncash methods have various incentive programs (rewards, discounts, and cash-back). It's pretty straightforward and seems like a good idea because we all love to feel that we are getting rewarded for spending our hard-earned money. If you go back just a few years, it was uncommon to use a credit card to buy anything that totaled less than $20. Now we pay without using cash nearly all the time. Sure, there are some places that still post a half-baked apology stating the minimum amount for a credit or debit card is $10 (see Figure 2-1 for a couple of examples of these notices), but there are far fewer barriers to using noncash payment methods today. We want to take a step back and make a point that is quite obvious to many: When cash eventually disappears, we will be paying for everything through a third party. Be it the banks (and their credit and debit cards) or the mobile applications (Apple, Google, Samsung, Venmo, etc.), it will still be controlled, contained, and above all viewable by these third parties and governments.

Let's see how cryptocurrencies compare to the third-party model. First of all, they are public networks and open to all. You do not need permission to join the network. The participants creating these cryptocurrency applications do not need permission to innovate; they are free to create new applications and they will immediately work. There is no central control. This does not mean that a user is powerless, it's that the power is shared by all of the participants. We think cryptocurrencies have a significant role to play in the replacement of real cash. Do you want to replace cash with a digital equivalent that is run, controlled, and monitored by a combination of the government and corporations? Or do you want a digital equivalent to be independent of any central entity? After all, banking is an application; does it really need an institution?

 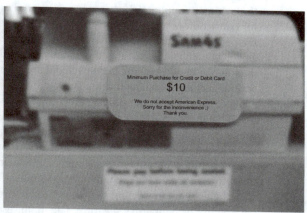

FIGURE 2-1   Credit/debit card minimum

Digital Tokens

Another common conversation point in discussions around blockchain is tokens, or digital tokens to be more specific. A digital token can be any kind of digital asset or any digital representation of a physical asset. Within Ethereum a digital token can represent any fungible, tradable good, such as currency, reward points, gift certificates, and so on. All Ethereum-based tokens implement baseline functionality in a standard way, known as the ERC20 token standard. These tokens remain compatible with any other client or contract that relies on and uses the same standards.

The significance of digital tokens is that in recent years it was venture capital companies and institutional investors that had invested in digital currency startups, to the tune of approximately $1 billion. This was one of the typical ways that a startup raised money. Traditionally, companies raise money in three ways:

- **Equity**   The company sells shares (ownership) in exchange for funds.
- **Bond**   The company borrows cash and promises to repay the amount with interest.
- **Presell product or service**   The company takes orders and payment for a product or service that does not exist, isn't complete, or is not available yet, such as event tickets, mobile or console games, or Kickstarter projects.

With these traditional approaches there is a greater degree of government regulation put in place to prevent investors from being scammed by swindlers and crooks.

What was happening in the funding aspect of these digital currency startup efforts? A new method, called an initial coin offering (derived from IPO, initial public offering), provided another way for a company or project to raise capital. These new projects raised money by creating and then selling their own digital tokens through crowdfunding on a blockchain. Some interesting aspects to this approach are that the tokens are the currency that is used in the company/application that is being created or developed. The developers of the application (or contributors) are paid in these tokens. The tokens can be converted to any currency at the prevailing market rate when needed. This really provides the ability to create and launch a project using a decentralized business model (DBM). There is a significant difference and divergence between these decentralized approaches to raising money and the traditional centralized ways. In effect, these ICO/DBM projects create their own financial ecosystem in order to drive the development, innovation, and delivery of the project.

This model is decentralized in several ways. There is no central control structure gatekeeping or preventing participation; it has shared contributions and ownership by all participants. This business model is facilitated by platforms that are already in place—the Internet and cryptocurrencies. This really is being tried for the first time and is looking like the future model of blockchain and the applications that will be created to run on it. It is nonetheless very important that these tokens are structured in a way that prevents them from coming under regulatory scrutiny. The main tests that regulators apply when scrutinizing these arrangements come from the U.S. Supreme Court case *Securities and Exchange Commission (SEC) v. W. J. Howey Co.* This 1946 case established the test for whether an arrangement involved an "investment contract." The case concerned an offer of a land sales and service contract that the court upheld to be an investment contract (in other words, a security) within the meaning of the Securities Act of 1933. In terms of tokens on the blockchain, the following three items must be true for a digital token to be considered an investment contract (security):

1. An investment of money
2. In a common enterprise or business
3. An expectation of profits predominantly from the work of others

A full and detailed document is available at https://www.coinbase.com/legal/securities-law-framework.pdf that attempts to lay out a process and best practices to help application builders—that is, those who want to create and sell tokens to the public—avoid such tokens being classified as a financial security.

Financial Services Use Cases

Blockchain will continue to transform the financial services industry because of the benefits and features it can provide, some of these being faster throughput, reduced costs, less room for error, transparency, and a multitude of "ities"—quality, reliability, simplicity, and traceability. The financial institutions that find ways to adopt and apply blockchain technology will gain the competitive advantages of delivering solutions with a faster time-to-market at a reduced cost. We will now examine use cases that will show you how blockchain can be applied to real-world challenges in the financial services industry.

Know Your Customer (KYC) Use Case

Problem: Know Your Customer (KYC) is the process by which a financial institution gathers information about a customer. The main purpose of this process is to ensure that institutions' services are not misused, and this process takes place when a customer opens an account. The process varies because each financial institution is responsible for being in compliance with the requirements laid out and specified by their local regulatory body. The process typically requires the passing of documents back and forth between the customer and financial institution. There is very little automation; financial institutions dedicate a huge amount of resources to the process, but it is still very time consuming. These delays are frustrating for a customer who wants to use the institution's services immediately. So how does blockchain technology help here? See Figure 2-2 for a blockchain solution.

Solution: The customer's personal information, KYC documentation, and data are encrypted and added as a block in the blockchain. The customer's block is validated using a consensus model running on the network. When the customer wants to open an account with a bank or financial institution (FI) for the first time, the FI directs them to their block and authorizes them with access. The FI can access all of the validated KYC information and move the customer along the on-boarding process. The single source of KYC (identifying) data that can easily be shared between financial institutions and external agencies will eventually result in much faster account opening, reduced resources, and therefore lower costs. This can all be done while maintaining the privacy of data, because the owner of the data (the customer) strictly controls its access. Initially, there would still be a role for a third party (e.g., the initial bank),

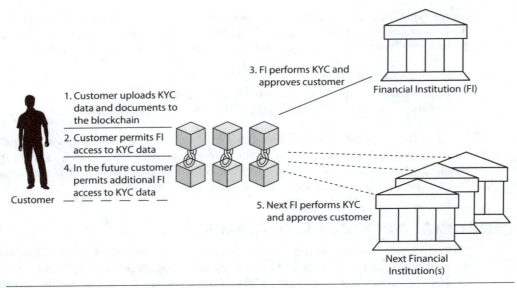

FIGURE 2-2   Know Your Customer (KYC) use case solution

and they might be rewarded for doing the initial physical work of adding information to the blockchain. This would happen at least until a decentralized attestation system was created as the process evolved.

Asset Management Settlement Use Case

Problem: Typical back-office trade processing and settlement methods can be awkward, risky, and time consuming. This is especially the case when manual steps are involved, such as during matching and reconciliation tasks. Every entity in the value chain keeps its own copy, or view, of the transactions that have taken place. These processes continue to get more complicated as new instruments are being developed and traded. In short, mistakes and associated costs are rising in proportion to the complexity of the tasks and involvement of resources to deal with them. See Figure 2-3 for a solution to asset management settlement.

Solution: The transactions can be stored in a blockchain and made available to all parties. This would drastically simplify and streamline this entire process for all parties. It would lead to automation of the trade life cycle, facilitate easier management of the data, and provide transparency as well as substantial infrastructure and resource reductions. These improvements would lead to minimal reconciliation and ultimately faster processing times. While all of the transactions may be visible to everyone, it is possible to arrange and set up so that only certain parties are privy to this information.

Insurance Claims Processing Use Case

Problem: Have you ever needed to make a claim on an insurance policy? If you have, you'll be able to relate to this problem. The claims process is complex and often drawn out and lengthy. Insurance contracts are typically difficult to understand, because over time they have evolved into a complex web of legal language in reaction to prior unfavorable outcomes. So when

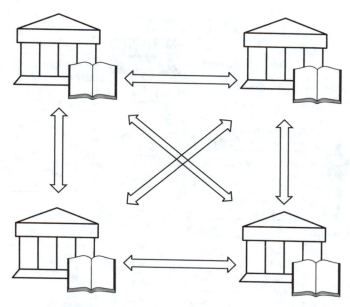

A blockchain solution will remove the need for intermediaries and provides a trusted and shared (with permission) view of data:

• Increase availability—no downtime

• Reduce costs because there are fewer reconciliation issues

• Speed up settlement because validation is fast

• Improve transparency and ability to monitor

FIGURE 2-3   **Asset management settlement use case solution**

you need to make a claim, it takes a while for the process to complete. Insurance companies are composed of many separate department silos, such as underwriting, policy issue and administration, claims, actuarial and statistical, accounting, investment, legal, and audit. When you add manual processes, legacy models, and disjointed data elements to the daily onslaught of fraudulent claims, it stands to reason that "speedy" is not the word typically associated with customer outcomes. See Figure 2-4 for a solution to insurance claims processing.

Solution: Create insurance policies using a smart contract on the blockchain. The qualities of a smart contract (control, transparency, and traceability) would allow for much more automation. A smart contract would provide the customer and insurer with the ability to manage claims in an open, speedy, and indisputable way. The contract (policy) is uploaded to the blockchain and validated by the network. Similarly, claims are then uploaded to the blockchain and applied to the smart contract. That being said, blockchains cannot access data outside their network. This data can represent external conditions such as temperature, payment, price change, or RFID presence trigger. An oracle (or data provider) is a third-party service designed for use by smart contracts. An oracle provides the necessary external data and pushes it onto the blockchain. Then the contract and the network will be able to validate and enforce the claim and either automatically reject or accept it. When the correct conditions are met, a payment is automatically triggered.

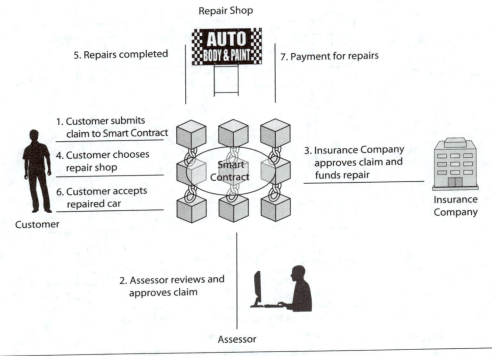

FIGURE 2-4   Insurance claims processing use case solution

Trade Finance (Supply Chain) Use Case

Problem: *Trade finance* refers to financial transactions, both domestic and international, that relate to trade receivables finance and global trade. Trade finance is a core business function for all global banks, especially tier 1 banks. Given its importance, it still lags in its application of technology and still resorts to using very manual processes for its document-centric flows. This leads to interruption in business cycles, and the lack of transparency leaves the door open to financial crime. Supply chains between many parties are complicated, distributed, and lack trust, therefore they are very slow and need many third parties such as banks and clearinghouses to facilitate the trust aspect and allow the commerce supply chain to flow. See Figure 2-5 for a solution to supply chain finance.

Solution: Blockchain will hold all of the necessary information in a smart contract, updated instantly and viewable by all members on the network. The smart contract can be used to automate the transfer of title to goods and money. This automation and network validation remove the need for third-party facilities, such as letters of credit (LCs), and will help to streamline the whole process and measurably reduce costs by eliminating the third parties and their associated fees. Applying smart contracts results in:

- Faster cycle time. Reducing and eliminating human intervention yields a more efficient process, resulting in much shorter cycles.
- Reduced fraud. The open and auditable transactions available in the distributed ledger reduce or eliminate supplier fraud.

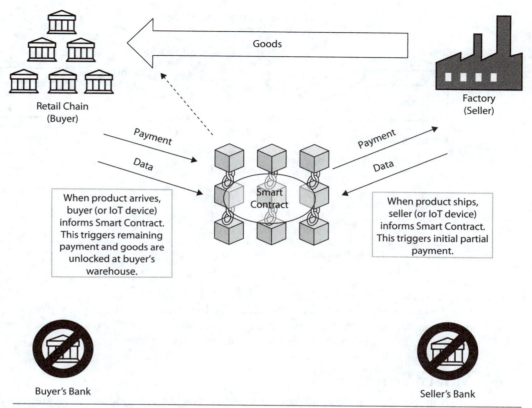

FIGURE 2-5   Trade finance (supply chain) use case solution

- Reduced costs and fees. The shared ledger is available to all banks, rating agencies, and suppliers participating in the chain, reducing processing and storage costs and fees. Payments between institutions in the network can potentially be made through a cryptocurrency. This will eliminate the need for higher-cost third-party payment networks.

Global Payments Use Case

Problem: It can take days to transfer money from a party in one country to a party in another country. The global payments business is a large, slow, costly, and error-prone industry. It is also attractive to those who wish to engage in money laundering because it is not completely traceable. See Figure 2-6 for a solution for cross-border payments.

Solution: Blockchain payment technologies can add tremendous value in this space by (a) reducing the multi-day payment cycle down to real time, (b) enhancing currency conversions, and (c) providing transparency to improve anti–money laundering capabilities. Aside from Bitcoin, there are several other cryptocurrency solutions that are gaining popularity in the

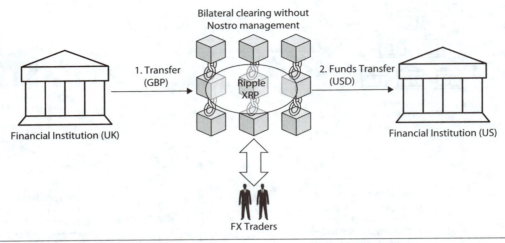

FIGURE 2-6   Global payments use case solution

payments space, notably the Ripple network and Ripple XRP. Santander became one of the first banks to apply blockchain to payments, enabling customers using their application to make overseas payments that clear within 24 hours. Blockchain will eventually enable real-time payments while reducing operational costs, human error, and fraud.

Smart Property

Smart property is really the extension of smart contracts reaching out into the practical and interactive world that includes the Internet of Things (IoT). We'll cover smart contracts later in this chapter, but feel free to to jump ahead and read about them first and come back to this section.

We've all seen (or, if not, certainly read about) actual physical objects being connected to the Internet. For example, with home automation the smart home has smart light bulbs, smart locks, and a smart refrigerator and a smart oven. All of these items are called smart because they have computer technology embedded within, they are programmable in some way, and they are connected to the Internet. So, in the case of a light bulb, it can be customized, scheduled, and controlled remotely. See Figure 2-7 for additional examples of smart property.

Smart property is all about ownership, access, and control of things using the blockchain network. Smart property can be in the physical world, such as a vehicle, tablet, or even real estate. In the virtual (non-physical) world, smart property can be a financial instrument, trademark, copyright, or patent. The real advantage to making property smart is that it can be traded, accessed, and controlled in a near trustless way, reducing cost as well as fraud. This will open up and expand commerce, making everything more competitive and at the same time less expensive. Think about this: smart property can be used as collateral by a borrower when they borrow money from a lender using a smart contract. We envision the blockchain becoming a tool for inventory, tracking, and exchange of assets in the future.

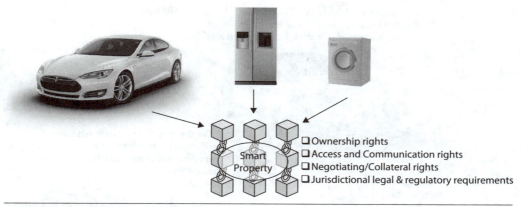

FIGURE 2-7   Smart property

Transferring Ownership of Smart Property

While simple forms of smart property exist, such as the combination of your car ignition and the car key, more advanced forms will be needed in the future to allow transfer of ownership. We will now distill a smart property approach to the ownership of a car. When the manufacturer builds the car, the car is given a digital certificate signed by the manufacturer and an identification key containing the public part of the certificate. The car has built in enough technology so that it can provide valid proof of its existence, and other valuable data like ownership, build date, maintenance history, and distance traveled or hours used. The car would also contain a small amount of cryptocoins (C) deposited on the ownership key to facilitate transfer in the future. See Figure 2-8 for an example flow for transferring ownership of smart property.

Now let's look at the steps involved when the car gets sold:

1. The buyer generates a random number (nonce) and passes it to the seller and asks in return for the car data.
2. The seller takes the buyer's random number and passes it to the car (probably implemented via a touchscreen or an application on the seller's phone that is paired to the car already).
3. The car returns a signed (via identification key) data structure that contains the buyer's random number, the car's public key, any pertinent data (mileage, age, etc.), the current owner's public key, and the transaction details of the prior ownership transaction. This data structure provides sufficient information for the buyer to know what they are buying and who the seller is.
4. The seller identifies the key to receive payment (*SellerKey*) and price required (*P*).
5. The buyer generates a new ownership key (*BuyerKey*) and creates a skeleton transfer transaction containing a pair of inputs and a pair of outputs. Note that the transaction is not completely valid and cannot be fully executed because only Input#1 is signed:
   - Input#1 is a signed entry for P cryptocoins.
   - Input#2 identifies the ownership key (holding the C cryptocoins).

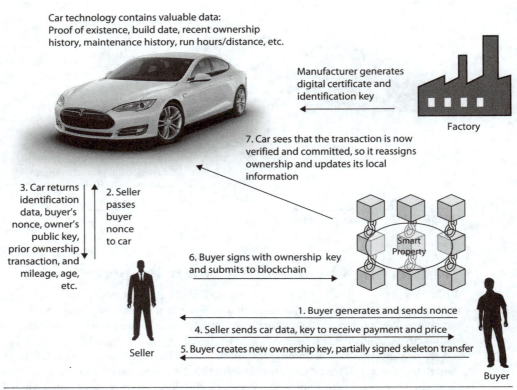

Car technology contains valuable data:
Proof of existence, build date, recent ownership history, maintenance history, run hours/distance, etc.

Manufacturer generates digital certificate and identification key

Factory

7. Car sees that the transaction is now verified and committed, so it reassigns ownership and updates its local information

3. Car returns identification data, buyer's nonce, owner's public key, prior ownership transaction, and mileage, age, etc.

2. Seller passes buyer nonce to car

6. Buyer signs with ownership key and submits to blockchain

Smart Property

Seller

1. Buyer generates and sends nonce

4. Seller sends car data, key to receive payment and price

5. Buyer creates new ownership key, partially signed skeleton transfer

Buyer

FIGURE 2-8 Transferring ownership

- Output#1 is an instruction to send P cryptocoins to the SellerKey.
- Output#2 is an instruction to send C cryptocoins to the BuyerKey.

6. The buyer passes this partially signed transaction back to the seller. The seller signs Input#2 with the car's current ownership key, commits the transaction to the blockchain, and waits for it to be validated.

7. The buyer presents the car with the verified blockchain transaction. This is a Merkle branch hash of the block header of the transaction and enough additional block headers to fill in the gap from the car's current ownership transaction. The car sees that the new transaction reassigns ownership and updates its ownership information.

8. The buyer now owns the car.

As we mentioned earlier, there will most likely be a touchscreen in the smart car and an application on the buyer's and seller's phones to facilitate identification and the transfer. It is highly likely that our smartphones become even more integral with our lives and even become part of the keys to our smart property along with some biometric or additional authentication/ authorization methods.

Using Smart Property as Collateral

While transferring ownership of smart property is an obvious necessity, using it in other ways will also be possible. For example, what if you could leverage your smart property and use it as collateral in another contract? This isn't transferring ownership, although penalties for not fulfilling a contract may lead to transferring ownership of the smart property, but while it's being used as collateral you will most likely want to continue to use the smart property. What would be the sense in metaphorically sticking it in a drawer where it would do nothing for the life of the contract? So let's flesh this out a little with an example. You want to borrow money. In exchange, the people lending you the money want something pledged as security for repayment of the loan, to be forfeited in the event of a default. You put up your smart property as collateral, but the wrinkle is that you still want to use the smart property while the loan is in place. See Figure 2-9 for an example flow for using smart property as collateral for a loan.

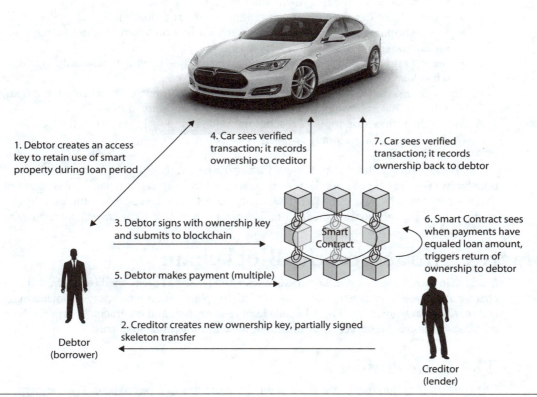

FIGURE 2-9   Using smart property as collateral

So how will we do this in practice? As we said earlier, smart property can manage ownership, access, and control. These are the basic capabilities. In this scenario we will use the ability to program into the contract the state of ownership and access for the life of the loan. Here is a high-level digest of how a loan contract using smart property as collateral might be set up:

1. The debtor creates an access key for the smart property so they can keep using it for the duration of the loan provided that they maintain the payments.
2. The creditor generates a key (*CKey*) that is to receive payments to repay the loan amount (*LAmt*).
3. The creditor generates a new ownership key (*OKey*) and creates a skeleton transfer transaction (*Tran*) containing three inputs and two input/outputs. The creditor passes this transaction to the debtor. Note that the transaction is not completely valid and cannot be fully executed because only two of the inputs are signed:
   - Input#1 is a signed entry for LAmt (loan amount).
   - Input#2 identifies the repayment amount (initially zero).
   - Input#3 identifies the current ownership key (smart property).
   - Input/Output#1 identifies the DKey and an instruction to send LAmt to DKey and assign ownership of smart property to OKey.
   - Input/Output#2 signs entry OKey and an instruction to assign ownership to DKey when loan is repaid.
4. The debtor signs Input#3 with the ownership key and Input/Output#1 with the DKey.
5. The debtor makes payments to the loan by adding amounts to Input#2.
6. When the transaction Input#2 reaches the value in Input#1, the instruction to take back ownership of the smart property is executed.

There are some additional conditions that would be attached to this contract, namely time limits. The creditor can revoke the access token if the loan is not repaid by a certain time, because they have the ownership key. The smart property can then be taken and used by the creditor or sold to recoup the loan amount. Now let's take a look at the smart contract itself.

Smart Contracts on the Blockchain

Blockchain technology handles cryptocurrencies and tokens as mentioned earlier in this chapter and throughout the book; it is the underlying platform for a new way of organizing and managing relationships. These include legal relationships and contracts. In order to best explain what a smart contract is, we must first look into the problem of trust.

The Trust Problem

The trust problem has been around since the dawn of time. In order to progress, a society or group of people has to cooperate with each other. When people cooperate they can do more collectively that they could individually. However, in doing so they are also opening themselves up to being deceived, misled, and subsequently disappointed. To attempt to address this issue, societies have instituted rituals, passed laws, and even installed governance processes. All of these elaborate techniques are in place to address the trust problem. To better explain the trust problem, let us use an example. A man frequently uses his credit card to pay for goods and services. He can walk into a store, pick an item, go to the checkout, and pay with the credit card. The store allows the purchase because the credit card, when swiped or inserted into the chip reader, checks with the bank to see if the shopper is a good risk for them to authorize the purchase and confirm that he is the person to whom the card was issued. The bank will actually collect the payment from the shopper some time later when it bills him. So, you see, there is trust all around here. The store trusts the bank and the shopper, and the bank trusts the store and the shopper, and the shopper trusts the store and the bank. The shopper can carry around a small piece of plastic instead of a wad of cash. If he loses the card, he can have it replaced within a few days. If he had to carry the cash equivalent, he might lose it or get robbed and would never get it back. Having the trust element makes it easier to purchase items, and that's also good for merchants, who always want and need to sell more items. As the barriers to payment come down, a whole lot more commerce occurs. That brings us back to the original point that trust is needed for cooperation, which in turn leads to progress.

Trusted Third Party

One way to solve the trust problem is to use a trusted third party. The bank and credit card example given above is this exactly. The transactions between the customer, the merchant, and the shopper are passed through and logged by a bank (credit card issuer). The bank facilitates the transaction; see Figure 2-10 for a diagram depicting a trusted third party. The bank can also step in and resolve a dispute in the event that a customer finds a transaction on their monthly statement that they didn't make.

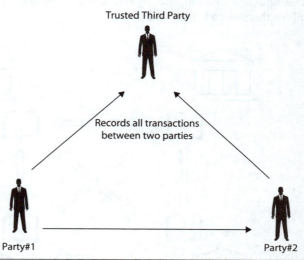

FIGURE 2-10   Trusted third party

Distributed Ledger and Consensus

What we have just described is still a centralized way to solve the trust problem. There is another way to solve it using a distributed ledger (or shared ledger) and combining this with a consensus methodology. Figure 2-11 depicts a ledger that is distributed across multiple parties. So, instead of logging transactions with a single third party, you send a single copy of each transaction to all parties in the network. All parties in the network would be required to keep an ongoing ledger of all transactions. Therefore, every party in the network would have the exact same set of transactions. At a point in time, everybody would know how much the shopper owes the merchant. If a dispute arises, the consensus majority (51 percent) of the network of ledger keepers would decide what he owed.

Blockchain technology follows this distributed ledger and consensus method. It is a network for resolving the trust problem through a distributed (decentralized) and publicly verifiable (open) ledger.

Blockchain Details

Blockchain leverages and combines the networking capabilities of computers with cryptographic technology to store and process data. Any computer on the network (known as a node) can be located anywhere with Internet connectivity. It's really outsourcing of intelligent computing resources to the cloud. These resources provide a platform for developers to build applications. It can be likened to other Platform as a Service (PaaS) offerings that exist today. The blockchain platform logs, processes, saves, and verifies transactions. Because it is based on the shared ledger concept, each and every node on the network stores the same copy of the ledger and therefore all of the transactions taking place on the platform. It is this decentralized (shared) aspect of the ledger that makes blockchain the public, comprehensive, permanent, and verifiable authority for administering and storing records of transactions. Let's look at an example of how this shared ledger works.

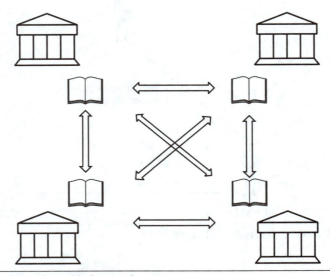

FIGURE 2-11   Distributed ledger and consensus

In this scenario, there are two parties who want to exchange money, with Party#1 wanting to give 100 cryptocoins to Party#2. As in the real world, each party will need a place to hold their cryptocoins—a digital wallet. Provided Party#1 knows the address of Party#2, they will be able to create a transaction that transfers the 100 cryptocoins to Party#2. This transaction is added to a temporary block of data that is then stored on the network. This block contains all of the transactions that took place on the network during a particular length of time, for example, the last few minutes. While it is recorded on the network, this block has not been verified. Once a set interval of time passes, all of the data collected in the temporary block is gathered and the network holds a competition among the participants on the network. The winner of the competition takes on the task of processing and verifying the transaction on the block and committing it to the permanent record by adding the block to the blockchain. Once they do this, the winner broadcasts the proof of work to the whole network; each node then checks that the proof of work is correct. If 51 percent of the nodes agree that the proof is correct, the block is added as a permanent block to the blockchain.

While the blockchain is often referred to as a trustless system, what that really means is that there is no need to place any trust in any human interaction because everything is taken care of by the platform technology. The only interesting point here is that the participants on the network give up their computing resources to this process. What is their incentive to do so? The winning participant is rewarded with a digital token for the underlying platform—that is, the winner gets a newly minted cryptocoin. So, are you ready to commit your home computer to the blockchain network and become a miner? Think again: to give yourself a shot at winning the competition requires a large amount of computing resources. Some of the largest companies or entities that participate are based in China, where electricity is state subsidized. This winner-takes-all approach could have been done in a more equal way where all participants could have shared the reward, but perhaps the competition is what made the platform so successful. Perhaps a future platform will take another look at the reward system to see if another way will work.

Smart Contract

In the real world, a contract is an agreement between parties that is intended to be enforceable by law. Within these contracts are agreements that lay out what each party is to do to fulfill the contract. In a two-party contract, the essence of this can be likened to an Aristotelian syllogism, which is a fancy way of saying "if this is true, then the following will happen, else the following will happen." If one party fails to carry out their obligation, they can be taken to court and ordered to carry it out or to provide financial compensation to the other party. In computer programming terms, these Aristotelian syllogisms are implemented using an "if … then … else …" construct. A smart contract is one or more of these conditions combined with the capabilities to enforce the obligations automatically. The distributed ledger system contains all of the data and theoretically the capabilities necessary for the smart contract to execute autonomously. The required conditions are coded in the smart contract and once they are met the contract obligations are automatically executed. In this digital case, though, there is no need for the courts or mediation—the facts are available to the contract, so it cannot make the wrong decision.

Example Smart Contract

The following is the sample code that Ethereum recommends will represent a digital token in their ecosystem. A token can represent any fungible and tradable good. This can be coins, reward for customer loyalty, certificates, and so on. Because digital tokens implement some basic data and functionality in a standard way, they will operate in a consistent way. If you use this code, the token, because it is ERC20 compliant, will be instantly compatible with the Ethereum wallet and any other client or contract that uses the same standards.

LISTING 2-1 **Ethereum Smart Contract Token (ERC20) Example (*Continued*)**

```solidity
pragma solidity ^0.4.8;

contract tokenRecipient { function receiveApproval(address _from, uint256 _value, address _token,
bytes _extraData); }

contract MyToken {
    /* Public variables of the token */
    string public standard = 'Token 0.1';
    string public name;
    string public symbol;
    uint8 public decimals;
    uint256 public totalSupply;

    /* This creates an array with all balances */
    mapping (address => uint256) public balanceOf;
    mapping (address => mapping (address => uint256)) public allowance;

    /* This generates a public event on the blockchain that will notify clients */
    event Transfer(address indexed from, address indexed to, uint256 value);

    /* This notifies clients about the amount burned */
    event Burn(address indexed from, uint256 value);

    /* Initializes contract with initial supply tokens to the creator of the contract */
    function MyToken(
        uint256 initialSupply,
        string tokenName,
        uint8 decimalUnits,
        string tokenSymbol
    ) {
        balanceOf[msg.sender] = initialSupply;       // Give the creator all initial tokens
        totalSupply = initialSupply;                 // Update total supply
        name = tokenName;                            // Set the name for display purposes
        symbol = tokenSymbol;                        // Set the symbol for display purposes
        decimals = decimalUnits;                     // Amount of decimals for display purposes
    }
```

LISTING 2-1   Ethereum Smart Contract Token (ERC20) Example (*Continued*)

```
/* Send coins */
function transfer(address _to, uint256 _value) {
    if (_to == 0x0) throw;                              // Prevent transfer to 0x0 address.
                                                        // Use burn() instead
    if (balanceOf[msg.sender] < _value) throw;          // Check if the sender has enough
    if (balanceOf[_to] + _value < balanceOf[_to]) throw; // Check for overflows
    balanceOf[msg.sender] -= _value;                    // Subtract from the sender
    balanceOf[_to] += _value;                           // Add the same to the recipient
    Transfer(msg.sender, _to, _value);                  // Notify anyone listening that
                                                        // this transfer took place
}


/* Allow another contract to spend some tokens in your behalf */
function approve(address _spender, uint256 _value)
    returns (bool success) {
    allowance[msg.sender][_spender] = _value;
    return true;
}


/* Approve and then communicate the approved contract in a single tx */
function approveAndCall(address _spender, uint256 _value, bytes _extraData)
    returns (bool success) {
    tokenRecipient spender = tokenRecipient(_spender);
    if (approve(_spender, _value)) {
        spender.receiveApproval(msg.sender, _value, this, _extraData);
        return true;
    }
}


/* A contract attempts to get the coins */
function transferFrom(address _from, address _to, uint256 _value) returns (bool success) {
    if (_to == 0x0) throw;                              // Prevent transfer to 0x0 address.
                                                        // Use burn() instead
    if (balanceOf[_from] < _value) throw;               // Check if the sender has enough
    if (balanceOf[_to] + _value < balanceOf[_to]) throw; // Check for overflows
    if (_value > allowance[_from][msg.sender]) throw;   // Check allowance
    balanceOf[_from] -= _value;                         // Subtract from the sender
    balanceOf[_to] += _value;                           // Add the same to the recipient
    allowance[_from][msg.sender] -= _value;
    Transfer(_from, _to, _value);
    return true;
}


function burn(uint256 _value) returns (bool success) {
    if (balanceOf[msg.sender] < _value) throw;          // Check if the sender has enough
    balanceOf[msg.sender] -= _value;                    // Subtract from the sender
```

LISTING 2-1   Ethereum Smart Contract Token (ERC20) Example

```
        totalSupply -= _value;                          // Updates totalSupply
        Burn(msg.sender, _value);
        return true;
    }

    function burnFrom(address _from, uint256 _value) returns (bool success) {
        if (balanceOf[_from] < _value) throw;           // Check if the sender has enough
        if (_value > allowance[_from][msg.sender]) throw;   // Check allowance
        balanceOf[_from] -= _value;                     // Subtract from the sender
        totalSupply -= _value;                          // Updates totalSupply
        Burn(_from, _value);
        return true;
    }
}
```

Blockchain IoT Protocol Projects

The Internet of Things (IoT) is a major buzzword, and there is little doubt that it is an industry with tremendous growth in its future. According to Gartner, the number of connected devices will exceed 20 billion by 2020, with a market worth of more than $3 trillion. A connected device can be as simple as a small sensor (think motion detector) or scale up to a much more complicated appliance (think house, car, boat, airplane), as depicted in Figure 2-12. One of the biggest concerns with these connected devices is security, and this breaks down into two aspects. The first is preventing unauthorized access to the device itself, and the second is unauthorized access to any data being exchanged with the device.

Additionally, as with all other data processing tasks, you will eventually run into scalability issues with a centralized approach, especially with the billions of transactions that are expected on these devices. Centralized servers can also be vulnerable to single point of failure conditions, making these devices susceptible to denial-of-service attacks where servers are flooded with traffic from compromised devices spread across the world. This is exactly how IoT systems that handle sensitive tasks will be impacted if they are not architected with resiliency from the start. That's where blockchain technology is being offered as a solution to the challenges of IoT. Each device would continue to manage and administer its own behavior, security roles, and the rules for interacting with other devices. Blockchain would be the platform to facilitate the transactions and the coordination between these devices. Blockchain technology will enable secure mesh networks to be created. The devices on the network can interconnect in a reliable way and prevent security threats that use techniques like spoofing and/or impersonation. If each valid point is registered on the blockchain, this will facilitate identification and authentication in a decentralized way, and the network will be scalable to support billions of anticipated devices.

In early 2017, a group of industry-leading startups and companies came together at a summit to discuss the challenges facing blockchain and IoT innovation and the potential for a collective effort to address them. This summit was the first step to explore and build a shared blockchain-based Internet of Things protocol. There were presentations that exchanged

FIGURE 2-12 Graphic depiction of IoT examples

ideas on applicable use cases, findings and feedback within the industry, and recognition of common requirements. The group agreed that security, interoperability, and integration would be essential for adoption. Going forward, a consortium of the meeting members will define the scope and implementation of a smart contracts protocol layer across several major blockchain systems.

Imagine a world where your washing machine can detect when you are running low on detergent, automatically engage with the market, negotiate the best price, and reorder the necessary product. The same goes with items in your refrigerator—milk, eggs, and so on. These smart devices will know your calendar and put off reordering if you are on vacation or away from home for a while. We're sure there will be some teething trouble with the first iterations of these devices and the smart contracts associated with them. As early adopters of this technology, we can imagine coming home to a pile of large boxes of fabric softener, enough to last a lifetime. But these devices and their associated intelligence will iterate and get it right for the mass market.

Summary

While blockchain technology is at the heart of cryptocurrencies like Bitcoin and Ethereum, and what they can do as decentralized, stateless currency and payment platforms, it clearly is a technology with widespread applicability in many sectors of business. This chapter gave some depth to real-world use cases in the financial services industry. These use cases ultimately lead to faster throughput, reduced costs, improved accuracy, greater transparency, and quality, reliability, simplicity, and traceability. The chapter also discussed smart property and smart contracts and showed how they can be used in conjunction in the not too distant world of blockchain technology. The chapter closed with how blockchain and the Internet of Things (IoT) will have a consortium of startups and companies to help define and refine security, interoperability, management, and coordination between connected devices. While IoT is still in its early stages of evolution and is currently composed mostly of technologies that either collect data or allow remote monitoring and control, this will change as devices become smarter and artificial intelligence is added. This network of things will transition toward becoming a network of autonomous devices that talk to each other and—hopefully—make smart decisions without the need for human intervention or interpretation. In short, we live in exciting times for blockchain technology.

3   Technology Use Cases

In the 1970s, the Internet was a small, decentralized collective of DARPA computers, called ARPANET. The personal-computer revolution that followed built upon that foundation, stoking optimism encapsulated by John Perry Barlow's 1996 manifesto "A Declaration of the Independence of Cyberspace" (www.eff.org/cyberspace-independence). Barlow described a chaotic digital utopia, where "netizens" self-govern and the institutions of old hold no sway. "On behalf of the future, I ask you of the past to leave us alone," he writes. "You are not welcome among us. You have no sovereignty where we gather."

This is not the Internet we know today. Two decades later, the vast majority of communications flow through a set of central servers run by a small group of corporations under the influence of those companies and other institutions. Netflix, for instance, now comprises 40 percent of all North American Internet traffic. Engineers anticipated this convergence. In the late 1960s, key architects of the system for exchanging small packets of data that gave birth to the Internet predicted the rise of a centralized "computer utility" that would offer computing much the same way that power companies provide electricity. Today, that model is largely embodied by the cloud-computing giants Amazon, Google, Azure, and other cloud-computing companies. They offer convenience at the expense of privacy. Internet users now regularly submit to terms-of-service agreements that give companies a license to share their personal data with other institutions, from advertisers to governments. In the United States, the Electronic Communications Privacy Act of 1986 (ECPA), a law that predates the Web, allows law enforcement to obtain without a warrant private data that citizens entrust to third parties, including location data passively gathered from cell phones and the contents of emails that have either been opened or left unattended for 180 days. Note that under the ECPA only a subpoena or an 18 U.S.C. §2703(d) order with little judicial review is needed to allow access to the aforementioned private data. As Edward Snowden's leaks have shown, this massive information set allows intelligence agencies to focus on just a few key targets in order to monitor large portions of the world's population. The National Security Agency (NSA) wiretaps the connections between data centers owned by Google and Yahoo, allowing the agency to collect users' data as it flows across the companies' networks. A lack of trust surrounds the U.S. cloud industry. The NSA collects data through formal arrangements with tech companies, ingests web traffic as it enters and leaves the United States, and deliberately weakens cryptographic standards.

The solution, as we have espoused in this book, is to make the Web and cloud computing less centralized and more distributed. For privacy advocates such as Access Now (accessnow.org), the goal is to make it harder to do surveillance. When you couple a secure, self-hosted platform with properly implemented cryptography, you can make NSA-style spying and network intrusion difficult and expensive.

While the peer-to-peer technology that Bitcoin and Ethereum employ is not new, its implementation is a breakthrough technical achievement. The system's elegance has led some to wonder: if money can be decentralized and somewhat anonymized, can we use the same model for other applications such as storage, communications, and computing? We will explore this as the chapter proceeds, but bear in mind this would require time and effort and lots of change to the existing infrastructure. Since the World Wide Web went mainstream in 1994, we've seen the network expand to encompass almost every aspect of human life. The infrastructure of the Internet and the services built on top of it are dependent on each other, one informing the other as new service use cases and technologies arise. There have been two clear generations in the web-based services and structure of the Web thus far, but today we are moving into a third generation.

We will look at the storage technologies that are likely to form its backbone: the decentralized storage network IPFS—the InterPlanetary File System—and its incentive platform Filecoin, and Swarm, an emerging Ethereum-oriented storage platform that uses IPFS. We will also look at decentralized supercomputers like Golem that are creating a global market for computing power, and messaging systems like Whisper, which facilitates secure and decentralized communications. These technologies and others will become the foundation for a new Internet.

Web Versions 1 and 2

Web 1.0, an extension of DARPA's ARPANET, was the first iteration of a new idea—a return to centralization after the distributed client server idea failed. Just before the Web came into use in the Wall Street business center, personal computers used by businesses had a "fat client" distributed setup, in which each user had all the application code and data on their individual machine. The "fat client" became expensive and impractical to synchronize all these machines and data. So corporate intranets started to emerge with HTML and Java servlets leading the way to the Web 1.0 idea: if we can connect all the computers in the world through a global network—the Internet—then we can trade and exchange assets and for humanity's sake make the collective knowledge universally accessible. For this mass of data to be usable, it needed to be indexed and browsable. This necessity was behind the innovation that led to the first generation of the World Wide Web. The Netscape browser was the tool used to search, find, and render the response data.

Web 2.0 furthered the use of this global resource. The pool of knowledge and content began growing at an extreme pace. Surface net data has grown fourfold since 2012. Programs could connect and use the Web to store information and communicate with each other. Centralized intermediates, such as Google, created large databases and messaging, offering scalable resources and routing traffic. While these new information-handling organizations have changed our way of life with convenience services, they also use their centralized position for profit and power.

These centralized intermediates (like Google) sell context-sensitive targeted advertising for huge profits and give back nothing more than a convenient messaging interface to the users—the content producers. In their paper "Swap, Swear and Swindle: Incentive System for Swarm," Viktor Trón, Aron Fischer, Dániel A. Nagy, Zsolt Felföldi, and Nick Johnson characterized this as: "We give you scalable hosting that would cope with any traffic your audience throws at it, but you give us substantial control over your content; we are going to track each member of your audience and learn—and own—as much of their personal data as we can, we are going to pick who can and who cannot see it, we are going to proactively censor it and we may even report on you, for the same reason."

So the bottom line is that new media organizations and content producers created immense value for their organizations, and we the users receive less than a quid pro quo in exchange.

To further exacerbate the problem, as the Web has grown it has been hampered by scaling limits. Central nodes or servers required increased bandwidth to handle increasing data flow. To compound the problem, the security available using Web 2.0 technology never achieved a level required for the new communications and commerce services provided through the Web. We see data breaches where nefarious syndicates steal our financial access data using SQL and code injection and disable financial, retail, and government websites and their services with denial-of-service attacks which take down these centralized servers almost weekly. According to Juniper Research, "the rapid digitization of consumers' lives and enterprise records will increase the cost of data breaches to $2.1 trillion globally by 2019, increasing to almost four times the estimated cost of breaches in 2015." (https://www.juniperresearch.com/press/press-releases/cybercrime-cost-businesses-over-2trillion) The stage is set for a paradigm shift with a host of new technologies emerging.

Web 3.0

Following the trend set by earlier iterations, and to correct some of the issues we have described, Web 3.0 proposes a change in the way content and programs interact. If central intermediaries like Google are removed from the picture, many of the issues we have today are removed with them. Blockchain technologies like Bitcoin and Ethereum use public key cryptography to secure the connection and communication between programs and data. This is an alternative to the centrally issued SSL certificates used today. There is no central intermediary routing traffic, so connections can dynamically find the most efficient pathway through the Internet and route around congestion or damage. Additionally, for the coming Web 3.0 there is a debate about what is the proper definition of its characteristics. See Figure 3-1, which depicts the evolution of the Web, its actors, and components.

For some, Web 3.0 is powered by the semantic web, where people can access linked information fast and easily. According to Tim Berners-Lee's explanations, Web 3.0 would be a "read-write-execute" web. Let's take a look at two things that will form the basis of Web 3.0: semantic markup and web services. Semantic markup refers to the communication gap between human web users and computerized applications. One of the largest organizational challenges of presenting information on the Web was that web applications couldn't provide context to data and therefore didn't really understand what was relevant and what was not. While this is still evolving, this notion of formatting data to be understood by software agents leads to the "execute" portion of our definition and provides a way to discuss web service. A web service is

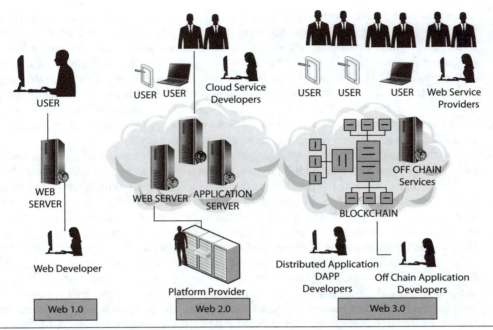

FIGURE 3-1 The evolution of the Web

a software system designed to support computer-to-computer interaction over the Internet. Web services are vendor agnostic. They are based on industry standards and can be interactive with all devices that can make service calls in standard APIs like SOAP or REST or any other emerging standard. The use and number of web services is trending up as it is a critical part of Web 3.0.

By combining a semantic markup and web services, Web 3.0 provides the potential for applications that can speak to each other directly and for broader searches for information through simpler interfaces. But now, with the emergence of a decentralized web powered by Blockchain technology, and since it enables unmediated transactions, there is a new focus on Web 3.0 based on the trustful nature of the blockchain. It is the "read-write-own" web. Here, the user owns and participates in owning the protocol. It is both peer-to-peer and machine-to-machine. And it is applicable to people, companies, and autonomous entities. For instance, the term Web 3.0 is used by Ethereum in a different context than that suggested by Berners-Lee. It is proposed as the separation of content from the presentation by removing the need to have servers at all. Stephan Tual, formerly Ethereum's CCO, defines that what makes Ethereum different from Web 2.0 is that "there are no web-servers, and therefore no middleman to take commissions, steal your data or offer it to the NSA, and of course nothing to DDoS." The transformation to blockchain distributed application (dapp) will happen over a period of years. The technology is currently unable to handle high-speed transactions for reasons discussed in later chapters.

Distributed Storage Systems

One of the fundamental open challenges for Web 3.0 is effective data storage. The socio-economic value and scale of information increases day by day, and Web 3.0 developers have been working to identify ways to ensure not only that digitally stored data endures but also that it is readily available, reliable, secure, and consistent. In recent years, the massive generation of data coupled with frequent storage failures has increased the popularity of distributed storage systems, which allow data to be replicated in different, geographically dispersed, storage devices. Due to the dissemination of data in multiple hosts, one of the major problems that distributed storage systems face is maintaining the consistency of data when they are accessed concurrently by multiple operations.

InterPlanetary File System

The InterPlanetary File System (IPFS) is a distributed file system that resulted from the evolution of prior peer-to-peer systems, including DHTs, BitTorrent, Git, and SFS. The contribution of IPFS is simplifying, evolving, and connecting proven techniques into a single cohesive system, greater than the sum of its parts (see https://ipfs.io/). IPFS presents a new platform for writing and deploying applications, and a new system for distributing and versioning large data. IPFS could even evolve the Web itself. IPFS is peer-to-peer; no nodes are privileged. IPFS nodes store IPFS objects in local storage. Described by Viktor Tron as "the Lego kit for the third web," IPFS is a new system for storing data on a large number of computers. It is transport layer agnostic, meaning that it can communicate through TCP, µTP, UDT, QUIC, TOR, and even Bluetooth. Instead of a central server, a peer-to-peer network is used to establish connections. IPFS implements a distributed hash table (DHT) that provides a lookup service similar to a hash table: (key, value) pairs are stored in a DHT, and any participating node can efficiently retrieve the value associated with a given key. Responsibility for maintaining the mapping from keys to values is distributed among the nodes in such a way that a change in the set of participants causes a minimal amount of disruption. This allows a DHT to scale to extremely large numbers of nodes and to handle continual node arrivals, departures, and failures.

IPFS Nodes

Nodes connect to each other and transfer objects. These objects represent files and other data structures. The IPFS protocol is divided into a stack of subprotocols responsible for different functionalities:

- Identities: Manage node identity generation and verification.
- Network: Manages connections to other peers, uses various underlying network protocols.
- Routing: Maintains information to locate specific peers and objects. Responds to both local and remote queries. Defaults to a DHT but is swappable.
- Exchange: A novel block exchange protocol (BitSwap) that governs efficient block distribution. Modeled as a market, weakly incentivizes data replication.

- Objects: A Merkle DAG of content-addressed immutable objects with links. Used to represent arbitrary data structures, such as file hierarchies and communications systems.
- Files: Versioned file system hierarchy inspired by Git.
- Naming: A self-certifying mutable name system.
- Applications can run over the Internet and leverage the principles and features of IPFS to create a web of Merkle links connecting data (objects and blocks) for business applications.

These subsystems are not independent; they are integrated and leverage-blended properties. However, it is useful to describe them separately, building the protocol stack from the bottom up.

Public key cryptography is built into the node addressing system, and content addressing is used to index content. Both node and content addresses are stored in a decentralized naming system called IPNS. Nodes in the peer-to-peer network each hold private keys and release public keys, just like in Bitcoin or Ethereum. Node addresses are derived through hashing their public keys. This allows connection verification through message signing. Their public keys can be used to encrypt data before it is transferred, preventing interception and theft. Solutions to today's security issues are built into this addressing system. There is no need for a trusted central certificate issuer to provide connection verification tools, and all connections can easily be encrypted by default.

IPFS Content Addressing

A content address is derived by hashing a piece of content. That content address is then hashed again to derive a key name (see Figure 3-2). The key name is associated with a human readable name in IPNS (the IPFS address registry). Today, if a file is moved, all links to that file need to be updated if they are to resolve. Because IPFS addresses are derived from the content they refer to, if the content still exists anywhere on the network, links will always resolve. This removes any need for duplication of content, except for the purposes of greater persistence security or for scaling up serving capabilities. So how do we grow a decentralized storage system to replace the current model? We need a way to incentivize the storage and serving of content. Filecoin is one prospective solution being developed by Protocol Labs. Swarm is another being developed by the Ethereum foundation. Both projects make use of IPFS technology but have different philosophies on how to incentivize participation.

So, as mentioned, IPFS creates a P2P swarm that allows the exchange of IPFS objects. The totality of IPFS objects forms a cryptographically authenticated data structure known as a Merkle DAG, and this data structure can be used to model many other data structures. We will introduce IPFS objects and the Merkle DAG and give examples of structures that can be modeled using IPFS.

IPFS Objects

An IPFS object is a data structure with two fields:

- Data: A blob of unstructured binary data of size less than or equal to 256 kB.
- Links: An array of link structures. These are links to other IPFS objects.

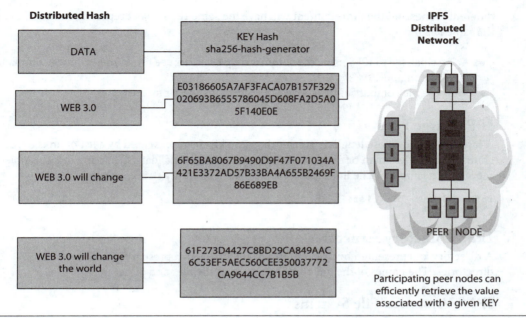

FIGURE 3-2   **Distributed hash table with content address derived by hashing content**

A link structure has three data fields:

- Name: The name of the link
- Hash: The hash of the linked IPFS object
- Size: The cumulative size of the linked IPFS object, including following its links

The Size field is mainly used for optimizing the P2P networking, and we're going to mostly ignore it here, since conceptually it's not needed for the logical structure.

IPFS objects are normally referred to by their Base58 encoded hash. All hashes begin with "Qm". This is because the hash is a multihash, meaning that the hash itself specifies the hash function and length of the hash in the first two bytes of the multihash. The data and named links give the collection of IPFS objects the structure of a Merkle directed acyclic graph (DAG) to signify that this is a cryptographically authenticated data structure that, as we noted above, uses cryptographic hashes to address content. Visualize an IPFS object by a graph with data in the node and the links being directed graph edges to other IPFS objects, where the name of the link is a label on the graph edge. Various data structures can be represented by IPFS objects, for example, a file system. IPFS can easily represent a file system consisting of files and directories.

IPFS Small Files

A small file—one whose length is less than or equal to 256 kB—is represented by an IPFS object with data being the file contents (plus a small header and footer) and no links (that is, the links array is empty). Note that the file name is not part of the IPFS object, so two files with different names and the same content will have the same IPFS object representation and hence the same hash.

- Add a small file to IPFS using the command `ipfs add`; see https://ipfs.io/docs/commands/ for all commands.
- View the file contents of the above IPFS object using `ipfs cat`.

IPFS Large Files

A large file—one whose length is greater than 256 kB—is represented by a list of links to file chunks that are less than or equal to 256 kB, and only minimal data specifying that this object represents a large file. The links to the file chunks have empty strings as names.

```
ipfs add ucny_dir/bigfile.js
```

IPFS Directory Structures

A directory is represented by a list of links to IPFS objects representing files or other directories. The names of the links are the names of the files and directories.

IPFS Versioned File Systems

IPFS can represent the data structures used by Git to allow for versioned file systems. The Git commit objects are described in the Git Book. The main properties of the commit object are that it has (like any good source control tool) one or more links with names parent0, parent1, etc., pointing to previous commits, and one link with a name object (this is called tree in Git) that points to the file system structure referenced by that commit.

IPFS Blockchains

So now for the most important use case for IPFS. A blockchain has a natural DAG structure in that past blocks are always linked by their hash from later ones. More advanced blockchains like the Ethereum blockchain also have an associated state database which has a tree structure that also can be emulated using IPFS objects.

As we saw in Chapter 1, in a simplistic model of a blockchain each block contains the following data:

- A list of transaction objects
- A link to the previous block
- The hash of a state tree/database

This blockchain can then be modeled in IPFS as shown in Figure 3-3.

Swarm

Swarm is a distributed storage platform and content distribution service, a native base layer service of the Ethereum web3 stack. The primary objective of Swarm is to provide a decentralized and redundant store of Ethereum's public record, in particular to store and

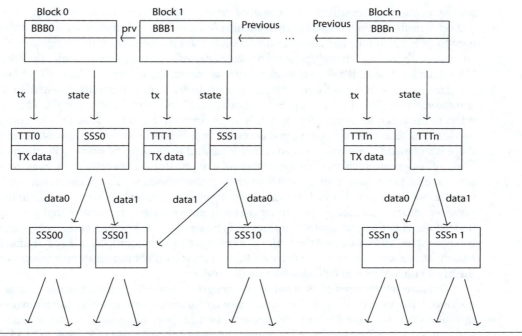

FIGURE 3-3 **Blockchain model**

distribute distributed application code (dapp) and data as well as blockchain data. Swarm and IPFS both offer comprehensive solutions for efficient decentralized storage layers for the next-generation Internet. Both high-level goals and the technology used are very similar. As a result both are well suited for replacing the data layer of the current Web 2.0. They both serve as storage layers for the Web 3.0 vision with all the required properties of distributed document storage:

- Low-latency retrieval
- Efficient auto-scaling (content caching)
- Reliable, fault-tolerant operation, resistant to node disconnections, intermittent availability
- Zero downtime
- Censorship resistant
- Potentially permanent versioned archive of content

Swarm's core storage component is an immutable content addressed chunk store rather than a generic distributed hash, i.e., DHT. As previously shown in Figure 3-2, IPFS uses DHT. IPFS and Swarm use different network communications layers and peer management protocols. Swarm has deep integration with the Ethereum blockchain, and the incentive system benefits from both smart contracts as well as the semi-stable peer pool, while Filecoin uses proof of retrievability as part of mining. The consequences of these choices are far reaching. So to continue, from the end user's perspective, Swarm is not that different from Web 2.0, except that uploads are not to a specific server. The objective is to create a peer-to-peer storage and serving solution that has the mentioned attributes such as denial-of-service resistant, zero downtime, fault tolerant, and censorship resistant as well as self-sustaining due to a built-in incentive system that uses peer-to-peer accounting and allows trading resources for payment. Swarm is designed to deeply integrate with the devp2p multiprotocol network layer of Ethereum as well as with the Ethereum blockchain for domain name resolution, service payments, and content availability insurance.

Two major features of Swarm that set it apart from other decentralized distributed storage solutions like IPFS are "upload and disappear" and the incentive system. The former refers to the fact that Swarm does not only serve content, it also provides a cloud storage service. Unlike in related systems, you do not only publish the fact that you host content, but there is a genuine sense that you can just upload stuff to Swarm and potentially disappear (drop off as a node, disconnect, or just operate without storage entirely) right away. Swarm aspires to be the generic storage and delivery service catering for all use cases ranging from serving low-latency real-time interactive web applications as well as acting as guaranteed persistent storage for rarely used content. The incentive system makes sure that participating nodes following their rational self-interest nonetheless converge on an emergent Swarm behavior that is beneficial for the entire system as well as economically self-sustaining. In particular, it allows nodes in the network to pool their bandwidth and storage resources in the most efficient way to collectively provide services.

The planned features of Swarm include integrity protection, random access (range queries), URL-based addressing, manifest-based routing on virtual hosts, domain name resolution via Ethereum Name Service, encryption support, plausible deniability, bandwidth and storage incentives, associated metadata, on-demand download of Ethereum blockchain state/receipts/contract-storage, auto-scaling by popularity (elastic cloud), auto-syncing, client side configurable redundancy/availability. A swarm-based Internet needs to provide solutions for web3 use cases with decentralized infrastructure, so broadly speaking, it is a project toward the ambitious goal of building the third web in the ethersphere.

Swarm was conceived of as a storage protocol tailored for interoperation with the Ethereum smart contract ecosystem. Like Filecoin, it will piggyback on Ethereum's consensus process in order to provide a decentralized alternative to our existing client/server infrastructure. Incentivizing persistent storage is a challenge, however. The downside of a node deleting data and losing some income is potentially much less significant than a user losing his or her valuable data. Swarm takes the approach of rewarding nodes for serving content. Because more often requested content is more profitable to store than rarely requested content, rewarding nodes only for recall would incentivize the trashing of rarely accessed data. Failure to store every last piece of a large data set can result in the entire set being rendered useless, so in these cases a solution must exist to balance this downside asymmetry.

Using content recall as the base reward mechanism and distributing content randomly among nodes, weighted for location, puts Swarm in a good place to start solving the persistence problem:

- Nodes offering "promissory" storage, or storage with a promise of persistence, must first post a security deposit covering the time for which they are offering storage.
- If data is lost during this period, the bond is forfeited.
- The smart contract infrastructure of Ethereum automates this whole process, making the "upload and forget" experience seamless.

Storj

Storj is a protocol that creates a distributed network for the formation and execution of storage contracts between peers. The Storj protocol enables peers on the network to negotiate contracts, transfer data, verify the integrity and availability of remote data, retrieve data, and pay other nodes. Each peer is an autonomous agent, capable of performing these actions without significant human interaction. In Storj, files are stored as encrypted shards. Sharding is a type of database partitioning that separates very large databases into smaller, faster, more easily managed parts called data shards. The word *shard* means a small part of a whole. So a shard is a portion of an encrypted file to be stored on this network. Sharding has a number of advantages to security, privacy, performance, and availability. Files should be encrypted client-side before being sharded. The reference implementation uses AES256-CTR, but convergent encryption or any other desirable system could be implemented. This protects the content of the data from the storage provider, or farmer, housing the data. The data owner retains complete control over the encryption key and thus over access to the data. The data owner may separately secure knowledge of how a file is sharded and where in the network the shards are located. As the set of shards in the network grows, it becomes exponentially more difficult to locate any given shard set without prior knowledge of their locations. This implies that security of the file is proportional to the square of the size of the network. Shard size is a negotiable contract parameter. To preserve privacy, it is recommended that shard sizes be standardized as a byte multiple, such as 8 or 32 MB. Smaller files may be filled with zeroes or random data.

Storj uses hash chains or Merkle trees, as they are sometimes called, to verify the contents of a file after it has been broken up into blocks or "leaves" off a master or root hash (see Figure 3-4).

Standardized sizes dissuade side-channel attempts to determine the content of a given shard and can mask the flow of shards through the network. Sharding large files such as video content and distributing the shards across nodes reduces the impact of content delivery on any given node. Bandwidth demands are distributed more evenly across the network. In addition, the end user can take advantage of parallel transfer, similar to BitTorrent or other peer-to-peer networks. Because peers generally rely on separate hardware and infrastructure, data failure is not correlated. This implies that creating redundant mirrors of shards, or applying a parity

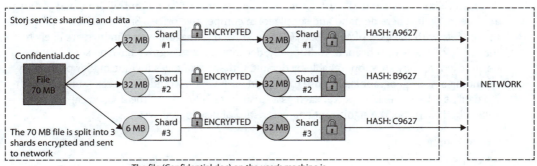

The file (Confidential.doc) on the user's machine is
protected before it is sent to the network storage provider

FIGURE 3-4 Storj service sharding and data transfer

scheme across the set of shards, is an extremely effective method of securing availability. Availability is proportional to the number of nodes storing the data. So, to summarize Storj:

- Files are encrypted.
- Encrypted files are split into shards, or multiple files are combined to form a shard.
- Audit preprocessing is performed for each shard.
- Shards may be transmitted to the network.

Decentralized storage services like Storj will most certainly evolve. They provide a peer-to-peer network that would "rent" unused capacity from a computer's hard drive as part of a cloud service to store files from other users. They will meet the Web 3.0 challenge to provide effective, available, reliable, secure, and consistent data storage.

Distributed Computation

Distributed computing is the science that studies and seeks to evolve the distributed systems model. In this growing paradigm, components located on networked computers/nodes communicate and coordinate their actions. These components interact with each other to achieve a common goal. As early as 1977, computer scientists like Gérard Le Lann described how networked distributed computing components could "solve user problems more satisfactorily … than centralized servers." (https://www.rocq.inria.fr/novaltis/publications/IFIP%20Congress%201977.pdf)

These days we are on the threshold of yet another revolutionary paradigm shift of supercomputers. As we have seen, blockchain technology allows developers to consider yet again reducing the price of high-performance computing services and making supercomputers—that is, networked computers—more accessible. A new model for decentralized clouds is a classic example of shared economy: the idea is about gathering users in a global peer-to-peer network where every machine acts as a provider of computation services by offering a part of its idling capacities. This distributed systems model promises a breakthrough for the industry coupled with profit for each user. Most of us do not even use half of our computers' capacities. By connecting these idle capacities to a network, users will be able to make money with their unused computing resources. Those who lease computing resources will also gain advantages in decentralized services. First, the service will be less expensive. Decentralized cloud platforms are free markets where demand and supply form competitive prices. Such services will be able to compete with the likes of Microsoft, Google, IBM, or Amazon, which in turn are likely to make relevant services cheaper. Additionally, decentralized structures have no single center to be attacked, so they are more reliable by default. Other advantages include higher probability of finding a node geographically close to the end user, which would also accelerate work with big data. It also may ensure power savings as distributed clouds use the unused capacities of subscribed users. So, the significant characteristics of distributed systems are:

- Resource sharing
- Openness
- Concurrency
- Scalability
- Fault tolerance
- Transparency

Golem

As we have been discussing, a supercomputer is a computer that performs at or near the currently highest operational rate for computers. The first supercomputers that were not networked emerged in the 1960s. They were unique monolith devices extremely powerful for their time and equally expensive. These supercomputers were used for scientific and engineering applications that handled large databases or performed a great amount of computation. Popular among supercomputers are traditional processors, interconnected and installed in given locations with the task of solving specific data problems. Examples of the top supercomputers in the world include:

- Jaguar, located at the Department of Energy's Oak Ridge Leadership Computing Facility in Tennessee (https://www.olcf.ornl.gov/).
- Nebulae, located at the National Supercomputing Centre in Shenzhen, China.
- Kraken, situated at the National Institute for Computational Sciences (NICS). The NICS is a partnership with the University of Tennessee and Oak Ridge National Lab.

  (www.datacenterknowledge.com/the-top-five-supercomputers-illustrated/)

With the emergence of decentralized technology, the design and installation of supercomputers appear to have shifted gears. Some engineers describe the decentralized supercomputer as "fog computing," where the fog exists in the singular. Fog computing can solve some of the most challenging tasks of humanity by joining the powers of personal computers, laptops, and even smartphones. Scientific calculations of any difficulty can be performed quite fast due to the opportunities fog computing provides. Solutions offered by decentralized supercomputers include the generous availability of processing power, uninterrupted uptime, and economic incentives.

Golem is touted as the first truly decentralized supercomputer, creating a global market for computing power. Combined with flexible tools to aid developers in securely distributing and monetizing their software, Golem hopes to change the way computer tasks are organized and executed. By powering decentralized microservices and asynchronous task execution, Golem is set to become a key building block for future Internet service providers and software development. By substantially lowering the price of computations, complex applications such as CGI rendering, scientific calculation, and machine learning become more accessible to everyone. Golem connects computers in a peer-to-peer network, enabling both application owners and individual users ("requestors") to rent resources of other users' ("providers") machines. These resources can be used to complete tasks requiring any amount of computation time and capacity. Today, such resources are supplied by centralized cloud providers which are constrained by closed networks, proprietary payment systems, and hard-coded provisioning operations. Core to Golem's built-in feature set is a dedicated Ethereum-based transaction system, which enables direct payments between requestors, providers, and software developers. The function of Golem as the backbone of a decentralized market for computing power can be considered both Infrastructure-as-a-Service (IaaS) as well as Platform-as-a-Service (PaaS). However, Golem's true potential may be adding dedicated software integrations to the equation. Any interested party is free to create and deploy software to the Golem network by publishing it to the application registry. Together with the transaction framework, developers can also extend and customize the payment mechanism, resulting in unique mechanisms for monetizing software. GNT (Golem Network Tokens) are Ethereum-based tokens used to fuel the Golem platform. The Golem supercomputers run when the user pays GNT tokens. These tokens are given to people who have rented out their extra computing power on the Golem network. GNT's coin supply is fixed, which means as the project becomes more popular, the price of GNT will likely increase (see Figure 3-5).

Zennet

Comparable to the Golem project is Zennet (zennet.sc), According to its founder, software engineer Ohad Asor, Zennet is a distributed supercomputing project that will use blockchain technology to remove the central administrators from the problem. Computation power is traded on Zennet's open market platform. Anyone can rent computation power and use it to run arbitrary tasks. Anyone can monetize their hardware by offering unused computation power for sale. Zennet allows "publishers" (those who need computation power) to run arbitrary computational tasks. Computation power is supplied by "providers" for a negotiated fee. A free-market infrastructure brings publishers and providers together. Publishers can

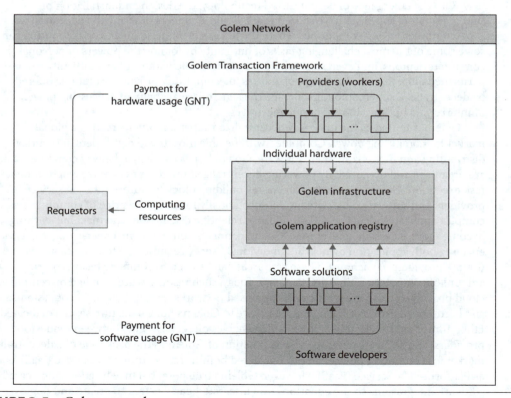

FIGURE 3-5   Golem network

hire many computers and run whatever they want on them safely, thanks to cutting-edge virtualization technology. Payment is continuous and frictionless, thanks to Blockchain technology. The network is 100 percent distributed and decentralized: there is no central entity of any kind, just like Bitcoin. All software will be open source. Publishers pay providers directly; there is no middleman. Accordingly, there are no payable commissions, except for regular transaction fees that are being paid to Xencoin miners. It is a totally free market: all participants are free to pay or charge by any rate they want. There are no restrictions. Hence, projects like Zennet put additional focus on customizability. Zennet allows advanced participants to control all parameters and conditions of their nodes in a versatile way. On the other hand, simplicity and automation are made possible by making the client software implement automatic risk-reward considerations by default.

Decentralized Communications

The decentralized communications model enables natively interoperable communications services that can trustfully use peer-to-peer connections without having to use central authorities or services. A wide range of distributed applications require confidential communication between users. The messages exchanged between the users and the identity of group members should not be visible to external observers. Classical approaches to confidential group communication rely upon centralized servers, which limit scalability and represent single points of failure. The use of confidential communication between a group of distributed entities is at the core of many applications. Examples include private chat rooms in social networks, information-sharing systems guaranteeing freedom of speech, control-flow and admission-control for pay-per view live streaming, distributed content indexes that should not be made public to prevent attacks, etc. The confidentiality of the messages exchanged between the members of a private group is typically achieved using encrypted channels that prevent malevolent parties from spying on the exchanged content. However, content encryption alone is insufficient for many of the applications mentioned above, which also require that the composition of the group remain secret—that is, one should not be able to determine whether a node belongs to a group. The existence of the group itself can also be hidden from unauthorized parties.

Computer networks typically use centralized solutions for supporting private group communication, such as by relying on dedicated servers. Virtual private networks (VPNs) allow nodes to create private communication channels with encrypted traffic. Group communication can leverage VPNs, for instance, as part of a multisite company infrastructure, with all communications between sites being routed through some VPN gateways. In large-scale dynamic settings, where sizable populations of nodes are interconnected in self-organizing and often loosely structured overlays, the use of VPN-based solutions is inadequate for implementing private group communications. The problem is that VPN gateways act as single points of failure. For this reason, they forfeit one of the major benefits of decentralized systems: their robustness to targeted attacks such as denial-of-service attacks. As soon as the attackers know the gateway, it is straightforward to disrupt communications within the private group by concentrating the attacks on the gateway. Further disadvantages of solutions based on VPNs or dedicated servers include their scalability to large numbers of users, their price, and their operating costs.

We should point out that these approaches do not keep the membership of private groups hidden from malevolent nodes; only the content of exchanged messages is protected. The process of hiding the communication partners, and hence the identity of the members of the group, must be provided by anonymizing systems such as The Onion Router (TOR). These systems rely on a set of dedicated servers that conceal the source of the message from the destination, typically using onion routing mechanisms. Here again, the cost of provisioning such a system with sufficiently many dedicated servers can be a hindrance in large-scale self-organizing networks. These observations make the case for a fully decentralized, autonomous, and self-organizing service to support confidential communications within groups of nodes in large-scale systems. Unlike existing approaches, this service should let private groups be created by ordinary nodes and emerge within the network, without relying on dedicated and trusted third-party servers. At the same time, it must hide communications between the members of a private group from the other nodes (content privacy), as well as keep the group memberships secret to external observers (membership privacy). This latter point is especially important, as it is impossible for an attacker to focus an attack on the members of a group without being able to determine their identity.

Existing Decentralized Communications

Bitmessage (bitmessage.org) is a peer-to-peer communications protocol used to send encrypted messages to another person or to many subscribers. It is decentralized and trustless, meaning that you need not inherently trust any entities such as root certificate authorities. It uses strong authentication, which means that the sender of a message cannot be spoofed, and it aims to hide "non-content" data, like the sender and receiver of messages, from passive eavesdroppers such as those running warrantless wiretapping programs. Bitmessage works by encrypting all the incoming and outgoing messages using public-key cryptography so that only the receiver of the message is capable of decrypting it. In order to achieve anonymity, Bitmessage replicates all the messages inside its own anonymous P2P network, therefore mixing all the encrypted messages of a given user with all the encrypted messages of all other users of the network, thus making it difficult to track which particular computer is the actual originator of the message and which computer is the recipient of the message.

Telehash (telehash.org) is a peer-to-peer data distribution and communications protocol that is designed to be decentralized and secure. The protocol is licensed under the Creative Commons public domain. Telehash is like BitTorrent Sync in that it allows users of the software to share data securely without any central server authority. There are implementations in C, Python, Ruby, Erlang, JavaScript, Go, and Objective-C. Similar in approach to BitTorrent, it routes to the recipient given its hash. Telehash uses DHT to do deterministic routing, therefore it may not be secure against simple statistical packet-analysis attacks.

Whisper

Whisper is fully decentralized middleware that supports confidential communications within groups of nodes in large-scale systems. (See "Whisper: Middleware for Confidential Communication in Large-Scale Networks" by Valerio Schiavoni, Etienne Rivière, and Pascal Felber.) Whisper builds upon a peer sampling service that takes into account network limitations such as network address translation (NAT) and firewalls. Whisper is a part of the Ethereum P2P protocol suite that allows for messaging between users via the same network on which the blockchain runs.

Some dapp use cases include:

- Dapps that need to publish small amounts of information to each other and have the publication last some substantial amount of time. For example, a currency exchange dapp may use it to record an offer to sell some currency at a particular rate on an exchange. In this case, it may last anywhere between tens of minutes to days. The offer wouldn't be binding, merely a hint to get a potential deal started.
- Dapps that need to signal to each other in order to ultimately collaborate on a transaction. For example, a currency exchange dapp may use it to coordinate an offer prior to creating transactions on the exchange.
- Dapps that need to provide non-real-time hinting or general communication between each other.
- Dapps that need to provide dark communication to two correspondents that know nothing of each other but a hash. This could be a dapp for a whistleblower to communicate to a known journalist exchange some small amount of verifiable material and arrange between themselves for some other protocol to handle the bulk transfer.

The Whisper architecture (see Figure 3-6) is a combination of layers. The Whisper communication layer (WCL) operates on top of the NAT-aware peer sampling services (PSS). It allows confidential communication between peers by protecting both exchanged content and relationship anonymity. This is still true even when relays should be employed for bypassing NAT limitations.

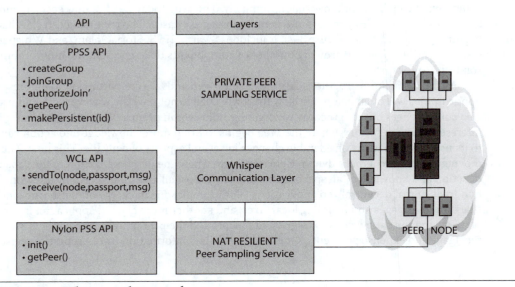

FIGURE 3-6   **Whisper architecture layers**

The private peer sampling service (PPSS) operates on top of the WCL. It provides the services of a PSS: it acts as a provider of a private view of live peers for the applications operating in the private group. It leverages the WCL to guarantee that communications with any node in the private view will remain strictly confidential. The PPSS also deals with group management and membership authentication, and ensures that confidential connections between peers can be maintained even when the destination node no longer belongs to the view of the source node. Whisper targets large-scale, Internet-wide networked systems in which a large majority of nodes reside behind NAT devices or firewalls. The Whisper algorithms exploit peer sampling as an underlying approach for organizing nodes in the network in a fully decentralized and autonomous manner. Whisper considers malevolent nodes that spy upon other nodes in the system, but that follow the protocol specification and do not exhibit other byzantine behavior.

Whisper implements confidentiality in two ways: it protects the content of messages exchanged between the members of a group, and it keeps the group memberships secret to external observers. Using multi-hop paths allows these guarantees to hold even if attackers can observe the link between two nodes or be used as content relays for NAT bypassing. Whisper supports the creation of confidential communication routes without the need for a trusted third party. It additionally provides membership management and overlay maintenance among private groups of nodes communicating in a confidential manner. Evaluation of Whisper in real-world settings indicates that the price of confidentiality remains reasonable in terms of network load and processing costs.

Summary

In this chapter, we introduced some of the components of the Web 3.0 architecture, including distributed networking and storage that are happening now and promise solutions that could save the global economy trillions annually. The Web today needs a new security model and an architecture designed around contemporary use cases. The technology stack is just beginning to emerge (see Figure 3-7). It includes Swarm, IPFS, Storj, Golem, and Whisper, just to mention a few of a growing number of components that represent the most ambitious solutions to this problem.

As the global infrastructure adapts to the new demands we are putting on it, unforeseen opportunities will open before us. New tools will change not only the way we work and use web conveniences but also the way we organize ourselves in groups. We are living in an interesting time in history, where the Web begins to bring more knowledge and action capacity to its users, resulting in considerable changes in several aspects of daily life. This new Web is moving fast toward a more dynamic environment, where the democratization of the capacity of action and knowledge can speed up business in almost all areas. Imagine a future with hundreds of real decentralized applications—for example, one in charge of registering land titles and mortgages and handling local taxes, and another more general application in charge of managing the supply chain of registered tenants and their monthly lease payments as well as mortgage and expense payments. One could easily link information from properties registered

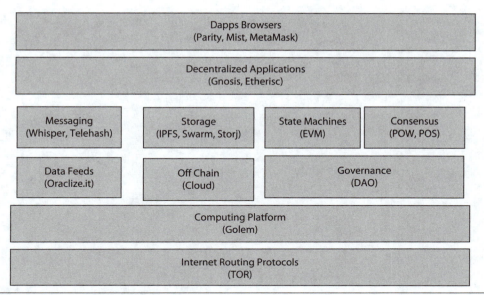

FIGURE 3-7   Web 3.0 technology stack

in the first application with tenants and their use of the properties registered in the second application. All this in an easy way, using the whole stack of semantic web technology and—something that is not possible to date—ensuring that all data is 100 percent true, guaranteed by the smart contracts. The real questions we must ask are: How will the world of Web 3.0 differ from the world of Web 2.0? How will this technology penetrate beyond the cultures that created it? One thing is for sure: the blockchain will be at the center of this new world.

4   Legal and Governance Use Cases

The legal industry will also be transformed and disrupted by blockchain technology and the associated scripting language and protocols known as *smart contracts*. As we have seen, this technology is already affecting the banking, financial services, and payments industries. They implement blockchain to facilitate transactions, save on fees, and approach instantaneous clearing of transactions. The fintech movement, which has embraced blockchain, is always looking to disrupt traditional banking models and the software that supports it to deliver increased convenience, efficiency for service consumers, reduced risk, and of course lower cost of operations for financial services providers. For too long, lawyers have been slow to adopt new technologies. This is all changing; lawyers need to understand how to communicate securely and protect their client data. In particular, they need to understand blockchain and smart contracts. The New York County Law Association as well as many bar associations nationwide provides legal technology education so their members can avoid potentially being at odds with the new American Bar Association (ABA) rules. ABA Model Rule 1.1, Comment 8 says:

> "To maintain the requisite knowledge and skill, a lawyer should keep abreast of changes in the law and its practice, including the benefits and risks associated with relevant technology, engage in continuing study and education and comply with all continuing legal education requirements to which the lawyer is subject."

Only recently, in response to demand and new standards, have lawyers started to use and rely on computing and communications tools. For example, e-discovery software is now a standard used to search email, documents, and other artifacts in the litigation discovery process. This process as well as other legal procedures would be facilitated with blockchain, which is an immutable and virtually infinite log. Blockchain when it is universally accepted will obviate most evidentiary issues. One question is how to treat blockchain data as evidence. In the U.S. judicial system, the standard for admissibility of evidence turns on whether a human has sworn under penalty of perjury that the information is true.

Stand-alone documentary evidence is usually not admitted. It's hearsay, "an out-of-court statement offered to prove the truth of the matter asserted." For example, to submit evidence from government or other sources, we produce the artifact and attach an affidavit to attest that the artifact was kept in the usual course of business and that the information in the artifact is true, to the best of the custodian's knowledge. Blockchain technology, an immutable log of events, will change the evidentiary rules. When we mature the technology both functionally and legally, blockchain can create a more efficient documentary evidence standard.

That said, law firms also are relatively weak in terms of information governance. Recent data break-ins at large law firms have resulted in stolen client information. Blockchain provides for use cases that can secure the information held in large law firms, especially contracts and other very confidential information. Futurists and technology vendors have already created the vision for how blockchain will change the way lawyers operate.

To put this in context, Janet Yellen, chair of the U.S. Federal Reserve at the time of this writing, recently said: "[blockchain] could have very significant implications for the payments system and the conduct of business [...]. I think innovation using these technologies could be extremely helpful and bring benefits to society." (See www.thinkconsortium.com/ on the topic "Think Consortium Blockchain, 2017 Outlook: Blockchain Impacts on Enterprise and Government.")

The *Harvard Business Review* in February 2017 had some thought-provoking insights:

> "Contracts, transactions and the records of them are among the defining structures in our economic, legal and political systems. They protect assets and set organizational boundaries. They establish and verify identities and chronological events. They govern interactions among nations, organizations, communities and individuals. They guide managerial and social action. And yet these critical tools and the bureaucracies formed to manage them have not kept up with the economy's digital transformation. They're like a rush-hour gridlock trapping a Formula 1 race car. In a digital world, the way we regulate and maintain administrative control has to change." (See https://hbr.org/2017/01/the-truth-about-blockchain.)

Blockchain Changes the Legal Landscape

"Code is law," as described in Lawrence Lessig's book *Code and Other Laws of Cyberspace*, refers to the idea that computer code has progressively established itself as a predominant way to regulate behavior to the same degree as legal code. (See updates to these ideas on http://codev2.cc//.) With the advent of blockchain technology, code is assuming an even stronger role in regulating people's interactions. However, while computer code can enforce rules more efficiently than legal code, it also comes with a series of limitations. With vast regulatory implications, blockchain applications have already raised many legal questions as they offer new capabilities to engage activities in ways that don't fit neatly into existing legal frameworks. Let's drill down and examine blockchain and its varied intersections with the law.

Cryptocurrencies as Legal Tender

Bitcoin, the world's most recognizable digital currency, uses encryption techniques to regulate the generation of units of currency and verify the transfer of funds, operating independently of a central bank. This means that this money has not passed through a bank or other financial institution, nor has it been screened by any government agency. If you have a major transaction that is normally required to be reported, it simply isn't. This leads to significant challenges, mostly concerning government regulators and current laws. As developers, it is important to at least be aware of this changing landscape.

As of late 2017, lots of new laws and regulations are being proposed and may be in place soon. That said, Bitcoin's "monetary policy" is written into its code: New money is mined and issued every 10 minutes. The supply is limited, and a hard money rule similar to the gold standard is applied, i.e., the money supply is fixed to a commodity and not determined by government. In the United States, bitcoin is deemed a commodity as per the Commodity Futures Trading Commission (CFTC) (see www.cftc.gov/). The CFTC has jurisdiction over local bitcoin exchanges. For the first time ever, the CFTC has given permission to a private company to exchange and clear any number of cryptocurrency derivatives. The New York–based startup LedgerX was granted a derivatives clearing organization (DCO) license allowing it to clear and provide custodian services for financial instruments backed by bitcoin, ether, and any number of blockchain-based cryptocurrencies.

Whether or not it's a currency under certain legislation might determine whether bitcoin transactions can be taxed (see www.irs.gov/pub/irs-drop/n-14-21.pdf). When it comes to taxes, the Internal Revenue Service has ruled that bitcoins and other "convertible virtual currencies" are "treated as property" and not treated as currency. According to the IRS, virtual currencies are property for tax purposes:

- There is capital gain or loss when disposing of virtual currency.
- Income is taxable, even if you are paid in virtual currency.
- Spending virtual currency is really two transactions in one: disposing of the virtual currency and spending the dollar-equivalent amount.
- Business transactions in bitcoin are subject to all the normal rules for sales tax, withholding, and information reporting.

The IRS definitions around virtual currency are:

- "Virtual currency is a digital representation of value that functions as a medium of exchange, a unit of account, and/or a store of value."
- Virtual currency "does not have legal tender status in any jurisdiction."
- "Virtual currency that has an equivalent value in real currency, or that acts as a substitute for real currency, is referred to as 'convertible' virtual currency."
- "Bitcoin is one example of a convertible virtual currency."
- "Bitcoin can be digitally traded between users and can be purchased for, or exchanged into, U.S. dollars, Euros, and other real or virtual currencies."

IRS tax treatment around virtual currency is:

- "For federal tax purposes, virtual currency is treated as property. General tax principles applicable to property transactions apply to transactions using virtual currency."
- "A taxpayer who receives virtual currency as payment for goods or services must, in computing gross income, include the fair market value of the virtual currency, measured in U.S. dollars, as of the date that the virtual currency was received."

- "Transactions using virtual currency must be reported in U.S. dollars" on the tax return.
- "Taxpayers will be required to determine the fair market value of virtual currency in U.S. dollars as of the date of payment or receipt."
- "If a virtual currency is listed on an exchange and the exchange rate is established by market supply and demand, the fair market value of the virtual currency is determined by converting the virtual currency into U.S. dollars . . . at the exchange rate, in a reasonable manner that is consistently applied."

At the state level, senators in Nevada have unanimously backed a proposal that would block local authorities from instituting taxes or fees on blockchain use (see www.coindesk .com/nevada-senators-blockchain-tax-ban/).

With respect to money laundering and other illegal monetary transactions, Bitcoin's blockchain has remained somewhat resilient to attack, and it supports a robust payment system. But this doesn't mean the people using this technology are always upstanding citizens. Blockchain actions are automated and fall outside of human legal action. So, despite their incentive structure flaws, mining pools account for more than 95 percent of Bitcoin's computation power. An adversary with a tiny amount of computing power and capital can execute an attack against mining pools in which a malicious party pays pool members to withhold their solutions from their pool operator (see https://eprint.iacr.org/2017/230.pdf).

In 2013, regulatory bodies responsible for preventing financial crimes introduced new regulations to bring Bitcoin within the scope of its enforcement. In 2013, 22 Bitcoin companies and investors were subpoenaed by the New York Department of Financial Services (NYDFS), culminating in federal agents shutting down their operations. The Silk Road (see https://silkroaddrugs.org/) also created a "Bitcoin is for criminals" narrative. The Silk Road illegal marketplace was accessible only via the "dark web," an anonymous network that requires specialized software to use, such as the Tor browser. As Silk Road grew in popularity, so did recognition that bitcoins could be used for illicit activity, and so did the government's interest in it. The government shut down Silk Road and many other bitcoin operations.

Lawmakers in West Virginia have deemed it a felony to use bitcoins or other cryptocurrencies for money laundering, with an update to the state's anti–money laundering (AML) statutes. The law specifically created a definition for cryptocurrency that is recognized as a "monetary instrument" in the state. Striking the right balance in these new regulations to promote growth but stifle illegal activity is a continuing challenge. See the Uniform Regulation of Virtual-Currency Businesses Act (www.uniformlaws.org/), which will give you an idea of how many of these challenges there are.

As mentioned, one of the key innovations of Bitcoin and other virtual currencies is the ability to transact pseudonymously. Most virtual currency transactions do not require the transacting parties to know each other, meet face-to-face, or directly interact to exchange value. Florida House Bill 1379 (flsenate.gov/Session/Bill/2017/01379) defines virtual currency and prohibits its use in laundering criminal proceeds. The bill adds the term "virtual currency" to the definition of "monetary instruments" under Florida's Money Laundering Act. The act defines digital currency as a "medium of exchange in electronic or digital format that is not a coin or currency of the United States or any other country." Previously, the act only applied money laundering to legacy financial transactions of various types, including bank deposits, investments, and wire transfers. The resulting outcome is that criminals using cryptocurrencies will be charged with money laundering as well as the underlying criminal activity. In most countries, financial services need to comply with rules pertaining to "know your customer" (KYC) and AML. Over time, blockchains and various new payment networks will not be exempt from such requirements. As such, some countries have severely restricted or even banned cryptocurrencies.

Blockchain and Privacy Laws

Blockchain, like any formal ledger, will become the official record for tracking the history and validity of transactions and other information. That record will effectively be visible to all, even though individual elements of the transactions are encrypted and not publicly visible. Here, the division of what information is public and what is private on a blockchain is especially interesting.

For example, your passport or other identity information might be securely encrypted, but the proof of the validation could be used publicly on a blockchain to prove that you are you for purposes of that transaction, without revealing the underlying private data. To that end, the startup ObjectTech (http://objecttechgroup.com) provides a digitized passport that incorporates a feature called self-sovereign identity for privacy protection, which it claims allows passengers to control which parties can view their passport information.

In addition to these typical technology issues, the sale of illegal goods has also put a dark cloud over the blockchain cryptocurrency Bitcoin. Public or unpermissioned blockchains provide an opportunity for nefarious transactions such as facilitating the sale of illegal goods and supporting the ransomware payment model, given the anonymous nature of participants. Blockchains could raise challenges where financial institutions are forced to comply with certain privacy laws. Some financial organizations are required by law to be able to permanently remove data when required to do so by a court. As of late 2017, the United States with its patchwork of privacy legislation has not determined how blockchain will be regulated. With respect to protected health information we are not sure how blockchain technology will match with privacy and security rules under the Health Insurance Portability and Accountability Act of 1996 (HIPAA/HITECH, U.S. Public Law 104–191). The soon to be enacted European privacy "right to be forgotten" laws will also present a challenge. Data privacy legislation in Europe as of May 2018 will be dictated by the EU General Data Protection Regulation (GDPR). The GDPR's "right to erasure" presents issues that need to be addressed when personal information is stored in blockchain-based storage systems like IPFS, which was discussed in Chapter 3. We will need to consider some of the following issues. Information stored in blockchain cannot be altered or deleted once added. Any application will need to address how to comply with the data protection principles of accuracy and an individual's right to correct data; see GDPR Rec. 39; Art. 5(1)(e).

> "Personal data must be kept in a form that permits identification of data subjects for no longer than is necessary for the purposes for which the personal data are processed. Personal data may be stored for longer periods insofar as the data will be processed solely for archiving purposes in the public interest, or scientific, historical, or statistical purposes in accordance with Art. 89(1) and subject to the implementation of appropriate safeguards."

Assuming personal information is encrypted before it is written to a blockchain, destroying the key renders the data unreadable. Is this enough to comply with the GDPR if the data is technically still there? The destruction of a key as an erasure for the purposes of the GDPR should probably suffice so long as the destruction is done in accordance with best practices and in an auditable way.

Another risk exists where blockchain applications are implemented across multiple jurisdictions without a single entity responsible for their operation in any jurisdiction. Any application will need to address cross-border data flows, and wider legal questions of enforceability, liability, dispute resolution, discovery, and extraterritorial application. An amended Rule 41 of the Federal Rules of Criminal Procedure by the United States Department of Justice facilitates U.S. law enforcement and intelligence agencies to get authorization to hack into Americans computers and electronic communications devices. The U.S. has many diplomatic arrangements in place with other countries to cooperate in investigations that cross national borders, including Mutual Legal Assistance Treaties (MLATs). The new version permits a federal judge to approve a single warrant for accessing multiple computers remotely. This amended Rule 41 ignores the fact that "remotely" could mean in a different country. This clearly has some serious implications for blockchain-based storage services providers operating overseas and their customers, as blockchain can be regarded as anonymizing technology. This FRCP Rule 41 states:

FEDERAL RULES OF CRIMINAL PROCEDURE

Rule 41. Search and Seizure

(b) Authority to Issue a Warrant. At the request of a federal law enforcement officer or an attorney for the government:(6) a magistrate judge with authority in any district where activities related to a crime **may have occurred** has authority to issue a warrant to use remote access to search electronic storage media and to seize or copy electronically stored information located within or outside that district, if:

(A) the district where the media or information is located has been concealed through technological means; or

(B) in an investigation of a violation of 18 U.S.C. § 1030(a)(5), the media are protected computers that have been damaged without authorization and are located in five or more districts.

This rule, effective December 2016, allows law enforcement in the U.S. to circumvent probable cause and chain of custody by allowing a federal magistrate judge to issue law enforcement a warrant to hack or deploy malware on any number of computers/servers, even those tangentially related to their investigations. The only prerequisite is that some effort has been taken by the suspected party to obscure the location of said computers. Obviously, Tor ("the onion router") browser users are a prime candidate for abuse with this change (see https://www.torproject.org). The vague wording and broad application means it could also apply to virtual private networks (VPNs), which are the preferred access by banks and businesses to secure their critical data. The change is the law enforcement equivalent of a blank check, enabling unchecked surveillance to be applied to blockchain-based transactions.

Tor directs Internet traffic through a free, worldwide, volunteer overlay network consisting of more than 7,000 relays to conceal a user's location and usage from anyone conducting network surveillance.

In summation, open source protocols that empower individuals to conduct business can be targeted by law enforcement. Blockchain and Bitcoin users should take notice and issue with these events. Many parallels can be drawn between the current state of Tor and Bitcoin. Rule 41 sets a difficult precedent for what the government deems acceptable when it comes to other distributed, open source, privacy enabling protocols that it has a vested interest in stopping—namely blockchain. This can stunt the growth and evolution of blockchain technologies as businesses must assess these risks as part of their implementation.

Legal Ramifications of Blockchain Records

Owing to its stringent encryption techniques, blockchain will have more legal bearing in court. Courts have already begun to evaluate computer-generated information, albeit in a limited capacity as evidence. In *United States v. Lizarraga-Tirado*, the U.S. Federal Court for the Ninth Circuit analyzed the use of a Google Maps entry of a crime scene in an immigration case (see 789 F.3d 1107 [9th Cir. 2015]). Federal prosecutors introduced as evidence a Google Maps screenshot with a computer-generated GPS "thumbtack" stuck to the alleged scene of the defendant's apprehension within U.S. borders.

Delaware, the corporate-friendly state, has laid the foundation for companies doing business there to use blockchain technology for company record-keeping. Delaware General Corporation Law (DGCL) marks a key milestone in the Delaware Blockchain Initiative to encourage the use of blockchain technology and smart contracts in business (see http://legis.delaware.gov/BillDetail/25730). The Delaware amendments provide for corporations to keep their "books and records" on a blockchain or distributed ledger. Sections 219 and 224 of the DGCL would be amended to permit the corporation to rely on the contents of a distributed ledger itself as the stock ledger. Vermont bill H868 (http://legislature.vermont.gov/bill/status/2016/H.868) makes records verified through blockchain technology admissible as evidence in court. Laws such as this create a kind of legal backing for blockchain-based information. In Nevada, a bill has deemed smart contracts and blockchain signatures acceptable records under state law. Nevada Senate Bill 398 specifies, "If a law requires a record to be in writing, submission of a blockchain which electronically contains the record satisfies the law."

As blockchain ledgers and systems become more common, their possible use in cases as evidence and discovery becomes more likely. This means lawyers will need to know such records exist as well as how to access and handle that evidence—that is, what specific information to request.

As we mentioned earlier, property ownership is obviously an excellent use case for a blockchain application. In many developing countries, wealth is created through ownership. Unfortunately, one of the most challenging aspects is determining who owns a certain piece of land, and disputes often occur when corrupt governments or individuals take advantage of the undereducated.

Having a public blockchain ledger would allow everyone to be aware of who owns which parcel of land, and it would make the exchange of ownership much easier and more equitable. This streamlined proof of ownership would create a better base for authentication, and governments could fairly tax individuals and businesses. To understand the potential of a blockchain land registry system, analysts argue one must first understand how property changes hands. When a purchaser seeks to buy property today, he or she must find and secure the title and have the lawful owner sign it over. This search has become more difficult. For a large number of residential mortgage holders, flawed paperwork, forged signatures, and defects in foreclosure and mortgage documents have marred proper documentation of property ownership. The resulting situation means that the property no longer has a "good title" attached to it and is no longer legally sellable, leaving the prospective buyer in many cases with no remedies. These issues are even more pronounced outside the United States. For example, in Haiti, natural disasters, forced evacuations, and the corruption of dictatorships have made the prospect of figuring out who actually owns the land one lives on impossible. This was remedied by an Ethereum-based blockchain (see https://media.consensys.net/how-blockchain-can-help-haiti-recover-b1657b609ad1). In the Gaza Strip, land speculation is made problematic by conflicting claims by both the Israeli government and the Palestinian Authority, as well as the possible intervention of third parties. Blockchain can help. The Republic of Georgia teamed with the Bitfury Group (http://bitfury.com), a provider of blockchain infrastructure, to use the Bitcoin blockchain to validate property-related transfers, marking the first time a national government used the Bitcoin blockchain to validate and secure government actions. Blockchain technology has also be tapped to improve land ownership in developing countries. A team of blockchain technology pioneers from Ghana, Denmark, and the U.S. launched the Bitland initiative (see http://landing.bitland.world) to establish usable land titles and free up trillions of dollars for infrastructure development in West Africa. The Bitland initiative will educate the population about technology and provide the benefits of documented land ownership to those who don't have it. It will begin in Ghana and expand throughout Africa, with hopes of catapulting infrastructure development and strengthening democracy.

The Beginning of Autonomous Law: Smart Contract

A computer scientist, legal scholar, and cryptography expert named Nick Szabo is credited for developing the concept of a smart contract. He defined a smart contract as "a set of promises, specified in digital form, including protocols within which the parties perform on these promises." (See Nick Szabo, "Smart Contracts: Building Blocks for Digital Markets," 1996, www.alamut.com/subj/economics/nick_szabo/smartContracts.html.)

So, a smart contract is a computerized algorithm (yet another way of describing it), which performs the terms of the contract. However, this definition does not differentiate smart contracts from some already well-known contractual constructs implementing automated performance, such as vending machines.

Vending machines are defined as self-contained automatic machines that dispense goods or provide services when coins are inserted or payment by, let's say, a credit card is made. Vending machines are programmed with certain rules and perform by these rules.

If there is no principal difference between vending machines and smart contracts, then smart contracts are as old as Roman law itself. In the first century CE, a Greek engineer and mathematician, Hero of Alexandria, documented the first vending machine in the published journal *Pneumatika*. His machine accepted a drachma coin and then dispensed holy water (for the mechanical details, see www.google.com.pg/patents/US95577400). Fast-forward to the 1980s. We essentially programmed financial smart contracts for Merrill Lynch when Paul and I used designated order turnaround (DOT) to perform automated program trading—trades frequently executed not by a trader himself but by a computer system based on a trading strategy implemented as a COBOL/C/SQL–based program. As of 2014, more than 75 percent of the securities traded on stock exchanges originated from automated trading system orders. So, smart contracts per se are not new.

Smart Contract Evolution

Most of today's legal contracts are created using word processing templates customized by attorneys and other legal professionals. They contain standardized legal languages which specify terms and conditions, e.g., manifest within a Word document. They rely on third parties for interpretation and enforcement. This process is time consuming and redundant. Moreover, if issues occur, the parties to the contract rely on arbitrators and the courts to remedy the situation. This is also time consuming, as well as hard to predict and expensive. The solution is the smart contract—i.e., a computer program that can carry out the contract. It contains code (e.g., Ethereum JavaScript Solidity) that is capable of executing the terms and conditions of an agreement. The contract code defines the terms and conditions as a set of if/then/else syllogisms in the same way that a legal document would. The conditions can be validated and confirmed by RPC calls to other smart contracts or initially to "off-chain" oracles. In this way smart contract code can then be automatically executed on the blockchain. Smart contracts will herald the dawn of new attorney and legal professionals who by necessity will need to be versed in both law and computer programming.

For example, a contract that automatically calculates the payments that are due and the goods to be delivered between the parties, and then automatically arranges for those payments to be made and the goods to be delivered, relies on software code (see Figure 4-1). The contract terms are expressed in logic statements such as if buyer Joe orders a guitar of a particular brand, make, and year, which becomes available via seller Gibson, then Joe's party pays money to Gibson's party's bank account, and the guitar is delivered to Joe's home.

As we shall see in the next chapters containing smart contract code examples, it is critical not only that the code is developed and tested but also that it is written with security checks on the identity of the parties.

Smart Contract Components

As the smart contract evolves, there initially will be hybrids built with separate components: on the blockchain and off the blockchain. Eventually, as blockchain technology becomes mature and widely accepted, smart contracts will be on-blockchain-only components.

Here are some of the possibilities:

- Smart contract code, for example, Ethereum Solidity code that is stored, verified, and executed on a blockchain.
- Smart legal contracts written as a specification for using smart contract code as a complement or complete substitute for legal contracts.

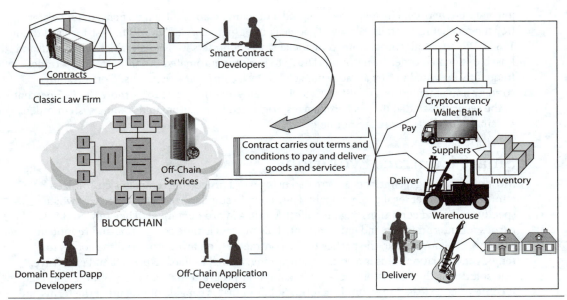

FIGURE 4-1   Smart contract flow

- An actual contract may initially be a smart contract and some off-chain logic and execution; as the concept evolves it will become a fully blockchain-executed smart contract. A very simple contract can be fully automated. Other contracts may require both self-executing terms and terms that are outside the software code. This is because not all decisions or steps in a contract can be reduced to logic statements, especially for complex contracts.

To the dapp programmers, a smart contract is just a well-written program that executes the contract, i.e., a contract written in code. They would say all programs are really contracts anyway.

To lawyers, the concept of a contract has a different meaning. It requires offer and acceptance, consideration, and specific terms and conditions. They are hard pressed to believe that code can be law.

Smart Contract Benefits

Like any new technology, there are benefits and risks to smart contracts. As we have seen in Chapter 1, the benefit of a distributed blockchain is that it provides a more trustworthy ledger than relying on one trusted central ledger. With blockchain technology there is more security, traceability, and transparency of records and transactions for participants and regulators as well as lower operational costs. The combination of smart contracts with blockchain adds certainty, security, and resilience. Terms can be verified by independent parties. Moreover, the information stored on the blockchain is protected from security threats as it is maintained on multiple nodes where more than 51 percent of the nodes would have to be compromised before any problematic issue would be manifest.

Smart Contract Challenges

The success of blockchain, as we'll cover in Chapter 9, will depend on whether it can be implemented practically and which applications are proper candidates. Briefly, the key deployment risks and challenges are listed here:

- **Performance**   The computing resources and performance required for transaction processing, validation, and fraud detection will determine which banking, financial, and payment services it can best be applied to. Currently blockchain is not performant enough to handle thousands of transactions per second. It will be relegated to asset transfers that are not time dependent, such as buying/selling a highly traded and volatile security.
- **Interoperability**   Ensuring interoperability between different blockchain implementations so they can talk to one another. What is the cost to achieve that? This will be determined by the alliance groups who will hopefully develop standards.
- **Scalability**   Each node in the particular blockchain network must know about every single transaction that occurs globally, which may create a significant drag on the network. The goal is to perform all transactions with a higher efficiency, but in a way that doesn't sacrifice the decentralization and security that the network provides.

Smart Contract Risks

The use of evolving smart contracts and blockchain technologies does create a number of potential risks, including governance, deployment, risk management, regulatory, and legal. These risks and how they are managed fundamentally underpin market confidence in the technology. We will discuss them in more detail in the sections that follow. To be effective, blockchain and smart contracts require standards, i.e., a set of common rules by which all participants operate, in order to ensure accuracy and trustworthiness. The decentralized model poses challenges when you need to change the rules, because those changes need to be agreed upon and accepted by all participants to function consistently. A governance framework will be required to implement and operate blockchain as a legal application and needs to take into account oversight and monitoring functions, rule setting, and acceptance and change control management. Governance in general will be a requirement not only for legal but for all technologies that manage information. This transformation to some common rules for information governance is not only critical to blockchain but to other pursuits like e-discovery and cybersecurity. Governance standards around the blockchain (see http://hbr.org/2017/04/who-controls-the-blockchain) will contribute to market confidence in the technology and the legal and regulatory environment. This will accelerate the adoption and success of the smart contract.

Smart Contract Legal Challenges

Smart contracts also raise a number of interesting and challenging legal questions. For starters, has a legally binding contract been formed? As mentioned, the current hybrid nature of a smart contract combined with a traditional nonprogrammed or manual contract, e.g., Word document with terms and conditions, creates some new issues as to its validity. Whether a smart contract is legally binding will depend on a number of factors, including the specific use case, the type of smart contract being used, and the applicable law.

As we have seen, some states like Delaware and Arizona have passed legislation to recognize the smart contract. Seeking to avoid any legal uncertainty surrounding blockchain transactions and smart contracts relating to certain digital assets, in 2017 Arizona passed the amended Arizona Electronic Transactions Act (AETA), HB 2417, which includes a very specific definition of blockchain technology as a "distributed, decentralized, shared and replicated ledger, which may be public or private, permissioned or permission less, or driven by tokenized crypto economics or token less" and provides that the "data on the ledger is protected with cryptography, is immutable and auditable and provides an uncensored truth." HB 2417 also includes a definition of smart contracts as an "event driven program, with state, that runs on a distributed, decentralized, shared and replicated ledger that can take custody over and instruct transfer of assets on that ledger." Forward-thinking states like Delaware and Arizona enact such legislation to encourage blockchain development in their respective states. That said, the electronic nature of smart contracts is unlikely to be a barrier to establishing contractual formation in many jurisdictions.

The legal requirement of "certainty" might not be satisfied easily, as not all smart contracts operate in conjunction with natural language contract terms. How will the parties to a smart contract get notice of its terms and conditions? When will they get to see those terms prior to or after the smart contract is agreed and executed? How will we address those contracts that are required by law to be in writing? Is computer code a writing? How do we deal with the formal execution requirements for deeds, i.e., in writing and signed by specified individuals/roles?

There is a spectrum of possible smart contract models. On the one hand, there are those who promote the "code is contract" approach. On the other hand, there are those who see smart contracts as consisting of digitizing the performance of business logic, e.g., payment, which is happening today and may or may not be associated with a natural language contract. In between these two extremes a number of permutations are likely to emerge, including, for example, a "split" smart contract model under which natural language contract terms are connected to computer code via parameters.

There are jurisdictional variations on whether smart contracts can give rise to legally binding contractual relations under the laws of a number of key contracting jurisdictions. The answer may vary significantly depending on the jurisdiction. Certainty as to what constitutes the contractual terms and whether they are comprehensive enough is often a critical factor necessary to establish the formation of a legally binding contract in many jurisdictions. Smart contracts that purely digitize a process but do not include, or operate in conjunction with, contractual terms may not satisfy such requirements.

- **Enforceability**   Where a smart contract has a legally binding contractual effect, the technology within which it is deployed may sometimes give rise to problems in relation to legal enforceability. There may be no central administering authority to resolve a dispute. Dispute resolution mechanisms could address enforceability and jurisdictional variations. Inserting a dispute resolution mechanism into a smart contract will be pro forma to address the issues around enforceability and jurisdictional variations.
- **Transparency**   Blockchain can involve a level of transparency. But what if the parties don't want the details divulged? How do you keep parts of the contract private and retain the other benefits of blockchain?

- **Changes**   How do you unwind transactions that shouldn't have happened—for example, if there has been duress—or it is a contract that is for some reason (or is somewhere) illegal or in breach of regulatory requirements? This has already occurred on the Ethereum platform, with a technical "hard fork" response (a split in the blockchain where non-upgraded nodes cannot validate blocks created by upgraded nodes following new consensus rules).
- **Coding limitations**   Contracts often deal with the unknown and have clauses that aren't easily reduced to code or that can execute automatically as a simple "if this, then that" procedure. Force majeure is a good example. Contracts often include concepts of subjective judgment, reasonableness, and acting in good faith. These concepts currently cannot be readily translated into logic statements. That said, there will be code services that can provide "reasonability" tests, which have been used in securities trading for years.
- **Liability for mistake, error, or fraud**   If something does go wrong with the execution of the contract and someone suffers a loss, where do they go for recourse? We will need a court system that is tech savvy. The courts have started to recognize blockchain not only for cryptocurrency but also for how it can improve the administration of law. Just as the courts got technical with e-discovery, they will need to be able to work with blockchain evidence.

Blockchain as Evidence and Digital Signature

In addition to the benefits, challenges, and risks, for blockchain applications to have bearing in the real world, digital signatures need to be as binding as pen and paper, and evidence recorded on blockchains needs to be admissible in court. Courts have complex rules of evidence about what information can come in and in what format. Right now in most legal systems, blockchain evidence can be considered but only with the help of expensive expert witnesses to explain what it means. This process would eliminate the potential efficiencies gained through use of blockchain technology, and would instead increase court costs and decrease access to justice.

Under U.S. Federal Rule of Evidence 901, "[t]o satisfy the requirement of authenticating or identifying an item of evidence, the proponent must produce evidence sufficient to support a finding that the item is what the proponent claims it is." This requirement is important to ensure litigants do not try to introduce falsified or tampered evidence. How does this work in practice? Typically, transaction and other business records can be admitted into court proceedings, but a witness typically must testify to authenticate the records. For example, if you are involved in a dispute with a security exchange over a trade, the exchange could introduce its computer records of your account and trades, but one of its techies would need to testify about the authenticity of the data. Thus, transaction records generally require a witness to explain what the transaction record is, how it is kept or was generated, and what it represents.

On the blockchain, if signature data is kept, it is easier to later authenticate the transaction record by referring to the digital signature used to validate the transaction. This will help meet the evidentiary requirement that the blockchain record "is what the proponent claims it is," i.e., the blockchain receipt for the specific transaction. Not all digital signatures are born equal. Sometimes there is a good reason to choose one system over another, like avoiding a system that has been poorly designed or modified by a surveilling agency (see https://privacyinternational.org/node/51). But other times it's completely arbitrary.

Governments have set complicated standards for digital signatures to give them the same weight as pen and paper (see https://www.nist.gov/). The process of signing electronic documents is full of friction. As discussed earlier, the Arizona Electronic Transactions Act (AETA) stipulates that records or signatures in electronic form cannot be denied legal effect and enforceability based on the fact that they are in electronic form. There is also a Federal E-Sign Act (15 U.S.C. § 7001), which generally provides that a signature, contract, or other transaction record may not be deemed invalid or unenforceable solely because it is in electronic form. It is to be determined whether the federal statute preempts AETA. Under AETA electronic records, electronic signatures and smart contract terms secured through blockchain technology and governed under U.C.C. Articles 2, 2A, and 7 will be considered to be in an electronic form and to be an electronic signature. The statute also provides that a contract relating to a transaction may not be denied legal effect, validity, or enforceability solely because that contract contains a "smart contract term."

The bottom line is that governments are looking to streamline rules of evidence to allow blockchain evidence to be deemed admissible without an expert. States are leading the way. In addition to Arizona, Vermont passed a bill that creates a presumption of admissibility of blockchain records that meet certain requirements. Admitted records can be used as evidence of contractual parties or terms, effective dates, ownership, money transfers, identity, authenticity of a document, or anything else. We can expect to see much more in terms of legal developments in 2018.

Smart Contract Design Example

So we see that smart contract development will require a team of not only Solidity and distributed application developers but also business and legal professionals knowledgeable in the law and regulation of the blockchain. Let's design a smart contract that is used by affiliate and social media marketing businesses to receive compensation for their marketing efforts. They are paid based on campaign performance metrics known as CPA and CPC.

CPA (cost per action or cost per acquisition) advertising is performance based and is common in the affiliate marketing sector of the business. In this payment scheme, the publisher takes all the risk of running the ad, and the advertiser pays only for the number of users who complete a transaction, such as a purchase or signup. This is the best type of rate to pay for banner advertisements and the worst type of rate to charge.

CPC (cost per click) is a payment option that compensates a publisher whenever their referred customers click on a link for an advertiser offer. CPC is also an Internet-marketing formula used to price banner ads. Some advertisers will pay publishers based on the number of clicks a banner gets. We will design a smart contract that accesses HitPath performance and payment data so that affiliate networks can streamline the entire performance-to-payment cycle for global affiliates to reduce friction. HitPath (see www.hitpath.com/) is popular advertising campaign tracking software which maintains a central ledger of activity around publishers. Table 4-1 depicts a list of data rows identifying the publisher, the offer, and whether the hit resulted in CPC and CPA. This performance tracking log for HitPath provides the basis for payment.

We will design a smart contract for the marketers to automatically receive compensation—cryptocurrency, USD, or tokens deposited in the wallet account—based on social media

TABLE 4-1   Publisher Performance Tracking Log for HitPath

Hitid	Offerid	Pubid	Action Date	IP	CPA	CPC
123	A	B	2017-09-23	65.52.100.214	Y	Y
124	A	B	2017-09-24	64.122.75.81	Y	Y
125	A	B	2017-09-27	65.52.100.212	Y	Y
126	A	B	2017-09-29	64.122.75.82	Y	Y

advertising campaigns that result in CPC or CPA. This will be accomplished and verified by using an oracle to access the HitPath performance and payment data. An oracle is an agent that finds and verifies real-world occurrences (such as HitPath activity) and submits this information to be used by our smart contracts. Smart contracts contain value and only unlock that value if certain predefined conditions are met, for example, if the publisher's lead generated CPA or CPC. When a particular value is reached, such as the end of the month, the smart contract changes its state and executes the programmatically predefined algorithms to determine how much to compensate the publisher, automatically triggering an event on the blockchain. The primary task of oracles is to provide these values to the smart contract in a secure and trusted manner. Blockchains cannot access data outside their network on their own. So, in short, oracles provide external data and trigger smart contract executions when predefined conditions are met. Oracles are part of multisignature contracts where, for example, the original trustees sign a contract for future release of funds only if certain conditions are met. Before any funds get released an oracle has to sign the smart contract as well (see Figure 4-2).

We can then take the number of CPA and CPC hits for our tracking period, multiply it by the agreed-upon rate, and transfer the payment to the publisher's address. Figure 4-3 shows an example contract. We have extrapolated the variables from the formal contract language using a web-based user interface. Figure 4-4 shows the advertising contract header.

Is an Advertising Payment Application a Blockchain Fit?

We will look at a practical application of blockchain technologies by designing a smart contract for advertisers to be paid in a smart contract automated way from scratch. We will lay out a very basic blockchain automated payment contract based on the advertising CPA and CPC we discussed earlier. Later, in Chapters 10 and 11, we will delve in great detail into the description and use of the JavaScript and Ethereum tools needed to create, build, and deploy an entire application using Ethereum Solidity. That said, not all applications are well suited for blockchain. What would be the advantages of using blockchain for our advertiser payment application?

- Cryptographically secure authentication
- Fast, frictionless, low-fee payments
- A network with 100 percent uptime
- Publicly verifiable and guaranteed code transaction execution

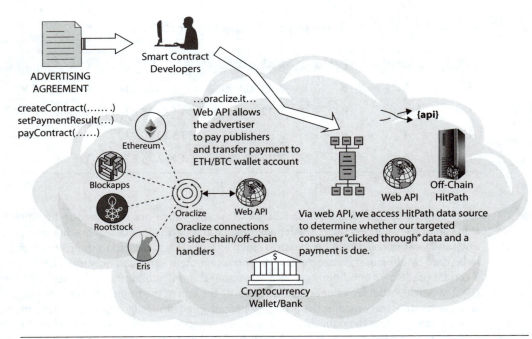

FIGURE 4-2 **Advertising smart contract flow**

There are no real disadvantages to using blockchain:

- The relatively slow blockchain network is not an issue as it is still faster than manual billing.
- The relatively limited transaction rate is not an issue as it is still faster than manual billing.
- Contract code deployment cannot exceed the block gas limit.

Let's take a look now at payment applications. Here are some required features:

- Frequent payment processing
- Handle contracts from multiple countries with different currencies
- Provide verifiable and consistent payment execution

These requirements are much better suited to a blockchain solution. One of the issues for advertising payment has been moving money around through wires and bank transfers. Network publishers must wait three to five business days to deposit or withdraw money from their bank accounts and must trust the advertiser site with their banking information. The sites in turn must secure this information, take appropriate security measures to protect their sites from hacking, and stay in compliance with a series of financial regulations in the various countries in which they operate. Additionally, transacting in different countries requires supporting a variety of different currencies and banks, all of which contribute to the complexity of the operation.

Affiliate Media Co., LLC   ADVERTISING INSERTION ORDER

Publisher:	Affiliate Media Co., LLC	Campaign Name/s:	Blockchain Demo
Advertiser:	Lifestyle Products, LLC	RateperCPA:	$3 per CPA
		RateperCPC:	$1 per CPC
City, State, Zip:	1234 Ethereum Rd, Blockchain, NY	Payable Action:	Unique Clicks
Contact:	John	Payment Terms: As described in Terms and Conditions	Prepay
Phone:	222-333-7777	Billing Contact:	Joe
Fax:	333-444-7777	Phone:	444-555-7777
Publisher Email:	John@affiliatepublisher.com	Advertiser Email:	Joe@lifestyleadvertiserinc.com
IM:		IM:	

CAMPAIGN DETAILS

Exclusive:	☐ True ☐ Network ☒ NO	Suppression File Retrieval:	Download via login or emailed
Channels:	☒ Email/Newsletter		
Regions:	English Speaking Countries		
Budget Cap?	☐ Daily ☐ Weekly ☐ Monthly	Dollar Amount: Initial $15,000 cap	
Lead Cap?	☐ Daily ☐ Weekly ☐ Monthly	Number of Leads: Based on spend amount above	
Start Date:	Upon Receipt	End Date (if applicable):	
Conditions:	All Creative requires approval from Advertiser Lifestyle Products, LLC prior to use (using non-approved creative will result in non-payment on leads generated). All email traffic must use approved from/subject lines that are not deceptive and are CAN-SPAM. Must include opt-out link and opt-out physical address in EVERY email along with a scrub against the suppression file before EVERY mailing. Publisher is responsible for its and its affiliates' actions.		

FIGURE 4-3   Example contract

THIS INSERTION ORDER IS SUBJECT TO THE TERMS AND CONDITIONS ATTACHED HEREWITH. THIS DOCUMENT SUPERSEDES ANY PREVIOUSLY AGREED TERMS AND/OR CONDITIONS.

THE SIGNATORY OF THIS INSERTION ORDER REPRESENTS THAT HE/SHE HAS READ, UNDERSTANDS, AND AGREES TO THE TERMS OF SUCH TERMS AND CONDITIONS, AND IS THE DULY AUTHORIZED AGENT OF PUBLISHER.

Publisher Signature:		Advertiser Signature:	

FIGURE 4-4   Advertising contract header

Using a blockchain solution allows advertisers and publishers to transfer money across borders easily for international betting sites and have a guarantee that their compensation will be paid out in a timely fashion. So we will need some functions to effect the contract:

- createContract(…various contract attributes as depicted in Figure 4-3…) will create our contract by pulling the variables specified in Table 4-1 and instantiating, i.e., breathing life into this contract to be referenced as contractid.
- setCPAPaymentResult((uint contractid)constant returns (uint)), setCPCPaymentResult((uint contractid)constant returns (uint)) will periodically access the HitPath tracking data to determine how many CPA/CPC hits we had during the billing period using the rate variables specified in Figure 4-3 to calculate the payment.
- payContract(uint contractid) will transfer an amount equal to the payment from the advertiser's address to the publisher's address and send notifications to each party that the transaction has been completed.

Defining Contract Data Structures

Before we can start coding our contract, we need to define the necessary data structures. This structure will house all the variables from our contract. See Table 4-1 and Figure 4-3 for a view of these variables from the contract and tracking sources. As we shall see in Chapter 10, a variable can have data types like string, integer, boolean, the address of a blockchain wallet account, an array of all these data types, or other structures. See Figure 4-3 for variables. In Ethereum Solidity, it will look something like this:

```
struct Contract {
string publisher;
string advertiser;
address advertiseraddress;
address publisheraddress;
string offerid    ;
string pubid   ;
string publisheremail    ;
string advertiseremail   ;
string campaignname      ;
int rate              ;
string payable action    ;
string paymentterms      ;
int ratepercpa        ;
int ratepercpc        ;
string billingcontact   ;
bool exclusivecontract          ;
string channels       ;
int budgetcap         ;
int leadcap           ;
```

```
uint startdate        ;  }
struct Payment {
uint amountcpchits; /* in wei */
uint amountcpahits; /* in wei */
Contract contract;
}
```

Smart Contract Events

As we shall see in detail later, Solidity events are used to log transaction activity to the blockchain. Event logs are less expensive than creating new entries in the state tree, so it is a best way to store read-only data. Logs are not accessible from within a contract (only variables are), but can be read by external client libraries like web3.js (more on this in Chapter 10). Ethereum transactions are asynchronous and usually do not mine for 15–30 seconds after they have been broadcast to the network. Because of this, transactions cannot return values. The only way a transaction can create an output is by modifying the state or adding an event log. Client libraries usually parse the logs to determine the output of a transaction.

A Solidity event is a schema for logs. Logs are automatically indexed by contract address and event type for efficient querying. In addition, Solidity events allow you to define three custom indexed fields. Only indexed fields can be queried when parsing logs.

```
event ContractCreated(uint indexed id, address indexed creator,
      Contract contract, uint64 locktime);
event ContractCPAMonth(uint indexed contract_id, address publisher,
      uint amount, uint timestamp);
event ContractCPCMonth (uint indexed contract_id, address publisher,
      uint amount, uint timestamp);
event PaymentCalculated(uint indexed Contract_id, int cpcamount,
      int cpaamount,  uint timestamp);
event PaymentMade(address indexed user, uint amount, uint timestamp);
```

There is an event associated with each of the major state modifications that can occur in our contract. Together, they provide a history of the actions taken by the contract on the blockchain.

Smart Contract Functions

Let's create a list of the functions we will be defining in our application. Functions, like variables, can be either public or private. Public functions can be accessed by other contracts and client libraries and are listed as part of the application binary interface (ABI), which is basically how you call functions in a contract and get data back. Private functions are only accessible by other functions in the same contract. Web3.js is Ethereum's JavaScript API to interact with the Ethereum node. It contains a host of modules to facilitate blockchain functionality.

```
var web3 = new Web3(new Web3.providers.HttpProvider("http://localhost:8545"));
```

When we get an ABI, and have saved it in a separate file abi.js, we can load it from the application into the abiArray variable. We also need the smart contract address, in the advertiserContract variable. We can then get hold of a JavaScript instance for the contract:

```
var advertiserContract = web3.eth.contract(abiArray).at(contractAddress);
var pubBalance = advertiserContract.getPubBalance.call();
var advBalance = advertiserContract.getAdvBalance.call();

var balanceWei = web3.eth.getBalance(account).toNumber();
var balance = web3.fromWei(balanceWei, 'ether');
```

Once we have our web3 object, we can start calling some APIs to find out what is going on in the blockchain, like getting your balance in wei and converting it to ether.

In addition, there are constant functions that read from, but do not modify, the blockchain. Public constant functions return immediately with their result, do not send a transaction to the network, and do not consume any gas when called.

Here are the public functions we will need:

```
pragma solidity ^0.4.0;
contract AdvertiserContract  {
function createContract(…………..)
function setCPAPaymentResult(uint contractid)
      constant returns (uint) {return cpapayment};
function setCPCPaymentResult(uint contractid)
      constant returns (uint) {return cpcpayment};
function payContract( uint contracted, int cpapayment, int cpcpayment){...}
}
```

Once the contract has been created, we emit a ContractCreated event to log the state modification we just made and return a variable to indicate that there were no errors. You will probably need some public constant functions such as:

```
getActiveContracts constant returns (uint[])
```

Once a number of contracts have been created, we need to be able to identify active contracts.

In addition, we will be defining some private functions for our own internal use:

```
getContractById(uint contract_id) constant private returns (Contract storage)
```

getContractById is a helper function we will use to get a pointer to a specific contract.

```
payContract(uint contract_id) private
```

Constant functions return a value whose type must be specified with the syntax above. So our advertiser smart contract will:

- Execute the createContract for each publisher we do business with:

  ```
  createContract(. . .)
  ```

- Calculate how many CPAs and CPCs occurred for this publisher during the current month:

```
function setCPAPaymentResult(uint contractid)constant returns (uint) {return cpapayment};
function setCPCPaymentResult(uint contractid)constant returns (uint) {return cpcpayment};
```

- Compensate each affiliate for CPAs and CPCs that occurred for this publisher during the current month:

```
payContract(Contract contract, uint contracted, int cpapayment, int cpcpayment)
```

The application will probably have a web-based front end and will require MetaMask, an extension for accessing Ethereum-enabled distributed applications, or dapps in your normal Chrome browser. The extension injects the Ethereum web3 API into every website's JavaScript context, so that dapps can read from the blockchain. MetaMask also lets the user create and manage their own identities, so when a dapp wants to perform a transaction and write to the blockchain, the user gets a secure interface to review the transaction before approving or rejecting it (see Figure 4-5).

This smart contract design must be coded to handle the functionality we enumerated here. In Chapters 10 and 11, we will detail and illustrate an entire application (betting) from the development setup all the way to production implementation, with explanations of the coding and execution as well as a web-based front end.

Smart Contracts in Practice

As we have seen in the previous sections of this chapter, there is confusion about what a smart contract means as well as its enforceability and evolving jurisdictional issues. Technologists come up with a programmable component that has the word "contract" in its name, and lawyers are intrigued and want to get involved in this new form of business and contract execution. Drafting actual standalone contracts is not what developers want to do.

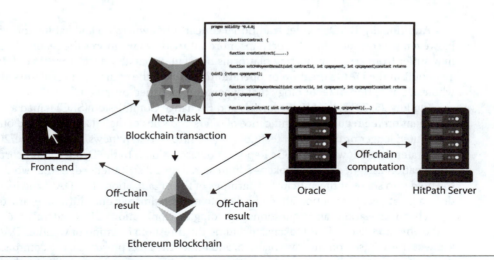

FIGURE 4-5   **Advertising contract oracle flow**

Developers build platforms and applications (see http://consensys.net/ventures/spokes/ for an array of existing applications). Smart contracts are just components. The traditional work of lawyers who draft contracts will change with widespread adoption of smart contracts. The new world where lawyers draft smart contracts will involve a team of legal and technology professionals. The makeup of these teams and the new contract development life cycle are incubating as we speak.

Decentralized Autonomous Organizations

A decentralized autonomous organization (DAO), also known as a decentralized autonomous corporation (DAC), is an organization that is run through rules encoded as smart contracts. A DAO's financial transaction record and program rules are maintained on a blockchain. The concept of a DAO entity is initially introduced in a document. There are several examples of this business model (see http://download.slock.it/public/DAO/WhitePaper.pdf). The use of blockchain, smart contracts, and DAOs raises significant legal issues. As these blockchain-based technologies become widely used, we will need laws and regulations to provide a legal framework within which blockchain can be utilized. As developers in this new paradigm, we need to understand these issues so we can build compliant blockchain applications. Some developing legal issues are as follows:

- When servers are decentralized and located around the globe, we will need to consider jurisdiction where a breach or failure occurred and then apply cross-border laws, which may cause expensive resolutions that undermine blockchain benefits.
- When the entity is essentially self-governing software engaging in or facilitating commerce, what legal status will attach to DAOs? Are they simple corporations or something else?
- What, if any, is the liability of DAOs and their creators? Who or what is claimed against in the case of a legal dispute?

Additionally, DAOs render traditional concepts of ownership and liability obsolete. However, we consider that this perhaps more futuristic view ignores the reality that coding may suffer from errors or hosting platforms may fail. What about the impacts of fraud at any point in the DAO's creation or operation? How will the courts and regulators allow the wholesale adoption of technology that bypasses established oversight?

On July 25, 2017, the U.S. Securities and Exchange Commission (SEC) issued a statement on the regulatory significance of offers and sales of digital assets carried out using distributed ledger or blockchain technology (see http://sec.gov/news/press-release/2017-131). That statement followed the SEC's Report of Investigation into the DAO, an unincorporated organization designed to issue tokens administered on a distributed ledger that would allow the holder to share in the anticipated earnings of the organization. The DAO and its structure drew a great deal of attention after a hacker stole approximately one-third of its assets.

The investigation raised questions regarding the application of U.S. federal securities laws to the offer and sale of DAO tokens, including the threshold question of whether DAO tokens are securities. Based on the investigation, and under the facts presented, the commission determined that DAO tokens are securities under the Securities Act of 1933 and the Securities

Exchange Act of 1934. The report reiterates these fundamental principles of the U.S. federal securities laws and describes their applicability to a new paradigm—virtual organizations or capital-raising entities that use distributed ledger or blockchain technology to facilitate capital raising and/or investment and the related offer and sale of securities. The automation of certain functions through this technology, smart contracts, or computer code does not remove conduct from the purview of the U.S. federal securities laws. See "Report of Investigation Pursuant to Section 21(a) of the Securities Exchange Act of 1934: The DAO," https://sec.gov/litigation/investreport/34-81207.pdf.

DAO and Jurisdiction

A DAO can cross jurisdictional boundaries as the nodes on a blockchain can be located in any country in the world. This poses complex jurisdictional issues which will require specialized consideration by lawyers versed in each country's law and the relevant contractual relationships. The principles of contract and title differ across jurisdictions and therefore identifying the appropriate governing law will be a first step in designing and implementing a DAO. In a decentralized environment, it will be critical to identify the appropriate set of rules to apply.

For starters, every transaction could potentially fall under the jurisdiction of the location of every node in the network. This could result in the blockchain needing to be compliant with a large number of legal and regulatory regimes. Some design constraints need to be identified early to facilitate the development of a DAO. In the event a fraudulent or erroneous transaction is made, pinpointing its location within the blockchain will be an important security consideration.

The inclusion of an exclusive governing law and jurisdiction clause is therefore essential. It should ensure that a DAO member has legal certainty as to the law to be applied to determine the rights and obligations of the parties to the agreement and which courts will handle any disputes. One vendor, Aragon (https://blog.aragon.one), has developed a DAO arbitration mechanism, which will be fully operational in 2018 (see Figure 4-6).

The Aragon Network Jurisdiction requires an individual who has a dispute to open a case and post a bond. The bond will be locked for the period of the arbitration process and returned if resolved in favor. If not in favor, the bond will be kept as a network reserve. Only applicants who have a legitimate reason for dispute will post a bond. In extreme cases, there may be cause to freeze operations of the organization—for example, when all stakeholder funds are at risk. Any organization shareholder can raise an issue if the company's contracts are frozen and moved to a state of review. When an arbitration begins, five judges will be randomly selected from a pool of individuals who have posted a bond indicating their interest in serving as a judge. The judges will vote on the final judgment of the case for this round. If the applicant is unsatisfied with the ruling of the decentralized court, they have the option to elevate the issue to the next realm. This is done by posting an even larger bond than before. For this round of court, Aragon uses a prediction market where all the judges of the network can take part, providing the applicant with a much larger audience.

If the applicant still finds the issue unsatisfactory, there is the supreme court of the Aragon Network Jurisdiction composed of the top nine judges by ANJ payout—in other words, these are the individuals with the highest ranking in resolving Aragon Network Jurisdiction cases.

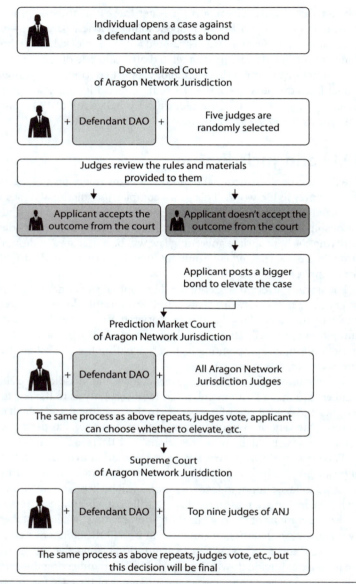

FIGURE 4-6   **Aragon arbitration mechanism**

This time the judgment will be final with no appeal process. The judges of the previous round will be rewarded or penalized according to the ruling of the supreme court. If the supreme court agrees with the previous round's judges, the judges from that round will be rewarded. The judges of that round are penalized for a call that was overturned. The Aragon Network Jurisdiction purports to provide the tools needed to solve all issues that are not accounted for in the smart contract code. It creates an incentive for Aragon organizations to join and take part in the network. All parties that want to interact with an organization are guaranteed that, in the case of a breach of trust not covered by the contract, their issue will be resolved. Also, if a bug is discovered that threatens the organization's existence, it can be stopped by opening an arbitration that freezes all activity until the issue is resolved.

DAO Service-Level Liability

An important aspect of DAO adoption is the willingness of vendors (like Aragon) to commit to performance assurances and service-level metrics. This will depend on considerations such as the vendor risk/reward profile, the service delivery model, and the "multiplication factor" of accepting significant liability for multiple customers at the same time. This is likely to mean vendors preferring to offer the technology and service on an almost "as is" basis, with a limited availability service level, and excluding warranties regarding performance of the services, leaving customers without any assurance that the technology will function as described or the service be reliable and available. For users who are utilizing the service as part of their business, this is unlikely to be an acceptable proposal. The balance of performance risk will therefore be a key issue.

DAO Liability for Contract Breach

The risk to customers of a systemic issue with trading related infrastructure such as blockchain could be material if trades are not settled or are settled incorrectly. Likewise, the risk relating to security and confidentiality will be toward the top of the risk issues for any prospective customer. Blockchain poses different risks because of the technology and manner of operations: one of the main issues affecting public blockchain is the inability to control and stop its functioning. In case of a private blockchain, the lack of control on the functioning of the platform does not apply, but whether this would be sufficient to trigger a liability of the company managing the platform has not yet been tested. So the allocation and attribution of risk and liability in relation to a malfunctioning blockchain service must be thought through carefully, not just at the vendor/customer level but between all relevant participants, in particular the parties affected by the issues.

DAO and Intellectual Property

There is value in the blockchain. The ownership of the intellectual property (IP) will form an important consideration. Given the amount of investment and the potential financial returns of blockchain technology, vendors will have to determine their IP strategy. Vendors will likely want to capitalize on any other commercial benefits to be generated from the blockchain, including commercialization of the underlying dataset. To the extent the dataset relates to the users, this will be a carefully negotiated area. Likewise, what of specific developments or solutions that overlay the core, developed to meet a customer's specific requirements? Possible IP options are no different from any other software development agreement and are likely to hinge on whether those specific requirements could give a customer a competitive edge and/or can be used by the blockchain vendor with another customer or by the customer with another blockchain vendor. Depending on the answer to these questions, a customer may insist on ownership of such developments or may only be willing to license them for the term of the agreement. A customer might restrict the vendor's ability to use such developments in some way based upon time, use, recipient, or a combination of all three. An "open innovation" approach is prevalent throughout fintech. Financial organizations are working toward a viable blockchain proof of concept and are developing a lot of code in-house. Traditionally, financial organizations have expected to own the IP in any software they develop. However, there appears to be a realization that technology will have to be shared in order for real value to be gained.

DAO and Who or What Is Responsible

DAOs are essentially online, digital entities that operate through the implementation of precoded rules. These entities often need minimal to zero input into their operation, and they are used to executing smart contracts and recording activity on the blockchain.

Modern legal systems are designed to allow organizations, as well as actual people, to participate. Most legal systems do this by giving organizations some of the legal powers that real people have—the power to enter into legal contracts, to sue, and to be sued. But what legal status will attach to a DAO? Are they simple corporations, partnerships, legal entities, legal contracts, or something else? Since the DAOs "management" is conducted automatically, legal systems would have to decide who is responsible if laws are broken. What, if any, is the liability of DAOs and their creators? Who or what is claimed against in the case of a legal dispute? Courts and regulators are unlikely to allow the wholesale adoption of technology that bypasses established oversight.

DAO Compliance with Financial Services Regulation

Many sourcing arrangements, including the use of certain technology solutions, require regulated entities to include in the relevant contracts a series of provisions enabling them to exert control, and seek to achieve operational continuity in relation to the services to which the contracts relate. With blockchain (as has been the case with cloud and certain fintech agreements) this may well be more of a challenge.

The DAO and Exiting a Contract

The need for exit assistance will be determined in large part by the specific solution and the extent to which the blockchain vendor holds the customer's data. If the customer does not have its own copy of the data, it will require data migration assistance to ensure the vendor is obliged to hand over all such data on expiry or termination of the agreement and a complete record of all transactions stored on the blockchain.

DAO Data as Property

In common law, as a general principle, there is no property right in information itself. But while individual items of information do not attract property rights, compilations of data may be protected by intellectual property rights. When a database of personal information is sold, if a buyer wants to use the personal information for a new purpose, to comply with data protection legislation (such as the EU's GDPR) they will have to get consent from the individuals concerned.

DAO and Due Diligence

Public companies and private investors have already begun to make significant capital investments in blockchain technology startups. This trend is likely to accelerate as commercial deployments of blockchain technology become a reality. Transactional lawyers who are tasked with performing due diligence on the buy and/or sell side of these investments need to understand blockchain technology and the emerging business models based on the technology. Traditional due diligence approaches may need to be adapted. For example, there will be unique issues concerning ownership of data residing on decentralized ledgers and intellectual property ownership of blockchain-as-a-service offerings operating on open-source blockchain technology platforms. These issues will need to be considered in the context of the business value proposition and competitive barriers to entry.

Summary

By now we see that smart contracts may be the most transformative current blockchain component. To that end, Marco Iansiti and Karim Lakhani of Harvard Business School offered some revealing insights for business and lawyers in "The Truth About Blockchain," in the *Harvard Business Review*, January–February 2017. In their view:

> "The implications are fascinating. . . . If contracts are automated, then what will happen to traditional firm structures, processes, and intermediaries like lawyers and accountants? . . . Their roles would all radically change. . . . [W]e are decades away from the widespread adoption of smart contracts. . . . A tremendous degree of coordination and clarity on how smart contracts are designed, verified, implemented, and enforced will be required. We believe the institutions responsible for those daunting tasks will take a long time to evolve. And the technology challenges—especially security—are daunting. . . . [L]aw firms will have to change to make smart contracts viable. They'll need to develop new expertise in software and blockchain programming."

In summary, blockchain, the distributed database technology with the capability to execute smart contracts, is more than a platform for cryptography. The universe of use cases, which we briefly covered, is expanding exponentially. As this technology continues generating new possibilities for the way we interact and exchange information, it brings forth challenging and complex legal issues and pushes the boundaries of existing laws. Our laws will have to adapt to blockchain technology, just as they adapted to the Internet, medical technology, e-discovery, and social media. There is a huge change before us as lawyers and as developers. We need to embrace it and be part of its evolution.

5 Technology on Ethereum

The simplest way to describe Bitcoin is to say that it is cryptocurrency or digital money. Bitcoin was released in January 2009, so for approximately nine years it has been used to transfer money in a peer-to-peer blockchain network. There is no central or world bank entity that controls the flow or functionality of Bitcoin; it is a decentralized digital currency. When compared to Bitcoin, Ethereum differs mainly in that it adds the functionality of the smart contract to its base cryptocurrency, known as ether. What does smart contract mean? Well, think of it as digital money that has logic associated with it. A smart contract can be set up to transfer value from one entity or account to another, and to do this if—and only if—certain conditions are met. Here's an example. Suppose you want to purchase a piece of real estate from someone. For those of you who have had the privilege of doing this, you know that there are almost too many third parties involved in the purchase, including real estate agents and brokers, lawyers, title searchers, home inspectors, surveyors, mortgage banks, and escrow agents. These external parties are what typically make the process incredibly slow and, of course, add cost. An Ethereum solution would have logic (or code) that could automatically transfer the ownership (title) from seller to buyer and the funds from buyer to seller after a deal is agreed upon in a far simpler way without needing as many third parties involved. See Table 5-1 for more Ethereum to Bitcoin comparison items.

Ethereum was created to serve as a platform for building blockchain-based, or decentralized, applications. It is developed by the Ethereum Foundation, a Swiss nonprofit, with contributions from great minds around the globe. Ethereum is well positioned for applications that need to be built quickly and that interact efficiently and securely in a blockchain ecosystem.

Ethereum uses blockchain technology, which is a transaction record that is independently verified by others and held on a distributed ledger. The same technology underpins Bitcoin. However, the Bitcoin blockchain is predominantly designed to do one thing: facilitate Bitcoin transactions. Ethereum, on the other hand, is designed to act as a programmable infrastructure. This means that Ethereum is a more adaptable and flexible development platform.

The Ethereum platform is often referred to as a Turing-complete virtual machine built upon the foundational functionality of blockchain. Ethereum allows one to construct smart contracts and applications with their own arbitrary rules for ownership, transaction formats, and state transition logic. A bare-bones version of a value application can be written in two

TABLE 5-1   Comparison of Ethereum to Bitcoin (Source: bitinfocharts.com)

Comparison	Ethereum	Bitcoin
Created	2015	2009
Market cap	Over $27 billion	Over $64 billion
Supply	94,832,363	16,588,550
Blockchain	Proof-of-work	Proof-of-work
Mining	GPU	ASIC
Initial distribution	ICO	Mining
Avg. blocktime	12 seconds	10 minutes
Avg. transaction fee	0.149 USD	3.18 USD

lines of code, and other protocols such as currencies and reputation systems can be built in under twenty.

Ethereum has its own token, called ether, which provides the primary form of liquidity allowing for exchange of value across the network. Ether also provides the mechanism for paying and earning transaction fees that arise from supporting and using the network. Ether has been the subject of speculation, and, as with Bitcoin, the price of ether has seen wide fluctuations. In the past two years, the price per ether ranged from US$10 to over US$400. It's now back to around US$300, but it has shown classic speculative characteristics. It is worth noting that ether is the financial incentive that pushes and fosters decentralization (and attracting miners), which makes the platform more secure.

Ethereum contains smart contracts. A smart contract is simply any agreement that can execute certain functions without human intervention. A smart contract in Ethereum is a cryptographically secured box containing logic and value. The logic has specific conditions that have to be met in order to release the value. It is the addition of logic and state that makes Ethereum a more powerful platform than what is available with other cryptocurrencies, including Bitcoin (and its scripting functionality). An example of a smart contract for insurance could automatically pay out to the insured entity based on a data feed showing that a payable event had occurred.

Smart contracts enable decentralized applications (dapps). Centralized applications are really centralized services. For example, when we interact with a third-party app on our smartphone, the app will communicate with centralized servers and services. A dapp can look exactly the same in terms of the user interface, but the backend services are replaced with smart contracts that run on the decentralized Ethereum network.

Ethereum also has decentralized autonomous organizations (DAOs). A DAO is a new form of entity or organization that can, for example, replace articles of incorporation and shareholder agreements with smart contracts.

Dapps and DAOs can also have their own digital tokens that serve a variety of functionality by acting as an internal currency. The development of dapps and DAOs is now being funded by selling these digital tokens in what is known as a token sale or an initial coin offering (ICO).

Ethereum Accounts

Within Ethereum, the current state is made up of objects that are commonly called accounts. The internal fuel on Ethereum is ether, and it is used to pay transaction fees (more on this later in the chapter). Ethereum can be viewed as a transaction-based state machine, starting with the genesis state and incrementally executing transactions that morph the state into a final state. The final state is what is considered the canonical "version" of the world of Ethereum. The state includes anything that can currently be represented by a computer, such as account balances, reputations, trust arrangements, and data representing information in the physical world. Transactions therefore represent a valid transition between two states. Each account within Ethereum has a 20-byte address (or identity) and the object is made up of four attributes or fields, which are:

- **Nonce**   Counter that is used to ensure each and every transaction can be processed once and once only
- **Ether balance**   The account's current value
- **Contract code**   An optional container for logic
- **Storage**   Empty by default

There are two types of accounts, externally owned accounts (EOAs) and contract accounts. EOAs, also known as normal accounts, have an ether balance, contain no logic, and are controlled by private keys. Contract accounts also have an ether balance but are controlled by their accompanying contract code (logic). All action on the Ethereum platform is set in motion by transactions fired from externally owned (normal) accounts. An externally owned account sends messages by creating, signing, and submitting a transaction. When a contract account receives a message, its code activates and executes as instructed by the input parameters of the transaction. The code (or logic) can read and write to the internal storage and send additional messages or create contracts. The use of the term *contract* in Ethereum should not be confused with its typical everyday use such as needing fulfillment, completion, or compliance per se. It is used to indicate logic bound inside the Ethereum execution environment that is executed in a defined way (by contract) when "poked" by a message or transaction (more on transactions later in this chapter), and that controls its internal state (variables), which includes its ether value.

Ether the Cryptocurrency

Ether (ETH) is the name of the cryptocurrency that fuels the distributed application Ethereum platform. It is used as the form of payment made by the clients of the network to the actual machines that execute the requested tasks. As we mentioned earlier, ether is the financial incentive that pushes and fosters decentralization and therefore attracts miners. Additional miners make the platform more secure and viable. Ether is also the incentive ensuring that quality applications are created, because inefficient code will usually cost more, and that the network remains highly available and functional, because owners are compensated for their contributed resources (computing power and storage).

As with a fiat currency, ether comes in size denominations that have their own name, shown in Table 5-2.

In short, ether has two purposes: it is used to pay the fees associated with a transaction, and it provides the Ethereum platform with the liquidity to exchange value between the types of digital assets housed on the platform.

TABLE 5-2 Ether Denominations

Name	Unit	Typical Usage
wei	1	Transaction fees
szabo	10^{12}	Transaction fees and protocol implementation
finney	10^{15}	Microtransactions
ether	10^{18}	Regular transactions

Genesis Block

Ether (ETH) was first issued in order to get the Ethereum project and platform launched and off the ground. The launch of the platform used the crowdfunding approach and took bitcoin in exchange for ether. The fundraising started in mid-2014 and approximately 60 million (actually 60,102,216 ETH) ether units were issued at the price of 1,000–2,000 ether per bitcoin (BTC). Of the total amount sold, 9.9 percent were allocated to the organization to compensate early contributors and pay ETH-denominated expenses before the genesis block on July 30, 2015. Another 9.9 percent of the total amount sold will be maintained as a long-term reserve. This means that the total amount released prior to the launch was close to 72 million. The bitcoin received from the sale was used to pay salaries/bounties to developers and invested into various for-profit and nonprofit projects in the blockchain ecosystem.

Post-Genesis Block

Once the Ethereum platform was launched, the way to issue ether was defined and set in order to secure the future success and health of the platform. It was defined that the ether units to be released per year will be 26 percent of the initial 60 million raised during the fundraising phase. Ether is issued at a rate of 5 ETH per block on a blocktime target of 12 seconds. This means that the amount of ether released per year will be a constant 15.6 million ether units, and so by July 2020 around 52 percent of the total currency issued will have been mined. See Figure 5-1 for a depiction of the issuance model (at launch) at per year for the first five years.

The issuance model for ether is similar to bitcoin, where the inflation is front loaded into the first few years and deflation occurs down the road. The big difference is that bitcoin is capped and no further issuance will occur. This may not matter as much given the Bitcoin Cash (BCC) spinoff, but with ether there will continue to be an issuance of 15.6 million units each and every year, which is marginal but nonetheless an increase in the fuel supply.

Obtaining Ether

There are multiple options to obtain ether, the fuel that drives transactions in Ethereum. You can

1. Buy it
2. Mine it
3. Accept it as payment

Description	Launch	Year 1	Year 2	Year 3	Year 4	Year 5
Crowdfunded/Issued (%)	119.8%	145.8%	171.8%	197.8%	223.8%	249.8%
Currency Issued	71,880,000	87,480,000	103,080,000	118,680,000	134,280,000	149,880,000
Early Contributor Holding (%)	8.264%	6.790%	5.763%	5.005%	4.424%	3.963%
Reserve Holding (%)	8.264%	6.790%	5.763%	5.005%	4.424%	3.963%
Miners (%)	0.00	18%	30%	39%	46%	52%

Issuance Agreement	Ether (ETH)
Crowdfunded	60,000,000
Early Contributors/Expenses (9.9%)	5,940,000
Reserve (9.9%)	5,940,000
Annual Increment (26%)	15,600,000

FIGURE 5-1   Ether (ETH) issuance model

In terms of mining, this can be done within a private environment or on the public test network (testnet). This is simple enough, but to mine within the production live environment (mainnet) requires significant dedicated GPU time and horsepower set up locally and connected to the Internet or to similarly powerful infrastructure available in the cloud (e.g., AWS, GCP, Azure, etc.). To purchase ether you will need to get it via an exchange. As different regions have different exchanges, you will need to perform a search in order to find the latest and greatest information on the best exchange for you.

Mining in Ethereum

The Ethereum blockchain is similar to the blockchain for Bitcoin. The main differences are in the design of the blocks. The Ethereum blocks contain a copy of both the transaction list and the most recent state (see Figure 5-2). The Ethereum blocks also contain values for the block number and the difficulty.

In its basic form, the Ethereum validation algorithm is as follows:

1. Check the following:
   - Prior block reference exists and is valid.
   - Timestamp of the current block is later than the prior block referenced and also less than 15 minutes later than the prior block timestamp.

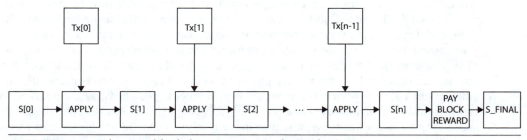

FIGURE 5-2   Ethereum blockchain transaction list and state

- The block number, difficulty, transaction root, uncle root, and gas limit are valid.
- The proof-of-work on the block is valid.
- If any of the above is not true, then return an error.

2. Set the zero-index state (i.e., S[0]) equal to the state at the end of the previously referenced block.
3. Set TX list equal to the block's list of n transactions. Loop through the transaction list and apply the transaction to the appropriate state, i.e., for all i in 0...n-1, set S[i+1] = APPLY(S[i],TX[i]). If any call to APPLY returns an error, or if the total gas consumed in the block up until this point exceeds the GASLIMIT, return an error.
4. Set S_FINAL equal to S[n], but adding the block reward paid to the miner.
5. Verify that the Merkle tree root of the state S_FINAL is equal to the final state root provided in the block header. If it is, the block is valid; otherwise, it is not valid.

It is important to note that while it looks like the entire state is stored with each block—an inefficient use of storage—this isn't so in reality. The states are stored in a tree structure, and after every block only a minority of the tree needs to be changed. Typically between two adjacent blocks the majority of the tree will be the same, and an optimization opportunity and technique is utilized. The data can be stored once and referenced twice using pointers (i.e., hashes of subtrees). This concept and approach with a tree is known as a Patricia tree. This combined with a modified Merkle tree allows for nodes to be inserted, deleted, and changed very efficiently. On the storage front, because all of the state information is part of the last block, there is no need to store the entire blockchain history, which results in a 5–20x savings in space when compared to the approach that Bitcoin uses.

A frequently asked question is where or when the code contained in a contract gets executed. The answer is that the execution of contract code is part of the definition of the state transition function (see later in this chapter), which is part of the block validation algorithm. Therefore when a transaction is added into a block, the code execution spawned by that very transaction will be executed by all nodes when they download and validate that same block.

GHOST Implementation

The Greedy Heaviest Observed SubTree (or GHOST) protocol was introduced in 2013 to blockchain platforms to combat the way that quick-blocktime blockchains, like Ethereum, suffer from a high frequency of stale blocks. Stale blocks are those that were propagated to the network and verified by some nodes as being correct but are eventually discarded because later, chronologically speaking, blocks get mined and propagated before the earlier ones do.

The GHOST protocol also combats the issue known as centralization bias—an example of which is, if miner X is a mining pool with 35 percent hash power and miner Y has 15 percent hash power, miner X will have a risk of producing a stale block 65 percent of the time and miner Y will have a risk of producing a stale block 85 percent of the time. So, if the block interval is short enough for the stale rate to be high, miner X will be substantially more efficient than miner Y simply by virtue of their pool size. In other words, the larger the pool and the smaller the block interval, the more often they are going to get a head start on other miners by producing the block themselves and then immediately starting the race for the next block.

With these two effects combined, blockchains producing blocks very quickly are highly likely to lead to a consolidated mining pool with a large enough percentage of the network hash power to take over the mining process. In Bitcoin, the probability of finding a block at the same time is more likely because the blocktime is 10 minutes and propagating a block to 50 percent of the network takes approximately 12 seconds. But in Ethereum, which has a much shorter blocktime (the target being 12 seconds), there is a need to reduce the incentive for pooled mining. This is where GHOST comes in.

GHOST solves the first issue of network security loss by including stale blocks in the calculation of which chain is the "longest." So the longest chain does not just take into account the parent and further ancestors of a block, but also the stale descendants of the block's ancestors ("uncles") are added to the calculation of which block has the largest total proof-of-work backing it.

GHOST solves the second issue of centralization bias by providing block rewards to stales. In Ethereum a stale block receives 87.5 percent of its base reward, and the nephew (child of the uncle) that includes the stale block receives the remaining 12.5 percent. Transaction fees, however, are not awarded to uncles.

The Ethereum version of GHOST is a simplified version that only goes down (or back) seven levels of the block chain.

- A block must specify a parent and its number of uncles (zero or more).
- An uncle included in a block must have the following properties:
  - It must be a direct child of the new block and less than seven blocks below it in terms of height.
  - It cannot be the direct ancestor of the block being formed.
  - It must be a valid block header; it does not have to be a pre-verified or even a valid block.
  - It must be different from all uncles included in previous blocks and all other uncles included in the same block (non-double-inclusion).
- For every uncle included in the block, the miner gets an additional 3.125 percent and the miner of the uncle receives 93.75 percent of a standard block reward.

This restricted version of GHOST (uncles includable only back seven generations) is used in Ethereum for two reasons. First, having an unlimited number of levels would include too many complications into the calculation of which uncles for a given block are valid. Second, unlimited levels with compensation removes the incentive for a miner to mine on the main chain as opposed to the chain of a malicious actor.

How Fees Protect

Every transaction that is published to the blockchain needs to be downloaded and verified by the network nodes. This feature (or burden) needs to be regulated in some way to prevent waste and abuse. In Bitcoin, the default approach is to have voluntary fees, where the miners set minimum fees and act as the gatekeepers. This market-driven approach uses the supply of miners and demand of transaction senders to make a market for the fee. But the issue here is that transaction processing on a blockchain is not a true market because it is not as simple as a single miner providing a transaction-processing service to a single sender. In actuality, every transaction that the miner includes in a validated and committed block needs to be processed by every node in the blockchain network. This means that the majority of the cost of processing a transaction is spread to the whole network, while it is the miner that makes the decision to include it or not that gets the reward.

Mining Issues

The mining algorithm in the Bitcoin network has the verifying nodes (miners) compute a SHA256 calculation on slightly modified versions of the block header. Simultaneously repeating this calculation millions of times over and over again, eventually one miner comes up with a version whose hash is less than the target. This presents a vulnerability to two forms of centralization. Let's examine this further.

Centralization   The first issue is that the hardware that the miners used became dominated by ASICs (application-specific integrated circuits). These are computer chips designed to be much more efficient at Bitcoin mining. By definition this stopped making mining a level playing field and meant that it became necessary to invest higher amounts in order to buy these specialized chips in order to compete. The second issue is that most Bitcoin miners do not actually perform block validation locally; they use a centralized mining pool to provide them with the block headers. The word "centralized" in the mining pool name should give it away, but in any case there is potentially a much worse problem than the specialized chip issue. The top three mining pools are all in China, and they indirectly control roughly 50 percent of processing power in the Bitcoin network. The miners still have the ability to switch mining pools, and this does present a mitigation strategy in the event of collusion when a pool or coalition attempts a 51 percent attack.

Ethereum Handles Centralization   Ethereum is set up to use an algorithm where miners are required to fetch random data from the state, compute some randomly selected transactions from the prior N blocks in the blockchain, and return the hash of the result. This has a couple of benefits. First, smart contracts can include any kind of computation, so an Ethereum ASIC would essentially be a CPU for general computation, or GPU. Second, mining in Ethereum requires access to the entire blockchain, forcing miners to store the entire blockchain and at least be capable of verifying every transaction. This more importantly removes the need for centralized mining pools and the risk and issue of centralization.

Ethereum Work

Ethereum has essentially one way for work to begin and that is via a transaction. A transaction in Ethereum is a cryptographically signed data packet that contains a message sent from an externally owned account. Let's take a closer look at the transaction and message objects.

Transactions

There are essentially three types of transactions that can be found on Ethereum:

- A transfer of value from one entity to another
- The creation of a smart contract
- The invocation of a smart contract

A transaction is made up of attributes, or fields, which are:

- **From**   A signed address for the sending account. It is signed in order to prove that the sender intended to send the transaction to the recipient.

- **To**   The destination address of the transaction, this is left undefined for a transaction that creates a contract.
- **Value**   The amount of value to be transferred (always expressed in wei). For a transaction that creates a contract this field will typically hold the endowment.
- **Gas**   This is sometimes referred to as the Start Gas field. It is the amount of fuel to use for the transaction and represents the maximum number of computational steps for the transaction. Any unused fuel will be refunded to the sender. See more on this field below.
- **Gas Price**   The price of gas for this transaction (specified in wei—more on this later in the chapter). This defaults to the mean network fuel price and represents the fee the sender pays per computational step. See more on this field below.
- **Data**   This can be omitted or defined as a byte string containing data for the message. For a transaction that creates a contract, this may contain the initialization logic.
- **Nonce**   This can be used to overwrite pending transactions that use the same nonce.

As you can see, the first three fields are those that are needed for any financial transaction that transfers value. The Data field has many purposes depending on the type of transaction—as we've already mentioned this can be initialization logic or data. It all depends on what is needed to fulfill the transaction.

Network Fuel (Gas)

In order to process transactions there needs to be sufficient fuel (ether) in the account from which the transactions are being sent. Ether is needed to pay the execution cost for the Ethereum client that performs the transaction work on behalf of the sender, committing the result to the Ethereum blockchain.

Interestingly, it is the Gas and Gas Price attributes on the transaction that are key components to the denial-of-service (DoS) prevention design built into the Ethereum network. To combat infinite loops or computational waste (whether intentional or not), each transaction is required to specify a limit to the number of computational steps a transaction can take to complete. The unit of computation in Ethereum is known as gas, and each operation in Ethereum has an associated gas cost that depends on how intensive it is from a computing power perspective (see Table 5-3 for the gas cost associated with the majority of Ethereum's opcodes/instructions).

Some operations cost higher amounts of gas simply because they are computationally resource intensive. In addition to compute power fee, there is also a fee of 5 gas for every byte in the transaction data. As we've stated earlier, the intent of the fee structure in this model is to ensure that senders pay proportionately for every resource consumed, be it computation, bandwidth, and/or storage. So it stands to reason that resource-intensive contracts and messages must have an appropriately proportionate gas fee.

Messages

An Ethereum contract has the ability to send a message to another contract (it can do this multiple times). A transaction initiated by an externally owned account can contain values in the Data field that will go into a message. Within Ethereum a message is a virtual object that is

TABLE 5-3   Ethereum Opcode (Instruction) Cost (*Continued*)

Opcode (Instruction)	Gas
ADD	3
ADDMOD	8
ADDRESS	2
AND	3
BALANCE	20
BLOCKHASH	20
BYTE	3
CALLDATACOPYBASE	3
CALLDATALOAD	3
CALLDATASIZE	2
CALLER	2
CALLVALUE	2
CODESIZE	2
COINBASE	2
CREATE	32,000
CREATEDATA	200
DIFFICULTY	2
DIV	5
DUP	3
ECRECOVER	3,000
EQ	3
EXPBASE	10
EXPBYTE	10
EXTCODECOPYBASE	20
EXTCODESIZE	20
GAS	2
GASLIMIT	2
GASPRICE	2
GCALL	40
GCALLNEWACCOUNT	25,000
GCALLSTIPEND	2,300
GCALLVALUETRANSFER	9,000
GCOPYWORD	3

TABLE 5-3 Ethereum Opcode (Instruction) Cost (*Continued*)

Opcode (Instruction)	Gas
GLOG	375
GLOGDATA	8
GLOGTOPIC	375
GSUICIDEREFUND	24,000 refundable
GT	3
GTX	21,000
GTXDATANONZERO	67.75945113
GTXDATAZERO	4.234965696
IDENTITYBASE	15
IDENTITYWORD	3
ISZERO	3
JUMP	8
JUMPDEST	1
JUMPI	10
LT	3
MEMWORD	3
MLOAD	3
MOD	5
MSIZE	2
MSTORE	3
MSTORE8	3
MUL	5
MULMOD	8
NOT	3
NUMBER	2
OR	3
ORIGIN	2
PC	2
POP	2
PUSH	3
QUADCOEFFDIV	512 (divisor)
RETURN	0
RIPEMD160BASE	600

TABLE 5-3 Ethereum Opcode (Instruction) Cost

Opcode (Instruction)	Gas
RIPEMD160WORD	120
SDIV	5
SGT	3
SHA256BASE	60
SHA256WORD	12
SHA3BASE	30
SHA3WORD	6
SIGNEXTEND	5
SLOAD	200
SLT	3
SMOD	5
SSTORE (from zero to non-zero)	20,000
SSTORE (to zero or non-zero change)	5,000
STOP	0
STORAGEKILL	5,000, plus 15,000 refund
SUB	3
SUICIDE	0
SWAP	3
TIMESTAMP	2
XOR	3

never serialized per se and exists within the execution environment only. It is made up of the following fields:

- **Sender** The sender of the message (implicit)
- **Recipient** The recipient of the message
- **Amount** The amount of ether to transfer alongside the message
- **Data (optional)** An optional data field
- **Start Gas** A value

As you can see, essentially a message is very similar to a transaction. The difference is that it is produced by a contract and not an external actor (although it can be caused by one). When the code inside a contract executes and calls the CALLopcode function, it creates and executes a message. Similar to a transaction, the message is sent to the recipient account running its code. So you can see that contracts can interact with other contracts the same way that external actors accounts can. An important thing to note is that the gas allowance specified by a contract or transaction is the governing amount for the transaction and any and all dependent executions. So, for example, if account A sends (commits) a transaction to account B with 100 gas, B performs operations that consume 70 gas and then sends a message to C. C then performs operations that consume 25 gas before returning. Then B can use another 5 gas before running out of fuel (Out-of-Gas exception).

The Ethereum Block

The block in Ethereum is the collection of relevant pieces of information (known as the block header), H, together with information corresponding to the comprised transactions, T, and a set of other block headers, U, that are known to have a parent equal to the present block's parent's parent (such blocks are known as ommers2).

Below are the fields that exist in the block header:

- **parentHash**   The Keccak 256-bit hash of the parent block's header, in its entirety; formally Hp.
- **ommersHash**   The Keccak 256-bit hash of the ommers list portion of this block; formally Ho.
- **beneficiary**   The 160-bit address to which all fees collected from the successful mining of this block are transferred; formally Hc.
- **stateRoot**   The Keccak 256-bit hash of the root node of the state trie (Merkle Patricia Tree or radix tree), after all transactions are executed and finalizations applied; formally Hr.
- **transactionsRoot**   The Keccak 256-bit hash of the root node of the trie structure populated with each transaction in the transactions list portion of the block; formally Ht.
- **receiptsRoot**   The Keccak 256-bit hash of the root node of the trie structure populated with the receipts of each transaction in the transactions list portion of the block; formally He.
- **logsBloom**   The Bloom filter composed from indexable information (logger address and log topics) contained in each log entry from the receipt of each transaction in the transactions list; formally Hb.
- **difficulty**   A scalar value corresponding to the difficulty level of this block. This can be calculated from the previous block's difficulty level and the timestamp; formally Hd.
- **number**   A scalar value equal to the number of ancestor blocks. The genesis block has a number of zero; formally Hi.
- **gasLimit**   A scalar value equal to the current limit of gas expenditure per block; formally Hl.
- **gasUsed**   A scalar value equal to the total gas used in transactions in this block; formally Hg.
- **timestamp**   A scalar value equal to the reasonable output of Unix's time() at this block's inception; formally Hs.
- **extraData**   An arbitrary byte array containing data relevant to this block. This must be 32 bytes or fewer; formally Hx.
- **mixHash**   A 256-bit hash that proves, combined with the nonce, that a sufficient amount of computation has been carried out on this block; formally Hm.
- **nonce**   A 64-bit hash that proves, combined with the mix-hash, that a sufficient amount of computation has been carried out on this block; formally Hn.

The other two components in the block are simply a list of block headers (of the same format as above) and a series of the transactions.

State Transition Function (STF)

As with Bitcoin and other cryptocurrencies, the ledger of Ethereum is essentially the result of a state transition function (STF), which takes the state of the network prior to a transaction and, upon executing the transaction, produces a new state as the result. See Figure 5-3 for a graphical depiction of Ethereum state transition function.

The specifics of the Ethereum STF (i.e., APPLY(S,TX) -> S') are as follows:

1. Check the following, and if any are not true, then return an error:
   - Transaction is well-formed and has the correct number of values.
   - Signature is valid.
   - Nonce matches the nonce in the sender's account.
   - If any of the above is not true, return an error.
2. Calculate the fee for the transaction as Start Gas * Gas Price, and derive the sender's account address from the signature. Subtract the calculated transaction fee from the sender's account balance and increment the sender's nonce. In the event that there is an insufficient amount in the sender's account, return an error.
3. Initially set Gas equal to Start Gas, and take off a certain quantity of gas per byte to pay for the bytes in the transaction (this is the storage fee).
4. Transfer the transaction value from the sender's account to the receiving account. If the receiving account does not yet exist, create it. If the receiving account is a contract, run the contract's code either to completion or until the execution runs out of gas (Out-of-Gas exception).
5. If the value transfer failed because the sender did not have enough money, or the code execution ran out of gas, revert all state changes except the payment of the fees, and add the fees to the miner's account. Otherwise, refund the fees for all remaining gas to the sender, and send the fees paid for gas consumed to the miner.

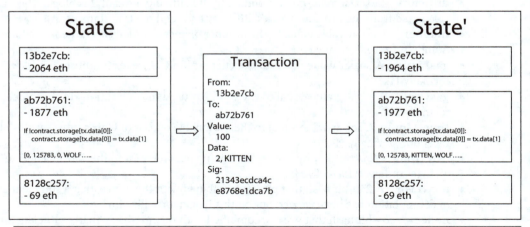

FIGURE 5-3 Ethereum state transition function (STF)

Now let's work through an example. Suppose that a contract's storage starts off empty, and a transaction is sent with 10 ether value, 4,000 gas, 0.001 ether gas price, and 32 bytes of data, with bytes 0–15 representing the number 4 and bytes 16–31 representing the string "KITTEN-AND-WOLF". The process for the state transition function in this particular example is as follows:

1. Check that the transaction is valid and well formed.
2. Check that the transaction sender has at least (4,000 * 0.001) 4 ether. If it does, then subtract 4 ether from the sender's account.
3. Initialize gas = 4,000; assuming the transaction is 120 bytes long and the byte fee is 5, subtract 600 from the gas, and that will leave 3,400 gas remaining.
4. Subtract 10 more ether from the sender's account, and add it to the contract's account.
5. Run the code. The code checks if the contract's storage at index 4 is used; if it is available, it sets the value to KITTEN-AND-WOLF. Imagine this takes 1,177 gas, so the remaining amount of gas is 3,400 − 1,177 = 2,223.
6. Refund (2,223 * 0.001) 2.223 ether back to the sender's account, and return the resulting state.

If there was no contract at the receiving end of the transaction, then the total transaction fee would simply be equal to the provided Gas Price multiplied by the length of the transaction in bytes, and the data sent with the transaction would be irrelevant. It is important to note that messages work the same way as transactions in terms of reverting—that is, if a message execution runs out of gas, the message's execution and all dependent executions triggered by the execution will revert, but the parent executions do not need to. This makes it okay for a contract to call another contract, so if X calls Y with F gas then X's execution is guaranteed to lose at most F gas. For the CREATE opcode, which is used to create a contract, its execution process is similar to the CALL opcode, except that the output of the execution determines the code (logic) of a newly created contract.

Code Execution

The EVM code that is contained in Ethereum contracts is a low-level, stack-based bytecode language. The code is a series of bytes that represent operations. Typically, code execution inside the EVM is an infinite loop of carrying out the operation at the current program counter (i.e., index beginning at zero) and incrementing this counter by 1 until one of three things happens: end of code, an exception, a STOP or RETURN instruction is encountered. While the operation is executing, it has access to four areas for reading and in most cases storing of data:

- **Stack**   This utilizes the LIFO (last-in-first-out) principle. Data is pushed to the top of the stack or data is popped from the top of the stack. This is reset when computation ends.
- **Memory**   This is an infinitely expandable byte array. This is reset when computation ends.

- **Storage**   This is the contract's key/value store. This persists when computation ends.
- **Other**   The executing code can read the value, sender, and data of the message. It can also access the block header data and optionally return a byte array.

The EVM execution model is straightforward. While EVM is running, its complete computational state can be defined by the following tuple (collection or row) of data:

```
block_state, transaction, message, code, memory, stack, pc, gas
```

where `block_state` is the top-level or global state containing all accounts, including balances and the storage. At the beginning of every step of execution, the current instruction is found by taking the `pc` (Program Counter) byte of `code` (or 0 if `pc` is set to a value greater than the length of the `code` item), and each opcode (or instruction) has its own definition in terms of how it operates on the tuple. For example, the `ADD` operation pops two items off the top of the stack, adds them together, and pushes their sum value to the top of the stack. It then reduces `gas` by 3 and increments `pc` by 1, and `SSTORE` (save word to storage) pops the top two items off the top of the stack and inserts the second item into the contract's storage at the index specified by the first item. It then reduces `gas` by 20,000 and increments `pc` by 1.

Turing Complete

The Ethereum virtual machine (EVM) is said to be Turing complete. What does that mean? It means that the EVM code can encode any conceivable computation and this includes looping. There are two ways that the EVM code can loop. The first way the EVM can loop is via two direct instructions: JUMP, which allows the execution to jump back to a previous location in the code, and JUMPI, which allows the execution to carry out conditional jumping (using if/then/else or while statements). The second way the EVM can loop is through recursive calls. For example, contract A can call contract B, which in turn calls contract A, and so on. This presents a problem whereby a malicious actor on the network can effectively shut down nodes and the network's associated mining by deploying contracts that contain logic that executes infinite loops. This issue is known in computer science as the halting problem, which is the inability to determine whether the program will finish running or continue to run forever. Ethereum deals with this issue using simple economics. When a transaction is committed to the blockchain, it contains a field, Gas (or Start Gas), that specifies the maximum number of computational steps that the transaction is allowed to take. Once this threshold is exceeded the computation is reverted, but the fees are still paid to the miner. The same mechanism is in place for messages. Let's work through some malicious actor scenarios to see how the design of the Ethereum platform handles them.

- The malicious actor builds and deploys a contract that contains an infinite loop. They send a transaction that activates the loop. The miner processes the transaction, which kicks off the infinite loop. Even though it runs out of gas and stops before completing fully, the transaction is still considered valid from the miner's perspective, and they claim the fee from the attacker for each computational step.

- The malicious actor again tries to create a very long infinite loop forcing the miner to keep computing for a long time. By the time computation finishes, more blocks will have come out, and it will not be possible for the miner to include the transaction in the block they are processing in order to claim the fee. This is where the Start Gas field, which limits the number of computational steps an execution can take, will be need to be set sufficiently and unusually high, giving the miner sufficient clues to the malicious intent of the transaction and a chance to reject it.
- The malicious actor reviews contract code that is something like:

```
send(A, contract.storage[A]); contract.storage[A] = 0;
```

  The malicious actor sends a transaction with enough gas to run the first step only—in other words, to withdraw an amount. But the part that sets the amount to zero does not execute. The network (and specifically the contract author) does not need to be concerned about handling and protecting against such assaults, because when the transaction runs out of gas, the changes will be reverted. Note that the miner will still get paid the gas that was used to process the first instruction, so the malicious actor still pays.
- A contract is created and deployed to work in the following way. It references seven data feeds and takes the average data value of the seven as a way to calculate a risk factor. A malicious actor finds a way to compromise one of the seven data feeds and changes its functionality so that it runs an infinite loop instead, the idea being to force any attempts to calculate a risk factor from the contract to run out of gas. However, the Ethereum feature of being able to set a gas limit on the message will prevent this scenario from causing a problem. Note that the function that combines the seven values into an average will still need to deal with one or more feeds from failing to respond and act appropriately.

In short, the halting problem and associated Turing completeness are surprisingly easy to manage with the Ethereum design and architecture.

Scalability

There is a concern about the scalability of the Ethereum platform. After all, it is based on blockchain, and the design is such that it has to replicate transactions and blocks to every node in the network, so just how scalable can it be? Let's recap on what scalability is. It's the capability of a system, network, or process to handle a growing amount of work, or its potential to be enlarged to accommodate that growth. At the time of writing, the Bitcoin blockchain size is around 159 GB and can grow by 1 MB approximately every 10 minutes. If the Bitcoin network had to process one of the major credit card companies' number of transactions it would potentially grow by 1 MB every 3 seconds or approximately 1 GB per hour or 8 TB per year. Each node would need to have some serious resource capabilities in order to process that amount of data at the speed necessary to handle the requests. The Ethereum blockchain size is 57 GB and would also suffer from the same growth pattern. It would be even more complicated by the fact that Ethereum is an application platform containing applications and code and not solely a cryptocurrency. Ethereum has some relief in that the full nodes only need to store the state and not the complete history. However, this relief is combined with a huge increase in blockchain size, so you will start to see fewer and fewer full nodes and more and more simplified payment verification (SPV) nodes, increasing the risk of centralization. The risk is that the full nodes could collude and cheat the platform by adjusting the reward in their favor. The SPV (or light) nodes would not detect the issue immediately. Aside from the spinoff of Bitcoin Cash (BCC), there are a few suggestions on how to alleviate the future scaling issue for Bitcoin. For the Ethereum platform, there are two strategies in place to help deal with the issue of scaling. First, because of the mining algorithm every miner is forced to be a full node. Second, after processing each transaction, an intermediate state tree root is saved to the blockchain. In the event of a centralization event, as long as there is a single honest miner on the network the issue can be addressed via a verification process. So if a malicious miner publishes an invalid block, the verifying node would run the same computation and see that the state generated does not match the state provided and reject the transaction.

The switch to Casper, a proof-of-stake (PoS) consensus algorithm, is also said to improve, among other things, the scalability issues that are associated with the current proof-of-work (PoW) consensus approach. In PoW-based blockchains, the consensus algorithm rewards nodes that solve cryptographic puzzles. The winning miners validate transactions and create new blocks. In PoS-based blockchains, a set of validators take turns proposing and voting on the next block, and the weight of each validator's vote depends on the size of their stake (or deposit). This PoS approach is said to be advantageous over PoW in terms of security, a reduced risk of centralization, and energy efficiency.

Infrastructure: Storage and Communication

At their core, all successful computer platforms need to *calculate*, *persist*, and *communicate* data in the most efficient and secure manner. The Ethereum Virtual Machine (EVM) covers the calculate (or compute) aspect, so let's take a look at what is used for persistence and communication.

- **Decentralized file storage (persistence)**   Swarm is peer-to-peer (p2p) file sharing that is paid for with micropayments of ETH. Within Swarm, data files are broken down into chunks, distributed, and stored across the network participating nodes. The applications and smart contracts that need to store and retrieve data compensate the nodes that persist and serve the data.
- **Communication**   Whisper is an encrypted messaging protocol allowing nodes to send messages directly to each other while hiding the sender and receiver and the message from third-party snoopers.

INFURA

INFURA is a scalable, standards-based, globally distributed cluster and API endpoint for Ethereum, IPFS (InterPlanetary File System), and other emerging decentralization infrastructures. Its mission is to provide secure, stable, robust, balanced, fault tolerant, and easily scalable Ethereum and IPFS nodes. In essence, INFURA is a shared infrastructure layer acting as a bridge to the blockchain. For Ethereum dapp developers, INFURA eliminates the requirement to install, configure, and maintain Ethereum nodes. Specifically for IPFS, which enables distributed storage, this can be accessed seamlessly without the hassle of managing the infrastructure. Figure 5-4 shows the high-level architecture for INFURA.

Here are highlights of INFURA capabilities:

- Exposes TLS (Transport Layer Security)-enabled endpoints to seamlessly access IPFS from decentralized applications running software locally.
- Presents TLS-enabled endpoints for Ethereum that support CORS (Cross-Origin Resource Sharing) and provides capabilities that available in the JSON-RPC API (including web3 and eth methods).
- Broadcasts signed raw transactions to Ethereum blockchain.
- Provides Ferryman, a reverse proxy that helps with caching, throttling, logging, scaling, and reliability, and provides intelligent request routing to a number of specialized backend clients such as EthereumH, Geth, Nethereum, Parity, Strato, or any other client that performs certain operations in an optimized way.
- Works on Ethereum Main Net (ETH), Ethereum Testnet (Morden), and the Ethereum ConsenSysNet.

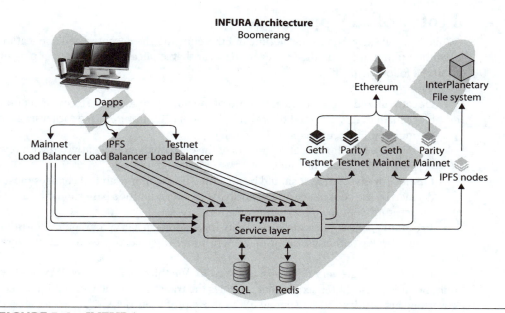

FIGURE 5-4   INFURA

Below are the steps necessary to start using INFURA:

1. Sign up for an INFURA access token at https://infura.io/register.html. Though the service is free, requests do need to be identified to the RPC provider endpoints.
2. Choose a network. This can be production or one of the many test networks.
3. Issue requests to INFURA. A list of available requests can be found at https://infura.io/docs/#supported-json-rpc-methods. (Note that if you omit the access token, calls will probably still work, but they are subject to more restrictive throttling and filtering of available JSON-RPC API calls.)
4. Or you can use the REST(ish) API that is documented at http://docs.infura.apiary.io/.

Decentralized Applications

A decentralized application (dapp) is like any other modern web-architected application, typically consisting of a user interface (UI) whose functionality is supported by backend services (reading and writing to persistent storage, processing, complex logic). These backend services typically make use of the Ethereum platform and in particular the smart contracts that are deployed to it. See Figure 5-5 for an example dapp.

Profile of a Dapp

While it is still early days in the lifetime of Ethereum and the decentralized applications that are built upon it, it is nonetheless becoming clear that applications that are popping up appear to fit the following profile:

- **Decentralized** The complete record of the operation must be stored on a public blockchain that is designed to prevent pitfalls of centralization (see earlier in the chapter for more on Ethereum's approach to this).
- **Incentivized** The validating miners of the blockchain are incentivized with rewards of cryptographic tokens or value.
- **Open source** Ideally, it should be governed by autonomy and all changes must be decided by the consensus, or a majority, of its users. Its code base should be available for scrutiny.
- **Protocol** The application community must agree on a cryptographic algorithm to show proof of value (either via proof-of-work or proof-of-stake, or a combination thereof).

In retrospect, the very first dapp was Bitcoin. We think of Bitcoin as a cryptocurrency only, but it is a distributed ledger that provides the transfer of value without intermediaries or governing authorities and satisfies all of the above profile entries.

There are now many examples of Ethereum-based dapps. If you navigate to the State of the Dapps website (https://dapps.ethercasts.com/) you will see there are more than 700 dapps in various states of development. Some of the most successful in terms of market cap are Augur (prediction market), Golem (distributed computation), and Melonport (asset management portal).

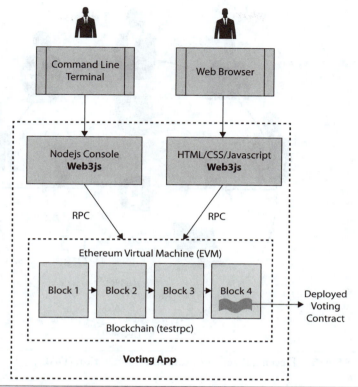

FIGURE 5-5   Ethereum dapp

Decentralized Autonomous Organizations

A decentralized autonomous organization (DAO) uses the same or similar thought processes applied to Bitcoin where it did away with central governing middlemen, and extends that to the corporate structure. The idea is that companies and other organizations can exist and operate without hierarchical management. A DAO attempts to codify (put into code) the rules that a company operates under. These rules include what projects are to be funded, how to accept investment, how to pay back investors, and how to amend and extend the governing rules (which most likely would be to fork the DAO code or make a new DAO and transfer value from old to new). Figure 5-6 shows an example DAO topology. Basically, a DAO works the same way as a typical company, but its rules are digitally encoded and automatically enforced and executed.

The biggest issue with a DAO is that when something unforeseen is encountered, its structure and current code base may not facilitate a fix or change to overcome or address the situation. It is still something worthwhile to keep an eye on and even participate in, so the kinks can be worked out and iterated on.

FIGURE 5-6   Decentralized autonomous organization (DAO)

Summary

With its state transition function, Ethereum provides an open-ended platform by design, and is well suited to serve as a framework for financial and nonfinancial decentralized applications. Regulation is still up in the air on this. How it may even apply to a global decentralized platform is unclear. Current laws and regulations will catch up and apply to these platforms. However, it is still important to work through any legal and regulatory impacts of particular applications. Businesses operating in regulated industries should seek guidance from their regulators before integrating critical, customer-facing, or data-handling processes with platforms like Ethereum. Large strides have been made in the financial services arena with private and consortium varieties of blockchain, and clearly this is an indication that financial institutions are playing in and watching the space very closely.

6

Fast-Track Application Tutorial

Whenever new technology comes along, especially for us developers, the first thing we want to learn is how to use the language to invoke its functionality and manipulate its data types. We want to know how to develop, validate, and deploy the application. The blockchain is no different. At the current time, the Bitcoin blockchain does not provide the comprehensive functionality required by lots of applications where blockchain can be applied and helpful. Ethereum, however, does provide a comprehensive functionality via its smart contracts capability using Solidity. In this chapter, we will introduce Solidity the language, a browser-based integrated development environment (IDE) to write and deploy Ethereum contracts. At the writing of this book mid-2017, Ethereum IDEs are not matured. That has been typical for new technologies and development, such as Java. When Java development started in the late 1980s, developers used tools like Notepad text editors to write Java programs and deploy them to application servers. It was a tough time for development. Ten or so years later, IDEs like Eclipse facilitate the development, testing, and deployment of Java applications. This evolution will no doubt take place with blockchain Ethereum and Solidity. It is merely a matter of time.

Introducing Solidity

Solidity the word means the quality or state of being firm or strong in structure. Solidity the language is a contract-oriented, high-level language whose syntax is similar to that of JavaScript. It is designed to target the Ethereum Virtual Machine (EVM). Solidity is statically typed and supports inheritance, libraries, and complex user-defined types among other features. This chapter provides a basic introduction to Solidity and assumes some knowledge of programming in general. You can start using Solidity in your browser, with no need to download or compile anything. This application only supports compilation—if you want to run the code or inject it into the blockchain, you have to use a client or blockchain gateway service such as INFURA.

Solidity Basics

As mentioned, Solidity is an object-oriented programming language for writing smart contracts. Developers ask the question, "Is Solidity Turing complete?" An imperative language is Turing complete if it has conditional branching (such as `if`, `while`, `for`), conditional looping statements, and the ability to change an arbitrary amount of memory, such as the ability to maintain an arbitrary number of variables. Since this is almost always the case, most if not all imperative languages are Turing complete if the limitations of finite memory are ignored. The commonly used development languages C, C++, C#, Java, Lua, and Python are all Turing complete, as is Solidity. That said, most of the control structures from C/JavaScript are available in Solidity except for `switch`.

Let's start with some basic code examples. The first question to ask is what is the current release of Solidity. When starting, one should always go to the GitHub site (https://github.com/ethereum/solidity/releases), which lists the releases and new functionality for Solidity. Once you know that, then the second statement in the contract would be the release. If you look at the sample code below, you'll notice the specification of the current release of Solidity at the time of this writing.

```
StorageState
// COMMENT Class or Contract named StorageState

pragma solidity ^0.4.16;
contract StorageState{
// COMMENT unsigned integer variable named statedData
    uint stateData;


/* COMMENT
 The setter and the getter for variable named stateData
*/
    function set(uint x) {
        stateData = x;
    }

    function get() constant returns (uint) {
        return stateData;
    }
}
```

As mentioned, the first line indicates that the source code is written for Solidity version 0.4.16. The keyword or directive `pragma` (from "pragmatic") is a language construct that specifies how a compiler or translator should process its input.

A contract in Solidity is code that includes the functionality and data that execute and record the state of the contract. The contract resides at a specific address on the Ethereum blockchain. This contract, StorageState, if it were written in Java would be a bean. Java beans declare some variables and include a getter and a setter for each of the variables used to modify or retrieve the value of the variable. The bean is usually a data structure that is passed around class to class containing data we wish to share. The line `uint stateData;` declares a state variable called stateData of type uint which is an unsigned integer of length 32 bytes. This contract, as mentioned, is a bean allowing anyone to store a single number that is accessible by anyone publishing this number. Just as in Java, by declaring the variable private we pose access restrictions such that only the internal contract code can modify the variable. As you would expect, single-line comments (//) and multi-line comments (/*...*/) are specified as depicted here.

Solidity Control and Flow Statements

As with most of the current computer languages, there are the familiar constructs: the Aristotelian conditional if-then-else, the loop functionality of while and for with the break, continue, return. See Table 6-1 for descriptions and examples.

TABLE 6-1   **Functionality and Control of Execution (*Continued*)**

Solidity Statement	Description	Notes/Example
import	Solidity supports import statements that are very similar to those available in JavaScript.	import "filename";

if (else	Use the `if` statement to specify a block of code to be executed if a condition is true.	if (condition) {
		   block of code to be executed if the condition is true
		}
		if (totalPoints > bet.line)
		   balances[bet.over] += bet.amount * 2;
		else if (totalPoints < bet.line)
		   balances[bet.under] += bet.amount * 2;
		else {
		   balances[bet.under] += bet.amount;
		   balances[bet.over] += bet.amount;
		   }

while	Loops through a block of code as long as a specified condition is true.	while (condition) {
		  code block to be executed
		}
		while (i >= 0 && bid.amount > 0) {
		   uint j = uint(i);
		if (matchStack[j].amount == 0) {
		// matched bids
		  i--;
		  continue;
		   }

TABLE 6-1   Functionality and Control of Execution

Solidity Statement	Description	Notes/Example

for	Loops through a block of code a number of times.
	
	start1 is executed before the loop (the code block) starts.
	
	condition2 defines the condition for running the loop (the code block).
	
	test3 is executed each time after the loop (the code block) has been executed.
		<pre>for (start1; condition2; test3) {
		    code block to be executed
		}
		for (uint i=0; i < bets.length; i++) {
		    Bet bet = bets[i];
		    if (bet.status == BetStatus.Paid)
		        continue;
		
		    bet.status = BetStatus.Paid;
		}</pre>

Data Types

Solidity is a statically typed language, which means that the data type of each variable (state and local) needs to be specified at compile time. The following data types are also known as value types because they will always be passed by value as opposed to reference, i.e., they are always copied when they are used as function arguments or in assignments. See Table 6-2 for descriptions and examples.

TABLE 6-2   Solidity Data Types and Related Functions (*Continued*)

Data Type	Description	Notes/Example
Boolean bool	Values are true and false	Comparisons (<=, !=, ==, etc.) always yield booleans.
Integer int, uint	Signed and unsigned integers of various sizes	The integer types are signed and unsigned integers of various bit widths (int8/uint8 to int256/uint256 in steps of 8 bits, where uint/int are aliases for uint256/int256) and addresses (of 160 bits).
Address	20 byte value (Ethereum address)	Address types also have members and serve as base for all contracts.

TABLE 6-2   Solidity Data Types and Related Functions (*Continued*)

Data Type	Description	Notes/Example

Members of address	`<address>.balance (uint256):`
	`<address>.transfer( amount):`
	`<address>.send( amount) returns (bool)`
	`<address>.call(...) returns (bool)`
	`<address>.callcode(..) returns (bool)`
	`<address>.delegatecall(..) returns (bool)`
		Query the balance of an address using the property `balance` and to send Ether (units of wei) to an address using `transfer`.
		
		send is the low-level counterpart of `transfer`. If the execution fails, the current contract will not stop with an exception, but send will return false. `delegatecall` is identical to `call` apart from the fact that the code at the target address is executed in the context of the calling contract and `msg.sender` and `msg.value` do not change their values. A contract can dynamically load code from a different address at runtime. Storage, current address, and balance still refer to the calling contract, only the code is taken from the called address. This facilitates the library feature in Solidity: reusable library code that can be applied to a contract's storage, e.g., in order to implement a complex data structure.

Fixed-size byte arrays
`bytes1,`
`bytes2,`
`bytes3,`
`.. bytes32.`
	1 to 32 byte array
	Index access: If x is of type bytesl, then x[k] for 0 <= k < lreturns the k th byte s
	.length yields the fixed length of the byte array (read-only)
		Bit operators: &, |, ^ (bitwise exclusive or), ~ (bitwise negation), << (left shift), >> (right shift)

Array	Variable and fixed-size arrays are supported in storage and as parameters of external functions.
	Assignment replaces the array; see example.
	If the new size is smaller, removed array elements will be cleared; see example.
		`bool[7][] mFlags;`
		an array of 7 boolean variables called mFlags
		`delete mFlags`
		delete the array
		`mFlags.length = 6`
		change length of array and kill 7th item
		`uint[7] mIntegers`
		an array of 7 unsigned Integer variables called mIntegers

TABLE 6-2 Solidity Data Types and Related Functions (*Continued*)

Data Type	Description	Notes/Example
String literals	String literals are written with either double or single quotes.	`"foo"` or `'bar'` or `'snafu'`
Hexadecimal literals	Hexadecimal literals are prefixed with the keyword `hex` and are enclosed in double or single quotes.	Their content must be a hexadecimal string and their value will be the binary representation of those values, e.g., `(hex"001122FF")`.
Enums	Data type consisting of a set of named values called elements.	`enum HairColor { Brunette, Blonde, Redhead}`
Structures	Define new data types in the form of structs. Struct types can be used inside mappings and arrays, and they can themselves contain mappings and arrays but not a member of their own type, although the struct itself can be the value type of a mapping member.	`struct DataStruct1 {address addr;` `uint amount;}` `struct DataStruct2 {` `    address addr2` `    uint amount2;` `    mapping (uint` `=> DataStruct1)` `datastruct2;` `    }` Note a struct type is typically assigned to a local variable. This does not copy the struct but only stores a reference. `DataStruct1 ds1 = datastruct[1]`
Mappings	Mapping types are declared as mapping (`_KeyType` => `_ValueType`). `KeyType` can be almost any type except for a mapping, a dynamically sized array, a contract, an `enum`, and a `struct`. `ValueType` can actually be any type, including mappings.	Mappings can be seen as hash tables which are virtually initialized such that every possible key exists and is mapped to a value whose byte-representation is all zeros: a type's default value. The key data is not actually stored in a mapping, only its keccak256(), an alias to sha3() hash used to look up the value. Because of this, mappings do not have a length or a concept of a key or value being "set."
Date and time	Putting a suffix like `seconds`, `minutes`, `hours`, `days`, `weeks`, and `years` after literal numbers can be used to convert between units of time where seconds are the base unit. The `now()` method returns the number of milliseconds since January 1, 1970 00:00:00 UTC.	`uint start` `uint hoursAfter` `if (now >= start +` `(hoursAfter * 3 hours))`

TABLE 6-2   Solidity Data Types and Related Functions

Data Type	Description	Notes/Example
Units of ether	A literal number can take a suffix of `wei`, `finney`, `szabo`, or `ether` to convert between the subdenominations of ether.	`2 ether` `2000 finney`
Current instance of class	`this` the current contract, explicitly convertible to `Address`	

Visibility Specifiers

Functions and storage variables can be specified as being public, internal, or private, where the default for functions is public and for storage variables is internal. In addition, functions can also be specified as external. See Table 6-3 for descriptions and examples.

TABLE 6-3   Visibility of Constants and Variables

Visibility	Description	Example
external	External functions are part of the contract interface and they can be called from other contracts and via transactions. An external function `f` cannot be called internally (i.e., `f ()` is invalid, but `this.f ()` is valid). All function parameters are immutable.	`function f(uint a) private returns` `(uint b) { return a + 1; }`
public	Public functions are part of the contract interface and can be called either internally or via messages. For public storage variables, an automatic accessor function is generated.	`uint public data`
inherited	Inherited functions and storage variables can only be accessed internally.	`function setData(uint a) inherited` `{ data = a; }`
private	Private functions and storage variables are only visible for the contract they are defined in and not in derived contracts.	

Block and Transaction Properties

There are special variables and functions that exist in the global namespace. They provide information about the blockchain. See Table 6-4 for syntax and descriptions.

TABLE 6-4 Block and Transaction Properties

Property	Syntax	Description
blockhash	`block.blockhash (uint blockNumber) returns (bytes32):`	
coinbase	`block.coinbase (address)`	Current block miner's address
difficulty	`block.difficulty (uint)`	Current block difficulty
gaslimit	`block.gaslimit (uint)`	Current block gas limit
	`block.number (uint)`	Current block number
	`block.blockhash (function(uint) returns (bytes32))`	Hash of the given block
	`block.timestamp (uint)`	Current block timestamp
	`msg.data (bytes)`	Complete call data
	`msg.gas (uint)`	Remaining gas
	`msg.sender (address)`	Sender of the message (current call)
	`msg.value (uint)`	Number of wei sent with the message
	`now (uint)`	Current block timestamp (alias for block.timestamp)
	`tx.gasprice (uint)`	Gas price of the transaction
	`tx.origin (address)`	Sender of the transaction (full call chain)

Order of Operations

The evaluation order of expressions is not specified (more formally, the order in which the children of one node in the expression tree are evaluated is not specified, but they are of course evaluated before the node itself). It is only guaranteed that statements are executed in order and short-circuiting for boolean expressions is done. See Table 6-5 for descriptions and operators.

TABLE 6-5   Order of Operations

Precedence	Description	Operator
1	Postfix increment and decrement	++, --
	New expression	new <typename>
	Array subscripting	<array>[<index>]
	Member access	<object>.<member>
	Function-like call	<func>(<args...>)
	Parentheses	(<statement>)
2	Prefix increment and decrement	++, --
	Unary plus and minus	+, -
	Unary operations	delete
	Logical NOT	!
	Bitwise NOT	~
3	Exponentiation	**
4	Multiplication, division, and modulo	*, /, %
5	Addition and subtraction	+, -
6	Bitwise shift operators	<<, >>
7	Bitwise AND	&
8	Bitwise XOR	^
9	Bitwise OR	|
10	Inequality operators	<, >, <=, >=
11	Equality operators	==, !=
12	Logical AND	&&
13	Logical OR	||
14	Ternary operator	<conditional> ? <if-true> : <if-false>
15	Assignment operators	=, |=, ^=, &=, <<=, >>=, +=, -=, *=, /=, %=
16	Comma operator	,

Solidity Functions and Parameters

A function is defined with the function keyword, followed by a name, followed by parentheses (). Function names can contain letters, digits, underscores, and dollar signs (same rules as variables). The parentheses may include parameter names separated by commas (parameter1, parameter2, ...). The code to be executed by the function is placed inside curly brackets {}. When the function reaches a return statement, the function will stop executing.

If the function was invoked from a statement, the contract will "return" to execute the code after the invoking statement. Functions often compute a return value. The return value is "returned" back to the "caller". See Table 6-6 for descriptions and examples.

Cryptographic Functions

A cryptographic hash function is a special class of hash function with properties that make it suitable for use in cryptography. It is a mathematical algorithm that maps data of arbitrary size to a bit string of a fixed size (a hash function), which is designed to also be a one-way function—that is, a function which is infeasible to invert. The only way to recreate the input data from an ideal cryptographic hash function's output is to attempt a brute-force search of possible inputs to see if they produce a match, or to use a rainbow table of matched hashes.

TABLE 6-6   **Functions and Parameters**

Functions	Description	Notes/Example

Function calls	Functions of the current contract can be called directly and recursively; e.g., we can invoke function x which takes an unsigned integer and calls y which recursively calls x passing an unsigned integer.	`function x (uint a) returns (uint ret)`
		`{ return y(); }`
		`function y() returns (uint ret)`
		`{ return x(7); }`

Function arguments	Function call arguments can be assigned by name, in any order; see example.	`contract a {`
		`function b(uint key, uint value) { ... }`
		`function c() {  b({value: 2, key: 3});}}`

The secure hash algorithms are a family of cryptographic hash functions published by the National Institute of Standards and Technology (NIST) as a US Federal Information Processing Standard (FIPS). See Table 6-7 for syntax and descriptions.

TABLE 6-7   Cryptographic Functions

Hash Function	Syntax	Description
sha3 is a subset of the cryptographic primitive family Keccak.	`sha3(...) returns (bytes32)`	Compute the SHA-3 hash of the (tightly packed) arguments; SHA-3: A hash function formerly called Keccak, chosen in 2012 after a public competition among non-NSA designers. It supports the same hash lengths as SHA-2, and its internal structure differs significantly from the rest of the SHA family.
sha256 is from a family of two similar hash functions, with different block sizes, known as SHA-256.	`sha256(...) returns (bytes32)`	Compute the SHA-256 hash of the (tightly packed) arguments. SHA-256 uses 32-bit words.
ripemd160 RIPEMD (RACE Integrity Primitives Evaluation Message Digest) is a family of cryptographic hash functions.	`ripemd160(...) returns (bytes20)`	Compute RIPEMD of 256. It is similar in performance to the more popular SHA-1. RIPEMD-160 is an improved, 160-bit version of the original RIPEMD, and the most common version in the family. RIPEMD-160 was designed in the open academic community, in contrast to the NSA-designed SHA-1 and SHA-2 algorithms.
ecrecover Verify a cryptographic signature from an Ethereum address key pair.	`ecrecover(bytes32, byte, bytes32, bytes32) returns (address)`	Recover public key from elliptic curve signature.

TABLE 6-8   Contract-Related Functions

Contract Function	Syntax	Description
this	`this (current contract's type)`	The current contract, explicitly convertible to address
suicide	`suicide(address)`	Suicide the current contract, sending its funds to the given address

Contract-Related Functions

All functions of the current contract are callable directly, including the current function. See Table 6-8 for syntax and descriptions.

Functions on Addresses

It is possible to query the balance of an address using the property balance and to send ether (in units of wei) to an address using the send function. See Table 6-9 for syntax and descriptions.

Constructor Arguments

A Solidity contract expects constructor arguments after the end of the contract data itself. This means that you pass the arguments to a contract by putting them after the compiled bytes as returned by the compiler in the usual application binary interface (ABI) format. The ABI is how you call functions in a contract and get data returned. An ABI is like an application program interface (API). It dictates how functions are called and in which binary format parameters are passed. An Ethereum smart contract is bytecode on the Ethereum blockchain. There are usually many functions in a contract. An ABI provides the specification regarding how functions in the contract are invoked, and a guarantee that the function will return data in the expected format.

From Ethereum's ABI specification, an example:

```
contract AbiEx {
    function abc(uint32 x, bool y) returns (bool r) { r = x > 32 || y; }
    function xyz(bytes name, bool z, uint[] data) {}
}
```

TABLE 6-9   Functions on Addresses

Address Function	Syntax	Description
.balance	`address x = 0x123;` `if (x.balance < 10)`	Balance of an address
.send	`x.send(10);`	Send ether to an address

If we wanted to call abc with the parameters 77 and true, we would pass 68 bytes total, which can be broken down into the following:

- The method ID: This is derived as the first 4 bytes of the Keccak-256 hash of the ASCII form of the signature abc(uint32,bool).
- 0x000000000000000000000000000000000000000000000000000000000000004D: The first parameter, a uint32 value 77 padded to 32 bytes.
- 0x0000000000000000000000000000000000000000000000000000000000000001: The second parameter, boolean true, padded to 32 bytes.

Using a higher-level library such as web3.js abstracts most of these details, but the ABI in JSON format still needs to be provided to web3.js.

ABI is an abstraction and not part of the core Ethereum protocol. Anyone can define their own ABI for their contracts. That said, it is simpler for all developers to use Solidity, Serpent, and web3.js, which all comply with the ABI above.

Accessor Functions

The compiler automatically creates accessor functions for all public state variables. The contract given below will have a function called data that does not take any arguments and returns a uint, the value of the state variable data. The initialization of state variables can be done at declaration.

```
contract test {
    uint public data = 42;
}
```

Layout of Storage

Statically sized variables (everything except mapping and dynamically sized array types) are laid out contiguously in storage starting from position 0. Multiple items that need less than 32 bytes are packed into a single storage slot if possible, according to the following rules:

- The first item in a storage slot is stored lower-order aligned.
- Elementary types use only as many bytes as are necessary to store them.
- If an elementary type does not fit the remaining part of a storage slot, it is moved to the next storage slot.
- Structs and array data always start a new slot and occupy whole slots, but items inside a struct or array are packed tightly according to these rules.

The elements of structs and arrays are stored after each other, just as if they were given explicitly.

Due to their unpredictable size, mapping and dynamically sized array types use a sha3 computation to find the starting position of the value or the array data. These starting positions are always full stack slots.

The mapping or the dynamic array itself occupies an (unfilled) slot in storage at some position according to the above rule (or by recursively applying this rule for mappings to mappings or arrays of arrays). For a dynamic array, this slot stores the number of elements in the array. For a mapping, the slot is unused, but it is needed so that two equal mappings after each other will use a different hash distribution. Array data is located at sha3 (p) and the value corresponding to a mapping key is located at sha3 (k . p) where . is concatenation. If the value is again a non-elementary type, the positions are found by adding an offset of sha3 (k . p).

So for the following contract snippet:

```
contract c {
  struct S { uint a; uint b; }
  uint x;
  mapping(uint => mapping(uint => S)) data;
}
```

the position of data[4][9].b is at sha3(uint256(9) . sha3(uint256(4) . uint(256(1))) + 1.

Run Ethereum Dapps in Your Browser

Prior to blockchain, the application development life cycle, which facilitated large "Web2" applications, was built using tools like HTML, CSS, JavaScript, REST web services, Java, SQL, and NOSQL data stores. Now it is being amended to integrate the blockchain onto that stack. Ethereum enables the decentralized web, referred to as "Web3." What makes it different from Web2 is that on Ethereum the web servers are gone except where used to access some verifiable condition needed to support smart contract execution. So the new dapp ("decentralized application") is just like most applications. It consists of two parts: classic front-end and back-end architecture. As you would expect the frontend is written to either handle web services like REST or provide an HTML/CSS user experience to handle user requests and provide a response. The other part of the application is the backend, which interacts with the blockchain, the new "database." So how does a web browser application converse with the blockchain?

MetaMask solves that key blockchain usability point of friction by providing a way for normal browsers to access the blockchain and propose transactions, to help anyone accomplish any action on the blockchain, easily and securely, enabling a new kind of web browsing experience.

MetaMask is a browser extension that injects the web3 API into every website you visit. Using MetaMask, you can use the browser you are comfortable with to browse the emerging decentralized web. The key advantage of using MetaMask is simplified key management. It encrypts your private key locally and asks users to confirm and sign transactions and messages as requested before relaying them to the Ethereum blockchain.

In order to interact with the blockchain, a client needs access to the entire chain. This implies that for MetaMask to interact with the blockchain, it would need to download the entire blockchain locally for use. To circumvent this, a "zero-client" gateway can be used for instant access via RPC to and from the blockchain. The JSON-RPC API was discussed in the previous chapter. MetaMask uses INFURA as its gateway, which allows for instant setup simply by installing an extension.

Installing MetaMask

MetaMask is currently available as a Chrome extension, with other browser support under active development. The technology is advancing rapidly that could ultimately allow for MetaMask to function within a browser without requiring an extension. To install MetaMask, simply visit the Chrome Web Store, search for and install MetaMask.

Developing a Contract Using MetaMask

After installing, you will see the MetaMask fox logo in the browser toolbar. The first time using the application you will need to generate your wallet public and private keys. The private key will be encrypted locally using a password you set. You will also be given a recovery seed phrase which you should save and store securely if you plan to use MetaMask to store real value. If you forget your wallet password, lose your computer, or otherwise can't get access to your MetaMask wallet, you will be able to restore to a fresh browser using this seed phrase.

The Ethereum wallet is a gateway to decentralized applications on the Ethereum blockchain. It allows you to hold and secure ether and other crypto-assets built on Ethereum, as well as write, deploy, and use smart contracts. MetaMask provides an Ethereum wallet inside your browser. Metamask hosts a wallet with your private key—an Ethereum wallet— and allows you to access sites directly in your Chrome browser and trade as if you had your wallet right there with you on the site. The MetaMask user interface is quite simple, as seen in Figure 6-1. Your Ethereum account address is available, with links to a more detailed view of the account activity on a popular blockchain explorer. When on the Ethereum Main Net,

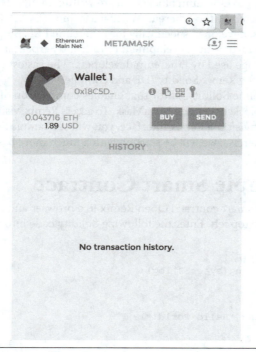

FIGURE 6-1 MetaMask user interface

you have the option to buy the ether token via integrations with popular exchanges such as Coinbase, where you can buy ether for fiat currency such as USD, or ShapeShift, where you can convert existing cryptocurrencies such as bitcoin to ether. You can send transactions as well, including sending the ether token to another account or smart contract.

In order to interact with the Ethereum blockchain, it is necessary to pay "gas" costs for each computational step a smart contract takes. Since this could become quite costly during development, test networks exist where the ether has no real-world value. In this way, development and testing can occur without risk of lost value. One such test network is called Ropsten. MetaMask supports Ropsten natively with INFURA on the backend communicating with the Ropsten chain. For now, you can switch MetaMask to use the Ropsten network on the top navigation bar of the MetaMask interface.

In the next step, we will start to write our first smart contract. To deploy that to the Ropsten test network we will need some Ropsten test ether. You can click the Buy button in MetaMask to get a link to the Ropsten faucet. At the faucet, you can request 1 ether. As soon as that transaction is included on the Ropsten blockchain, your ether balance in MetaMask will be 1. We will come back to this later when we deploy a smart contract.

MetaMask is the gateway that allows your web-based decentralized application to interact with the blockchain. Deployed smart contracts on the blockchain are the backbone of the decentralized web. Now that we have a gateway to interact with these smart contracts, we can look more closely at how to write and deploy them.

Remix/Browser Solidity

Smart contracts for the Ethereum blockchain are written in high-level languages and compiled to bytecode interpreted by the Ethereum Virtual Machine (EVM). Compilers exist for the following languages, developed specifically for Ethereum: LLL, Serpent, and Solidity. There are active efforts to further the development of LLL and Serpent, but for now Solidity is the most popular language used by Ethereum developers. The easiest way to get your feet wet with Solidity is through the Remix Solidity IDE and compiler.

Remix is an online Solidity editor that enables compilation of Solidity code and even deployment to the blockchain using MetaMask. To access Remix, visit https://remix.ethereum.org.

When you first visit the Remix interface, you will see sample Solidity code in the editor window. For this exercise, we will be starting with a much more basic smart contract.

Develop a Simple Smart Contract

Let's write our first smart contract! Open Remix in a browser and create an empty new file by clicking the + at the top left. Enter the following Solidity code into the editor:

```
contract HelloWorld {
    event log_string(bytes32 log);

    function () {
        log_string("Hello World!");
    }
}
```

This is a very simple smart contract that when executed writes "Hello World!" to the transaction log for that contract address. By default, Remix is set to autocompile as you are typing. When you have completely entered the code with no syntax errors, the Contract tab on the right side of the Remix interface will show the compiled bytecode and the application binary interface (ABI) needed to interact with the contract. The ABI is a JSON-formatted text string you will use in your code that interacts with a smart contract.

Remix provides a whole set of other features, including a debugger, formal verification, and of course links to complete documentation of the Solidity language. Remix has integrated deployment capabilities, which coupled with MetaMask make deployment painless.

Deploy the Smart Contract

As previously mentioned, the Remix compiler auto-compiles as you type into the editor window. When the smart contract is syntactically correct, the right panel Contract tab will provide the compiled bytecode; the ABI and web3 deploy JavaScript code on the Contract Details tab. You should see something similar to Figure 6-2. The bytecode is what is actually sent to the blockchain. This transaction must first be signed by your private key. MetaMask makes this easy.

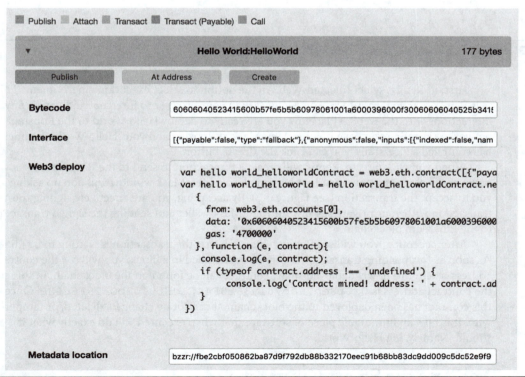

FIGURE 6-2   Remix compiler with smart contract Solidity code

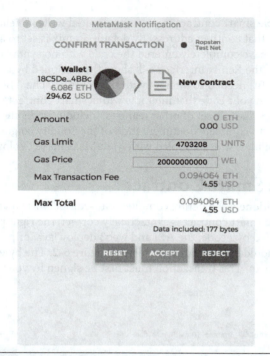

FIGURE 6-3   **MetaMask transaction signing**

First, in Remix, select Injected Web3 in the option to select execution environment. This tells Remix that you want to rely on MetaMask in your browser to intercept and handle any interactions with the web3 APIs. Now you are ready to deploy Hello World to the Ropsten network. Assuming you have pointed MetaMask at Ropsten and your Hello World contract has compiled successfully, you can click the Create button.

When you click Create, Remix will create a transaction to send to the Ropsten test network. That transaction must first be signed, so a MetaMask window will pop up asking you to accept the transaction (see Figure 6-3). By accepting, you are effectively signing the transaction with your private key in your MetaMask wallet and sending the signed transaction to the Ethereum blockchain.

After accepting, you will see Remix telling you that the transaction is waiting to be mined. As soon as this pending transaction is mined, or included in a block, you will see the contract address where this newly deployed smart contract can be found on the blockchain. In this case, the contract address is `0x2f8eb76Db701a36f8F44C1cEf0402bD329F6C03B`. Once this contract has been deployed to the blockchain, it cannot be changed, deleted, or tampered with. It is now an immutable piece of software that when executed will do exactly what it should. Namely, log Hello World.

Validate the Smart Contract

To validate that our Hello World smart contract has been deployed, we can look it up in a block explorer. Recall that a property of most blockchains is complete transparency to the blocks and the data in each transaction. A block explorer is like a search engine that allows you to look into all of the data contained on the chain. The leading explorer in the Ethereum ecosystem is Etherscan (etherscan.io).

Etherscan supports multiple test networks, in addition to the main Ethereum network. To search for your newly deployed contract, first select the Ropsten network in Etherscan. On the MISC menu, you will be able to choose Ropsten. Then you can search for the contract address you received from Remix when you deployed the contract. Etherscan should identify the address as a contract, as opposed to a user account. The contract is holding 0 ether and has had one transaction, which was the contract creation we just did. You'll be able to see what block this contract was created on as well, which can be useful in proving a timeline of activity. Furthermore, you'll see who created the contract—this is your MetaMask wallet address as MetaMask was the wallet that signed the transaction and sent it to the test network.

Now that we know the contract exists, let's execute it so we can validate that it behaves as we expect. To execute the contract, we need to send a transaction to the contract itself. There is no need to send any ether to the contract—in fact, if you do, that ether will be lost forever because the contract isn't written to do anything with any ether sent to it. Therefore, we can send an empty transaction to the contract address to execute it. How will we send a transaction? The answer again is MetaMask.

Back in MetaMask, ensure you are on the Ropsten network. You should still have plenty of ether left since the last transaction used just a tiny bit. To create a transaction, click Send in MetaMask. For the Recipient Address, enter the address of your smart contract. For Amount, leave that at 0 and click Send. Again, you will be prompted to accept the transaction. After acceptance, the transaction will be sent to Ropsten and eventually included in a block and written to the blockchain.

Back at Etherscan, you will notice now there are two transactions for this smart contract. The first is the contract creation, and the most recent is our transaction we just sent causing the code to execute. If we drill into the details for that most recent transaction, we see a handful of metadata about the transaction itself. In Etherscan, they also provide the event logs. In the event log for our contract, the data payload is stored in hexadecimal format. Etherscan conveniently provides a conversion to text, and we see what we are expecting to see: Hello World! Congratulations on successfully deploying your first smart contract!

Next Step: Try Truffle

If you're interested in some interesting tutorials or you want to start building web-based applications with the Ethereum blockchain, you will find the Truffle web framework to be a nice fit for your needs. For many types of dapps, Truffle does everything you could want: it compiles your blockchain contracts, injects them into your web app, and can even run a test suite against them! See http://truffleframework.com/ for documentation and tutorials.

Summary

In this chapter, we introduced the Solidity smart contract programming language and tools that make it simple and easy to fast-track deploy a smart contract to the Ethereum blockchain. In the next chapter, we will introduce tools that are a little more complex and support a development workflow to handle more complex development.

7 Ethereum Application Best Practices

Ethereum Blockchain Development

As we write this book in late 2017, integrated blockchain development environments (IDEs) are still emerging. Truffle (http://truffleframework.com/) is a development environment, testing framework, and asset pipeline for Ethereum.

Truffle provides:

- Built-in smart contract compilation, linking, deployment, and binary management
- Automated contract testing
- Scriptable, extensible deployment and migration
- Network management for deploying to any number of public and private networks
- Package management with EthPM and NPM, using the ERC190 standard
- Interactive console for direct contract communication
- The ability to build pipeline with configuration and tight integration
- Script runner that executes within a Truffle environment

Setting Up the Development Environment for Truffle

There are technical requirements to work with Truffle. You should install the following:

- Node.js (https://nodejs.org/en/)
- Git (https://git-scm.com/)

When developing your Truffle-based application, it is recommended that you use the EthereumJS TestRPC (https://github.com/ethereumjs/testrpc). It's a complete blockchain-in-memory that runs only on your development machine. It processes transactions instantly instead of waiting for the default blocktime—so you can test that your code works quickly—and it tells you immediately when your smart contracts run into errors.

You need the following two commands to install the TestRPC for Ethereum and Truffle:

```
npm install -g ethereumjs-testrpc
npm install -g truffle
```

Set Up a Truffle Project

To verify it installed, type

```
truffle list
```

in a console window to list all Truffle commands.
Then create a new project directory, cd to it and type:

```
truffle init
```

By default, `truffle init` gives you a set of example contracts (`MetaCoin` and `ConvertLib`) which act like a simple alt-coin built on top of Ethereum. You can use these contracts to learn quickly while navigating through the Getting Started guide, or delete these files and build a project of your own.

By default, `truffle init` creates a simple project for you so you can get familiar with writing, compiling, and deploying Solidity-based smart contracts.

Now start a client node in a new console window by running:

```
testrpc
```

Then in another command prompt window run the following commands to compile and deploy the code:

```
truffle compile
truffle deploy
```

Truffle Directory Structure

The default Truffle directory structure contains the following:

- `/contracts`: Contains the Solidity source files for our smart contracts.
- `/migrations`: Truffle uses a migration system to handle smart contract deployments. A migration is an additional special smart contract that keeps track of changes.
- `/test`: Contains both JavaScript and Solidity tests for our smart contracts.
- `truffle.js`: Truffle configuration file.

Beyond this brief overview, go to http://truffleframework.com/tutorials/ to try the latest Truffle tutorials and documentation to continue with your Ethereum blockchain development.

Ethereum Blockchain Development: Best Practices

Before plunging into code design and implementation, let's recap the properties that define the possibilities and constraints we need to consider when making contracts and applications and systems that utilize them.

The Ethereum blockchain is a second-generation blockchain. It contains all the properties of the first-generation blockchain, like an immutable block of transactions, proof of work, and cryptographic verification. In addition, the Ethereum blockchain contains a Turing complete virtual machine or EVM (Ethereum Virtual Machine). This allows for much richer applications than what Bitcoin has with transactions. The EVM is a simple 256-bit stack machine with a stack size of 1024. EVM code is deployed as smart contracts. All code is committed to the blockchain and accessed from the EVM as virtual ROM. Storage is word-addressable word arrays persisted as part of the blockchain system state.

The EVM can be considered a single instance of a worldwide virtual machine, synchronized across all nodes in the network. All code execution (transactions and smart contract function calls) is started by an external user—smart contracts do not execute by themselves. A code execution is considered a single transaction. Either all code is executed and the new state is persisted on the blockchain, or an error occurs and everything is reverted (except the mining reward), just like an ACID transaction in a relational database management system (RDBMS).

The EVM can be perceived as a cloud computer service, where the payment and execution are integrated. To execute EVM code and change blockchain state and storage, cash is provided as "gas" to the execution call. However, there is only a limited amount of execution gas available in each block. This implies that there is a finite and restricted amount of code that can be executed and storage to be changed in a single transaction. This is in sharp contrast to modern development where you have access to an almost infinite amount of resources at hand in the cloud.

The best mindset to have when programming smart contracts is to consider it as programming a microcontroller that is launched into space. There are very limited resources to execute, limited gas, and limited memory and stack size. If there is an error (bug) in the code, it's hard to fix, and one needs to think of the entire life cycle, with all of the future security and operational needs of the contract taken into consideration.

Blockchain Technologies

The EVM itself is only part of the whole decentralized ecosystem. In order to interact with and execute smart contracts, other components are needed. As mentioned in Chapter 3 on blockchain technology use cases, Web 3.0 components include:

- Dapps: decentralized applications
- Contracts: decentralized logic
- Swarm: decentralized storage
- Whisper: decentralized messaging

The simplest solution is a decentralized application (dapp). This form does not need a central server, only code running in a browser that interacts with the user and an underlying smart contract (or set of smart contracts). The browser code (web application) can be distributed either from a normal web server or from decentralized storage like Swarm or InterPlanetary File System (IPFS). For the remainder of this chapter we will mostly deal with applications that interact with traditional systems.

Solidity Basics Continued

We covered Solidity and the language constructs in Chapter 6. Now let's continue with a review of the basic language elements. Here is a contract showing constructor, modifier, and events for the Ownable pattern.

```solidity
pragma solidity ^0.4.8;
// module handling and transfer of contract ownership
contract Ownable {
  address public owner;
    function Ownable() {
        owner = msg.sender;
    }
    modifier onlyOwner {
        if(msg.sender != owner) revert();
        _;
    }
    function transferOwnership(address _newOwner) external onlyOwner {
        owner = _newOwner;
        TransferOwnership(msg.sender, _newOwner);
    }
    event TransferOwnership(address indexed _from, address indexed _to);
}
```

This is a good, simple base contract defining an onlyOwner modifier and function that allows the ownership to be transferred and issues an event when the ownership is changed. However, the transferOwnership function contains a danger. If it is called with a wrong address, the control of the contract is lost forever. One way of dealing with this is to transfer the ownership in a two-phase push/pull pattern. First, the old owner "pushes" a newOwner by calling the transferOwnership function. This does not transfer the ownership right away but rather stores the address in a contract variable in a pending state. Second, the new owner has to accept the ownership by calling acceptOwnership. This will "pull" the ownership to the new owner. Note that *only* the newOwner specified in the transferOwnership function can actually claim the new ownership, and the ownership is actually transferred *only* when the newOwner has called the acceptOwnership function. If the newOwner address is wrong or newOwner has lost access to the account, then the ownership is never transferred, thus avoiding the potential predicament from the first version of the contract.

In general, it is good practice to use a two-phase push/pull when dealing with irreversible functions with high implications like transfer of ownership, refunding, etc.

```solidity
pragma solidity ^0.4.8;
// module handling and transfer of contract ownership
contract Ownable {
    address public owner;
    function Ownable() {
        owner = msg.sender;
    }
    modifier onlyOwner {
```

```
        require(msg.sender == owner);
        _;
    }
    address newOwner;
    function transferOwnership(address _newOwner) external onlyOwner {
        newOwner = _newOwner;
    }
    function acceptOwnership() {
        if (msg.sender == newOwner) {
            var oldOwner = owner;
            owner = newOwner;
            TransferOwnership(oldOwner, newOwner);
        }
    }
    event TransferOwnership(address indexed _from, address indexed _to);
}
```

Calling Contracts from Contracts

A unique aspect of the EVM environment is the concepts of *gas* and *value*. As mentioned, the EVM can be conceived as a cloud computing service, where you need to pass payment to each call to pay for cloud execution. The payment for execution is added as gas, and the payment passed to accounts is added as value. As discussed, gas has a wei price (gasPrice) and can be calculated as a wei amount = gas*gasPrice. Both gas*gasPrice and value are taken from the caller's balance.

Consider the following contract:

```
contract A {
    function A(…)
    {
        …
    }
    function trade() public payable {
        // do some trade
        …
    }
}
```

Then to instantiate it from within another contract as

```
A a = new A(…);
```

if you simply now call

```
a.trade();
```

it will by default not pass any value to the function. You need to add a `.value(...)` argument to the calls like

```
a.trade.value(somevalue)();
```

When you call a function on a smart contract with a value, that contract will then own the value sent. It can in turn call functions on other contracts, transferring value to these and so on.

Let's see that in action. Consider a contract B:

```
contract B {
    A a;
    uint commissionPercent;
    address commissionWallet;
    function B(address _a, address _wallet, uint _commissionPercent)
    {
        a = A(_a);
        commissionWallet = _wallet;
        commissionPercent = _ commissionPercent;
    }
    function trade() public payable {
        var commission = msg.value * commissionPercent /100;
        a.trade.value(msg.value - commission)();
        commissionWallet.transfer(commission);
    }
}
```

and instantiate B as

```
B b = new B(a,wallet,10);
```

and then call

```
a.trade.value(sometradevalue)();
```

Within the trade function of B that now has `sometradevalue`, you can see an example of splitting this value passed to b.trade into a call to `a.trade()` with 90 percent of the value and passing 10 percent of the value to a commission wallet.

If you want to create a cloud service for the blockchain contracts that binds outside the EVM, this is a way to get paid by the caller directly, thus avoiding separate invoicing and so on.

However, please note that the `.value` call by default passes on all available (remaining) gas and should be considered unsafe against reentrancy. So be careful if you don't control the contract being called.

You can specify the amount of gas passed to a function by adding `.gas(someGasAmount)` to the function call:

```
a.trade.value(msg.value - commission).gas(40000)();
```

Calling `address.transfer` only passes 23000 gas. That is insufficient to do any reentrancy but might be insufficient for complex `function() payable` routines to complete.

Pitfall: Remember to forward gas and ether between contracts when calling payable functions.

Handling Events

EVM events are a central part of the smart contract ecosystem. We saw an example of an event in the Owner contract where the contract issues a `TransferOwnership` event each time the owner changes

Events allow users and especially applications to monitor smart contract changes on the blockchain. This is done by specifying filters and applying them on a blockchain node. Events can be filtered on topics, values, and block intervals, thus listing to new events or scanning through old events.

Users can be notified about changes to contracts they have interest in, such as changes to ownership, ERC20 tokens, changes to balances, notification of multisig wallets pending confirmations, etc. Likewise, enterprise applications that integrate to business logic and process flows in smart contracts can be notified when enterprise application actions are needed.

User actions on smart contracts can trigger enterprise services, and enterprise status updates on smart contracts can notify users, just like events in regular applications. In enterprise applications, a process needs to be put in place for events to be captured. Consider the event

```
event MyEvent(address indexed myidx, uint myval);
```

Adding `indexed` to the event argument `myidx` makes the event searchable through filters using `myidx` values.

In C#, using the Nethereum package monitoring for live events might look like this:

```
public class MyEventHelper
{
  MyContract _contract;
  int _sleep;
  bool _stop;
  public MyEventHelper(MyContract contract, int sleep)
  {
    _contract = contract;
    _sleep = sleep;
  }
  public void Start()
  {
    _stop = false;
    ThreadPool.QueueUserWorkItem(PoolEvents);
  }
  public event EventHandler<Exception> ErrorEvent;
  public event EventHandler<MyEventDTO> MyEvent;
  private async void PoolEvents(object state)
  {
    var event = _contract.GetEventMyEvent();
    var filter = await event.CreateFilterAsync();
    while (!_stop) {
     if (MyEvent != null) {
       var logs = await event.GetFilterChanges<MyEventDTO>(filter);
       foreach (var log in logs) {
```

```
        MyEvent(this, log.Event);
      }
    }
  }
  Thread.Sleep(_sleep);
}
...
```

The example below will set up an event listener that calls two functions whenever a new MyEvent event is seen on the blockchain.

```
var eventHelper = new MyEventHelper(contract, 100);
eventHelper.MyEvent += (model, event) =>
{
  ... execute business logic
};

eventHelper.MyEvent += (model, event) =>
{
  Console.WriteLine($"MyEvent idx={event.myidx} val={event._myval");
};
eventHelper.Start();
```

In NodeJS the syntax is a little simpler:

```
var event = myContractInstance.MyEvent()
// watch for changes
event.watch(function(error, result) {
  if (!error)
    console.log(result);
  ... execute business logic
});
```

If the service needs to process events from the past, they can be filtered by block interval as well as by filters on indexed parameters.

```
// watch for an event with {myidx: 'value'}
var myEvent = myContractInstance.MyEvent({myidx: 'value'},
    {fromBlock: 0, toBlock: 'latest'});
myEvent.watch(function(error, result){
  ...
});
// would get all past logs again.
var myResults = myEvent.get(function(error, logs){ ... });
...
// would stop and uninstall the filter
myEvent.stopWatching();
```

If an enterprise system needs to handle all events issued from a contract, it's a good idea to add a sequence number on each event.

```
event MyEvent(uint indexed eventId, address indexed myidx, uint myval);
```

This allows the enterprise system to easily track whether all events are handled and in case of breakdown efficiently recover/reprocess the missing events.

Remember that enterprise system event handlers can also call functions on contracts. This makes EVM events behave just like other kinds of events, thus allowing mixed cascade triggers through different systems. Imagine the following system flow (see Figure 7-1).

1. A user (web) app calls a function on a smart contract.
2. The smart contract function generates an EVM event.
3. This event is captured by a server monitor.
4. The monitor starts a job on a third-party system.
5. Retrieve the result from the third party when the job completes or some condition is met.
6. The monitor calls a function on a smart contract with the outcome and changes the status.
7. The smart contract function generates an event containing the outcome and the new status.
8. The user app captures this event and updates the UI with the outcome and new status.

As seen, this allows building of complex integrated systems without building complex infrastructures between trusted parties or agreements of cost share. It solely uses the blockchain of the infrastructure and payment platform. The user app and the server systems are independent of each other and do not need to establish complex agreements.

In a generalized form the server monitor acts like an intermediary between the blockchain and the real world; this is often referred to as an oracle.

As discussed, a smart contract can't trigger itself, since the blockchain needs to be deterministic. So it cannot depend upon or access the real world directly from the EVM. It needs to be activated by an external agent, as illustrated in Figure 7-2. An agent can be either a user or an oracle. Oracles comes in two forms. They can be "callable" from the smart contract

FIGURE 7-1   Example of enterprise system flow involving smart contracts

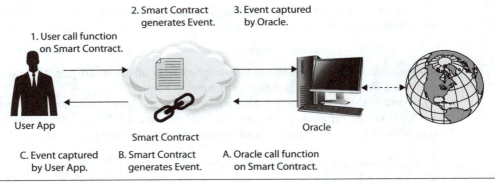

FIGURE 7-2 Application with a user, a smart contract, and an oracle

by generating an event with a request/reply interaction as shown in Figure 7-1. Or they can be trigger based where the oracle calls the smart contract when certain conditions are met. This could be when a currency hits a certain price or when an IoT sensor detects a certain value.

To include a third-party oracle in the smart contract flow, it needs to be trustworthy and reliable since its interaction with the blockchain is immutable and hence irreversible.

Smart Contract Design

All the virtues of modern design certainly apply to making smart contracts. In fact, even more so, because of the immutable nature of the blockchain: clear design, well-thought-out security, thorough tests, and life cycle management are musts. In this section, we will elaborate on some of the important virtues.

Modules and Interfaces

For traditional coding, it is a widespread best practice to divide the code into sections representing separation of concerns. This is especially relevant in writing smart contracts. There already exist a number of libraries containing typical modules that are needed when writing a contract. And it is preferable to reuse well-established modules. A good example of this is OpenZeppelin (https://github.com/OpenZeppelin/zeppelin-solidity). Their tagline formulates it very well: "Reduce the risk of vulnerabilities in your applications by using standard, tested, and community-reviewed code."

Using such modules whenever possible reduces the risk of error and frees valuable time to focus on the unique features of the contracts at hand. Even when a module needs to be modified to fit some particular needs, reuse of the corresponding tests to ensure nothing gets broken is highly recommended.

Don't over-engineer the contract or dazzle with fanciful coding techniques. Keep it simple, stupid—especially because most contracts used by the public are going to have the corresponding source attached on the blockchain for anybody to inspect and validate. Having a clear, simple contract that is easy to understand gains more trust and is actually less likely to contain flaws than a large over-engineered contract doing way more than actually needed, as its attach vector is much smaller.

Security and Roles

When designing smart contracts, it is important to think about security from the very start. Since contracts are public and visible on the blockchain, everybody can potentially call every function. Even if you do not submit the source code, there is still the bytecode so everyone with the right understanding of the EVM and proper endurance can figure out what the contract does and call it, so don't count on security by obscurity.

Most contracts implement the owner pattern that can be used to restrict the highest state "administrator" change functions, like `setup`, `start`, `stop`, and `kill`.

Consider the `kill` function:

```
function kill() onlyOwner {
  selfdestruct(owner);
}
```

Using the modifier signature, it becomes clear that the function is only allowed to be called by the owner and the function body contains only the business code. However, the private key of the owner should be stored somewhere safe and only used in major life cycle events for the contract.

More operational functions should be modularized and restricted to special roles different from the owner. The owner should then delegate these role rights to other addresses. The specialized roles often run on web services or staff computers, and need to contain the private key for their role address in order to execute. If a system is hacked and the private key of a role gets compromised, the implications are confined to that role's operations, and the system can more easily be recovered by the owner by changing the compromised role address.

Examples of roles could be:

- Minter: A role capable of minting new tokens in a token contract
- MigrationMaster: A role responsible for the migration process from an old contract to a new contract
- InvitedInvestor: A role given to invited addresses to make investments in a restricted ICO
- Trader/Executer: A role that executes trades or orders on behalf of customers

Each role can either be a single address role or multiple addresses, often referred to as whitelisted addresses.

As we saw in the Ownable contract, a modifier for a single address role can be as simple as

```
modifier onlyRole { require(msg.sender == roleAddress); _; }
```

A multiple address role can be implemented as a mapping like

```
mapping (address => bool) public roleWhitelist;
function setRoleWhitelist(address _addr, bool _status) onlySomeControleRole {
  roleWhitelist[_addr] = _status;
  RoleWhitelisted(_addr, _status);
}
```

And then the modifier would change to this:

```
modifier onlyRole { require(roleWhitelist[msg.sender]); _; }
```

The use of access control should not be implemented as part of the function itself, but the use of clearly defined modifiers on the function header is highly recommended. This is because it separates the access control logic from the function and also because it makes the functions easier to read since they only contain the business logic.

Single Contract Design

As a contract evolves and has more and more features added to it, it's easy to end up with a fat contract that does way too much and becomes difficult to manage. If nothing else is done, the development will end abruptly one day, simply because the combined cost of code deposit and create execution exceeds the total available gas within a single block execution. This is called block gas limit (BGL). The BGL on the public net is currently 4,712,388.

A way to keep an eye on this is to look at the gas estimates in the `json` output of the compilation. As seen here, the sum of the two numbers (code deposit and execution) exceeds BGL, so this contract will not be able to deploy.

```
"gasEstimates": {
    "creation": [
        329430,
        4264400
    ]...
```

In general, if the contract creation estimate comes anywhere near to BGL, the contract design should be revised.

Linked Contracts

Instead of putting all functionality into a single contract, it's often advisable to divide it into several contracts that act together. Ideally you can reuse already existing base contracts that have been well designed, well tested, and have stood the test of time. Such contracts could be standard tokens, multisig wallets, etc.

Let's say that you want to build an ICO contract, where investors are invited to buy tokens at a fixed price for a limited period of time. You want to collect all the ether into a secure wallet, and you want all the tokens to reside in a standard ERC20 token that eventually will be freely tradable on exchanges after the ICO. When the ICO is over and validated, the ICO contract is in fact not needed anymore as it has completed its life cycle.

How would you construct such an ICO contract system?

Well, there are a number of implementations of both multisig wallets and standard contracts, so no need to write those. Instead, we concentrate on writing our particular ICO process and then just bind it to a standard multisig wallet and a standard token contract.

Each contract is deployed as a separate transaction so the size of the total contract system can be much larger that a single BGL. Only the individual contracts need to be below BGL. Here is the pseudocode to create the contracts and bind them together.

```
// specify the token
uint initialAmount = 90000000;
string tokenName = 'MyToken';
```

```
uint8 decimalUnits = 18;
string tokenSymbol = 'XYZ';

// specify the ico owner and ico process auditor
address icoOwner = '0x…';
address auditor = '0x…';
// create a standard multisig wallet with ICO auditor as second confirmer
address[] public owners;
owners.push(icoOwner);
owners.push(auditor);
var multisigWallet = new Multisig(owners,2,0);
// create a standard token
var tokencontract = new StandardToken(
    initialAmount, tokenName, decimalUnits, tokenSymbol);
// create crowd sale contract with references to ERC20 and wallet
var crowdcontract = new MyCrowdsale(
    tokencontract, multisigWallet, start, end);
}
// transfer tokens from owner to crowd sale contract for sales
tokencontract.transfer(crowdcontract,salesAmount);
```

Once the contracts are deployed and connected, the ICO sales can start (here shown as explicit functions, often the ICO runs within a specified blockNumber range).

```
// START THE ICO
crowdcontract.startSales();
// token sales transactions on crowdcontract
…
crowdcontract.stopSales();
// THE ICO IS COMPLETE
```

When the ICO is complete, the ICO owner can request the funds.

```
// request transfer of crowd funding
var balance = address(multisigWallet).balance;
var h = multisigWallet.execute(icoOwner,balance,'');
// await auditor to confirm
```

The auditor can validate the ICO process and state and release the funds to the ICO owner.

```
// An AUDITOR confirms that all is fine and dandy
multisigWallet.confirm(h);
```

Now that the ICO is complete and the shares are stored in the standard contract, the ICO crowd contract can be destroyed.

```
// once the funding is done the crowd contract can be killed
crowdcontract.kill();

// and even the wallet can be killed
multisigWallet.kill();
```

User-Specific Contracts

Previously we saw an example where several (standard) contracts worked in conjunction, forming the whole system. If we want each user to have its own individual settings and peculiarities, then instead of polluting the core contracts with this complexity, it might be better to keep them as user-specific contracts. As we discussed earlier, polymorphism works well in Solidity with the interface specification.

Imagine we have a contract system that handles assets that is accessed within the main contract master only using an asset interface like this:

```solidity
pragma solidity ^0.4.11;
import "./Ownable.sol";
interface Asset
{
  function isActive() external returns(bool);
  function someAction(address _to) external;
}
contract Master is Ownable
{
    mapping (address => bool) public userAssets;
    function SetUserAsset(Asset _asset, bool _status) onlyOwner
    {
        if (_status && !_asset.isActive())
            revert();
        userAssets[_asset] = _status;
    }
    function someAction(Asset _asset, address _to) onlyOwner
    {
        if(!userAssets[_asset])
            revert();
        _asset.someAction(_to);
    }
}
```

Then different asset implementations can be developed even after the master contract is deployed.

```solidity
contract AssetBase is Asset
{
    address master;
    modifier onlyMaster {
        require(msg.sender == master);
        _;
    }
    function AssetBase(address _master)
    {
        master = _master;
```

```
    }
    function isActive() external returns(bool);

    function someAction(address _to) onlyMaster external;
}
contract MyAsset is AssetBase
{
    function MyAsset(address _master) AssetBase(_master)
    {
    }
    function isActive() external returns(bool)
    {
        return true;
    }
    function someAction(address _to) onlyMaster external


    {
        ... do some stuff
    }
}
```

Some later implementation of an asset contract:

```
contract MyAsset2 is Asset
{
    address master;
    modifier onlyMaster {
        require(msg.sender == master);
        _;
    }
    function MyAsset2(address _master)
    {
        master = _master;
    }
    function isActive() external returns(bool)
    {
        return true;
    }
    function someAction(address _to) onlyMaster external
    {
        ... do some other stuff
    }
}
```

This allows for the following deploy sequence.
Deploy master:

```
Master m = new Master();
```

Develop MyAsset, deploy it, and bind it to master:

```
var a = new MyAsset(m);
m.SetUserAsset(a,true);
```

Later, develop MyAsset2, deploy it, and bind it to master:

```
var b = new MyAsset2(m);
m.SetUserAsset(b,true);
```

Call some actions on the assets:

```
m.someAction(a,to);
m.someAction(b,to);
```

This also demonstrates that a system of linked contracts can be designed to upgrade and extend over time without a total redeployment—in this example, especially without redeployment of master, which address might be embedded in a lot of systems and users' wallets.

Handling Persistent Contract Addresses

In some situations, it may be desirable to keep a persistent contract address while maintaining the possibility of changing the implementation. For instance, if the contract address is imbedded in many other systems or registered with many users, changing the instance address may be an insurmountable endeavor and involve unmanageable synchronization issues.

This problem can be resolved by introducing a proxy contract that wraps the implementation contract. This is a well-known traditional technique that is especially relevant for this smart contract issue.

An implementation of a proxy goes like this:
You start with the interface of the desired functionality.

```
contract SomeInterface {
  // sample function
  function doSomething(address _arg1, uint256 _arg2) public;
  // sample event
  event DoneSomething(address _arg1, uint256 _arg2);

  // service functions
  function log(string _var, uint256 _value);
  event Log(string _var, uint256 _value);
}
```

Implement the proxy contract as callthroughs to the implementation contract functions. The `log` function is a helper function to issue events on the proxy contract level.

```
contract ProxyContract is SomeInterface, Ownable {
  SomeInterface public implementation; //current implementation class
  modifier onlyImplementation {
    if(msg.sender != address(implementation)) revert();
    _;
```

```
  }
  function setImplementation( SomeInterface _newimplementation )
    onlyOwner public
  {
    implementation = _newimplementation;
  }
  // this function must only be called from the implementation
  function log(string _var, uint256 _value) onlyImplementation
  {
    // add event at proxy level
    // triggering all event listeners at ProxyContract
    Log(_var,_value)
  }
  function doSomething(address _arg1, uint256 _arg2) public
  {
    // forward proxy call to current implementation
    implementation.doSomething(_arg1, _arg2);
    DoneSomething(_arg1, _arg2);
  }
}
```

The implementation class that implements the actual doSomething function is only allowed to be called from the proxy call.

```
contract ContractImplementation1 is SomeInterface, Ownable {
  SomeInterface public proxy;
  modifier onlyProxy {
    if(msg.sender != address(proxy)) revert();
    _;
  }
  function ContractImplementation1(SomeInterface _proxy)  {
    proxy = _proxy;
  }
  // actual function
  function doSomething(address _arg1, uint256 _arg2) onlyProxy
  {
    ...
    // fire event on proxy class
    proxy.log('_arg1',uint256(_arg1));
    proxy.log('_arg2',_arg2);
  }
  function log(string _var, uint256 _value)
  {
    revert();
  }
}
```

Set up the proxy.

```
ProxyContract proxy;
ContractImplementation1 impl1;
// create proxy class
proxy = new ProxyContract();
// set up the first implementation
impl1 = new ContractImplementation1(proxy);
proxy.setImplementation(impl1);
```

Correct call to implementation as a call to the proxy contract.

```
proxy.doSomething(this,0xFFF0);
```

This is not allowed:

```
impl1.doSomething(this,0xFF80);
impl1.log('arg',0xFF80);
proxy.log('arg',0xFF80);
```

If a change is needed, then change the implementation to a new class.

```
proxy.setImplementation(new ContractImplementation2(proxy))
```

Now the same proxy call will call the new implementation.

```
proxy.doSomething(this,0xFFF0);
```

Halting a Contract

If an unforeseen event happens, like a severe bug in the EVM or the discovery of a vulnerability within the code, the assets within the contract might be in danger. In this case it will be a good idea to have a halt functionally that stops most (but not all) of the activity within the contract while the situation is evaluated.

This can easily be accomplished by adding a notHalted modifier to the functions.

```
modifier notHalted {
    if(!halted) revert();
    _;
  }


// actual function
function doSomething(address _arg1, uint256 _arg2) notHalted
{...}
```

From a security perspective, the decision to halt the contract should be available for central system operators and security agencies, while the unhalt should be restricted to the owner—much like a normal emergency button where many people can stop the machinery, but only a few can start it again. Better safe than sorry.

```
function halt() onlyPrivilegedUsers { halted = true; }
function unhalt() onlyOwner { halted = false; }
```

Smart Contract Life Cycle: Migration

If case of bugs, vulnerabilities, or the need to add some new features, a new contract is needed and should replace the old contract.

The basic idea with a smart contract migration is similar to a normal application migration. The state of the old smart contract is transferred securely to a new smart contract, and the old contract becomes inert or is destroyed.

Here we have a trust issue. In the best-case scenario, the benign contract owner discovers a security issue, fixes the error and deploys a new contract, and as migration master puts the original smart contract into migration mode pointing to the new contract. Then each stakeholder transfers their state from the old contract to the new contract—that is, for a token contract the user transfers their tokens from the old contract to the new contract, and so on. Once all states (tokens, etc.) are transferred, the old contract can be destroyed or simply become an inactive void instance. Note that the *user* transfers the state, not the contract owner.

A migration interface could look like this:

```
// agent interface
contract MigrationAgent {
  function migrateFrom(address _from, uint256 _value);
}
```

When implementing the transfer function, we must ensure that it can only be called from the original smart contract.

```
// unsafe function can be called by anyone
function migrateFrom(address _sender, uint _value)
{
  balances[_sender] = balances[_sender].add(_value);
  ...
}
modifier onlyFromContract() {
  if (msg.sender != migrationFromContract || migrationFromContract == 0)
    revert();
  _;
}
// safe migrate function
function migrateFrom(address _sender, uint _value) onlyFromContract
{
    balances[_sender] = balances[_sender].add(_value);
    MigratedFrom(msg.sender, migrationFromContract, _value);
}
event MigratedFrom(address indexed _from,
                   address indexed _contract,
                                uint256 _value);

// each user calls the migrate function on the original contract
// to migrate the users' tokens to the migration agent
function migrate() external {
  if (migrationAgent == 0) revert(); // revert if not in migrate mode
  var _value = balances[msg.sender];
```

```
if (_value <= 0) revert(); // revert if not value left to transfer
// set the balance to 0 before the migrateFrom call
balances[msg.sender] = 0;
totalMigrated += _value;
// this is the only place migrateFrom is allowed to be called
MigrationAgent(migrationAgent).migrateFrom(msg.sender, _value);
Migrated(msg.sender, migrationAgent, _value);
}
```

Smart Contract Interaction with Users and Enterprise Applications

As we discussed earlier, smart contracts and blockchain are only a part of a whole solution. If the bulk of the business logic is within the contract(s) and only a simple user application is needed, it can easily be implemented as a dapp. In an enterprise solution, smart contracts can be thought of as an asynchronous web service or a batch job component of the system.

When integrating blockchains into an existing enterprise application, in many cases it is a good idea to expose the blockchain interaction through a standard web service. In this way, the "old" enterprise application developers don't need to deal with or understand the particulars of blockchain interaction. From their perspective, it's just an additional third-party component with normal async WEB-API behavior.

Debugging Your Smart Contract

Debugging is an essential part of application development. This is true for smart contract development as well. Unfortunately, in Solidity the `throw` keyword or calling `revert()` does not take any argument and cannot return any error number or error text. In non-trivial functions there can be several reasons for failure, and as a newbie or with complex contracts it can be difficult to quickly identify the reason for failure. This is a limitation of the current environment both during development debugging and debugging production problems. We hope this will be addressed in future versions of EVM and Solidity.

Pitfall: The low-level functions `send`, `call`, `delegatecall`, and `callcode` return *false* in case of an error; they do *not* throw an error. Take extra care when using these functions and test thoroughly.

Debugging Using Remix

As covered in Chapter 6, Remix Solidity IDE is one of the best debugging tools presently available. This tool allows you to code Solidity contracts, compile them, analyze them, and even run them. It is a great tool to try things out and to get acquainted with the mechanics and quirks of the Solidity and EVM environment. It also has a JavaScript VM that allows you to step through the function calls and identify problems and states, and is an indispensable tool to find those bugs that just elude your comprehension. Unfortunately, it currently only works well for small code bases. For large code bases containing many contracts, Remix becomes slow and even unworkable.

Debugging Using Events

Another way to debug your code is to (mis)use an event. If you add an event like this one,

```
event Debug(string text, uint value);
```

then you can add calls like this to your code:

```
... code that works
Debug('addr',uint(addr));
Debug('value',addr);
Debug('status',status?1:0);
return;
... some code that throws
```

You can then examine the values from the event log within your test environment.

Notice the premature `return` to prevent having the function throw, because otherwise all is reverted and no events are logged. It is the nearest thing to a `log.writeline` you can have in EVM. We often use this approach if we inadvertently introduce a throw bug that reveals itself within a complex Truffle test set, where the reason for the error is not obvious and is too cumbersome to reproduce in Remix.

Smart Contract Validation

Testing smart contracts is especially important since they cannot be changed once deployed. Therefore you definitely want to test and review every possible scenario that can unfold in the production network, including what happens when hackers are trying to steal the assets they contain.

Types of Tests

The relevant tests can be divided into separate types and domains and are described individually.

Functional Tests

Firstly, you have the traditional CRUD-like function tests that ensure you can create, read, update, and delete entries, roles, users, etc., within your contract. This is just business as usual.

Normal Life Cycle Flow Tests

These tests run through the different stages of a contract such as creating, preparing, running, halting, and terminating. They test that the contract can change stages correctly all the way from create to destroy. For each stage, it is tested that the functions for that stage can be called but also that functions for other stages *cannot* be called—for example, testing that `init` functions cannot be called in the running stage.

Vulnerability Tests

There are known vulnerabilities that need to be mitigated and tested.

Overflow and Underflow Attacks

Numbers like `uint` don't fail on overflow or underflow like most other high-level languages, but just wrap around, maxsize assembler style. Why this design decision was made is beyond us.

Consider the code:

```
uint a = 1;
uint b = a - 2;
uint c = b + 2;
```

Here a − 2 performed an underflow and becomes 115792089237316195423570985008687907853269984665640564039457584007913129639935.

And b + 2 performs an overflow and becomes 1. The same condition can be found for most other operations.

This constitutes an attack vector that may allow a user to call a function with a carefully designed value that triggers an arithmetic error, i.e., assigns a very large account value for an address. Normally these kinds of errors are mitigated by safe numeric operations like this:

```
library SafeMath {
  ...
  function add(uint a, uint b) internal constant returns (uint) {
    uint c = a + b;
    assert(c >= a);
    return c;
  }
}
```

and used in contracts like this:

```
contract XXX {
  using SafeMath for uint;
  ...
  uint a = 1;
  uint b = a.sub(2);
  uint c = b.add(2);
```

We don't understand why this is not the default behavior since everyone has to add it to their contract code.

Recursive Call Attacks, Reentrancy Exploit

Consider this code:

```
1) mapping(address => uint) balances;
2) function withdraw() public {
3)     uint amount = balances[msg.sender];
4)     if (!(msg.sender.call.value(amount)())) revert();
5)     balances[msg.sender] = 0;
6) }
```

This function withdraws all assets from an account (3), sends them to its owner (4), and updates the account balance to zero (5). However, since the `call.value` potentially hits a function at a sender's contract, this function can call the `withdraw` function again before it is set to 0, thus withdrawing the balance value again and again until the original contract is depleted.

Note that this attack might also be executed by calling a sequence of other functions on the original contract that exploit an incomplete state change. Normally this issue is mitigated by applying the Checks-Effects-Interaction pattern—that is:

1. First <u>Check</u> all preconditions,
2. Then perform all the <u>Effects</u> on the global state,
3. And finally do <u>Interactions</u> with other contracts

```
function withdraw() public {
    // Checks
    require(balances[msg.sender]>0);
    // Effects
    uint amount = balances[msg.sender];
    balances[msg.sender] = 0;
    // Interactions
    assert((msg.sender.call.value(amount)()));
}
```

Test Contract at Maximum Capacity

One consequence of the limited amount of gas in a block (BGL) is that you need to think about gas usage of the different functions when you keep adding items to the contract system. What happens at maximum capacity of the contract? Will the contract functions experience gas overflows at maximum capacity?

Loops and recursive calls are especially critical. Will the operations have enough gas to execute in worst-case conditions? Try to identify the longest run for loops and the deepest recursive call. In fact, it's best to avoid them altogether if possible. If that is not possible, ensure that they will have a defined upper limit within BGL.

Dry Run Using Private Nets

At the end of the day, testing with TestRPC and JavaScript VM isn't the real McCoy. To be blunt, each test daemon implements its own particular quirks and errors that are different from the quirks and errors in the production environment.

Therefore, it is prudent to do a dry run of the intended usage (and misusage) using the real daemon, such as Geth or Parity. The actual code is the same in all environments. The only difference between executing in dev, testnet, or production is the chainId. In many cases, especially during development, it is desirable to run in a private blockchain. You don't want to plaster testnet or production with half-baked contracts in your name. Fortunately, it's rather easy to launch a private blockchain. Here it's shown for Geth.

In a test cycle, it's preferable to start at the same state every time, so first delete all old chain information.

```
RD /S /Q "%~dp0\privChain\geth\chainData"
RD /S /Q "%~dp0\privChain\geth\dapp"
RD /S /Q "%~dp0\privChain\geth\nodes"
del "%~dp0\privChain\geth\nodekey"
```

Then initialize a new blockchain using a configuration file.

```
geth --datadir=privChain init genesis_dev.json
```

Finally, launch a node running your private blockchain.

```
geth --rpc --networkid=39318 --maxpeers=0

--datadir=privChain --rpccorsdomain "*"

    --rpcapi "eth,web3,personal,net,miner,admin,debug"

--verbosity 3 console
```

If you want your private node to run simultaneously with other nodes, add specification of the modified port like this:

```
--port 30304 --rpcport=8551 --ipcpath "devgeth.ipc"
```

Then connect to the private node using the URL, e.g., http://localhost:8551.

The configuration file that reflects production details might look like this:

```
genesis_dev.json
{
  "config": {
    "chainId": 39318,
    "homesteadBlock": 0,
    "eip155Block": 0,
    "eip158Block": 0
  },
  "nonce": "0x0000000000000042",
  "difficulty": "0x200",
  "alloc": {
    "12890d2cce102216644c59dae5baed380d84830c": {
      "balance": "1000000000000000000000"
    }
  },
  "mixhash":
  "0x0000000000000000000000000000000000000000000000000000000000000000",
  "coinbase": "0x0000000000000000000000000000000000000000",
  "timestamp": "0x00",
  "parentHash":
  "0x0000000000000000000000000000000000000000000000000000000000000000",
  "extraData": "0x",
  "gasLimit": "0x4c4b40"
}
```

Most are default values that should match production. The main values to set are the chainId and the alloc section where addresses can be prefilled with ether.

Autopsy of a Wallet Bug

On July 19, 2017, it was discovered that somebody had heisted three Parity multisig wallets. This resulted in a race where the community, with the White Hat Group (WHG) in front, tried to identify and mitigate the issue.

The constructor function looks like this:

```
contract Wallet is WalletEvents {
  // WALLET CONSTRUCTOR
  //    calls the `initWallet` method of the Library in this context
  function Wallet(address[] _owners, uint _required, uint _daylimit) {
    // Signature of the Wallet Library's init function
    bytes4 sig = bytes4(sha3("initWallet(address[],uint256,uint256)"));
    address target = _walletLibrary;

    // Compute the size of the call data : arrays has 2
    // 32bytes for offset and length, plus 32bytes per element ;
    // plus 2 32bytes for each uint
    uint argarraysize = (2 + _owners.length);
    uint argsize = (2 + argarraysize) * 32;

    assembly {
      // Add the signature first to memory
      mstore(0x0, sig)
      // Add the call data, which is at the end of the code
      codecopy(0x4,  sub(codesize, argsize), argsize)
      // Delegate call to the library
      delegatecall(sub(gas, 10000), target, 0x0, add(argsize, 0x4), 0x0, 0x0)
    }
  }
  ...
```

As you can see, it delegates the initialization to a _walletLibrary function initWallet by constructing the call directly in memory using assembly opcodes. This code is not for the fainthearted. This is pure brain surgery—you don't want to sneeze while writing this code.

Also, the wallet default function uses the fact that if you call a function not defined in the wallet contract itself, it will be caught by the default function.

The delegatecall to _walletLibrary is called with the original function call data. This means that you will have implicit access to *all* the functions in _walletLibrary as they were implemented directly in the wallet contract. This is a very powerful mechanism but potentially also very dangerous.

```
// gets called when no other function matches
function() payable {
 // just being sent some cash?
 if (msg.value > 0)
   Deposit(msg.sender, msg.value);
 else if (msg.data.length > 0)
   _walletLibrary.delegatecall(msg.data);
}
```

One of the functions in the WalletLibrary is the `init` helper function `initWallet` we saw called in the constructor of the wallet, and that is what it was meant for. However, since there are no checks or modifiers on it, and with the `delegatecall` call in the default function, this unfortunately means that *everybody* can call the `initWallet` at *every* moment of the wallet life cycle. Thus, they gain owner control over the multisig wallet, making transferring money out of it like stealing candy from a baby.

```
// constructor - just pass on the owner array to the multiowned and
// the limit to daylimit
function initWallet(address[] _owners, uint _required, uint _daylimit) {
  initDaylimit(_daylimit);
  initMultiowned(_owners, _required);
}
```

The fix was very simple, by just adding the missing modifier to control that the `init` helper functions can only be called in the initialization phase.

```
// throw unless the contract is not yet initialized.
modifier only_uninitialized { if (m_numOwners > 0) revert(); _; }
function initWallet(address[] _owners,
                    uint _required,
                    uint _daylimit) only_uninitialized
{ ... }
```

This clearly illustrates how important it is to think very thoroughly about each and every function:

- What are the preconditions?
- Who is allowed to call it?
- When in the life cycle is it allowed to be called?

Moreover, test that when you call it at the right moment as the rightful operator, it indeed does what it is supposed to do (normal unit testing). Even more important, test that if you are not the rightful operator or call it in the wrong state, it will do no harm and will in fact be rejected (security testing).

Writing thorough test cases is a job magnitude larger and more comprehensive than writing the contract itself.

The Future

One part of the smart contract development system that lags behind is automated testing. Using and extending the NatSpec comments could easily facilitate the generation of skeleton testing code that would significantly reduce the time spent on setting up unit and security testing.

However, the elephant in the room is the lack of scalability, which limits wide adaptation. It also makes blockchain vulnerable to denial-of-service attacks by flooding it with spam transactions. Also, to support microtransactions the transaction price needs to be lower. To become a universal and scalable platform, this problem has to be solved. One solution that tries to address the problem is the Lightning Network–like implementation for Ethereum called the Raiden Network. This work-in-progress project supplements the Ethereum blockchain with an offline chain to settle microtransactions. However, it requires preallocation of tokens/ether that are taken offline by transferring them to the Raiden Network before they can be utilized. This introduces a locking of assets offchain equal to the total liquidity needed. Also, it doesn't solve the scalability of general smart contracts. Other types of blockchain projects try to address this problem too. One example is the EOS Project, a generalized platform based on features from Steemit and Ethereum. This platform has no transaction fee and offers three-second block transactions without congestion by allowing parallelism in block execution and thereby introducing horizontal scalability beyond the 100,000 transaction per second mark.

Another example is the IOTA project, which is designed directly for massive microtransactions between IoT devices. In IOTA when you need to add a transaction, you need to validate two other transactions and check for conflicts before submitting into a tangle (connected graph), so you become your own miner, thus eliminating the need to pay somebody else for the validation. Strictly speaking, IOTA is not a chain of blocks containing transactions but rather a mesh of linked transactions. On the roadmap, IOTA will include smart contracts and oracles.

Absolute privacy is also an issue. Even though addresses are anonymous in the sense that the identities behind them are not normally registered, all transactions and balances are publicly available by design. If you use ether to pay to an address that uses some kind of KYC, either directly or indirectly, it is possible to back-trace your spending habits and wealth. Monero is an example of a blockchain that focuses on complete anonymity that is secure, private, and untraceable. It uses ring signatures where decoy addresses are added to the transaction, making it possible to hide the origin of a transaction. With stealth addresses (one-time addresses), the destination address is obscured. By using ring confidential transactions, the value of the transactions is hidden by cryptographical algorithms, but still verifiable. All in all, it ensures complete anonymity end to end. As yet they don't have Lightning Network or smart contracts, but those are on the roadmap.

Ripple XRP is a private centralized permission-based blockchain that acts like a worldwide transfer between bank accounts à la SWIFT. It's designed to scale to the same performance as VISA by implementing a peer-to-peer ledger network with a distributed agreement protocol. Instead of including the smart contract into the core blockchain, Ripple decided to implement a separate platform, Codius, for the smart contract and oracle part, which also allows cross-blockchain applications.

When looking at roadmaps for the different blockchains, it's clear that they have many of the same properties in mind. These include scaling the number of transactions to allow both volume and micropayments, as well as the inclusion of smart contracts and integration of oracles. All of these are where the best practices in this chapter will come in handy.

Summary

As we have seen in this chapter, the EVM provides a rich environment that enables development of solutions ranging from simple dapps, over simple interactions with oracles to fetch external information, all the way to full stack enterprise solutions. The smart contract platform includes all the features for creating modern code with multiple contracts calling and interaction with each other, including producing events to external systems. Also, we have recognized the importance of clear design in terms of modularity, roles and security, and life cycle management. Finally, because of blockchain's immutable nature, testing and validating of smart contracts need special attention prior to deployment on the blockchain.

8

Private Blockchain Platforms and Use Cases

Blockchain is a peer-to-peer distributed ledger technology, which makes it easier to create a more cost-efficient network with no central point of control. This is in contrast to the world where members of a business ecosystem maintain their own ledger or systems of record (SOR). These separate ledgers are continually being reconciled with one another in an inefficient, expensive, and often nonstandard way. Over time, these separate ledgers have been duplicated many times within each member's datacenters. It has gotten to the point where data governance, testing, release management, and in effect the complete software development life cycle (SDLC) is always hampered and more or less broken or damaged. It is no wonder that these institutions cannot innovate fast enough. It's like trying to run a race while dragging a trailer containing all the clothing you've ever owned throughout your lifetime!

However, recently the concept of private blockchains has become popular within the discussions on blockchain technology, particularly among financial institutions. Instead of having a fully decentralized network open to the public with anonymous parties, it is possible to create a system where each party is identified and granted permissions to change or read the blockchain. These private blockchains are also tackling the performance issue because consensus is performed on fewer nodes. In fact, it is likely that there will be many blockchain networks with each network serving a different set of goals and distinct business applications (see Figure 8-1).

It is important to note that there is some discussion that these private blockchains are compromising the central concept of decentralization. But for the purposes of this book let's take a look at the differences between the types or categories of blockchain.

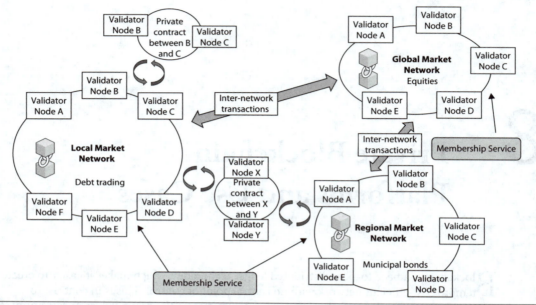

FIGURE 8-1   Many blockchain networks

Categories of Blockchain

Generally speaking, there are three categories of blockchain-like database applications: public, consortium, and private.

- **Public**   Anyone can read or submit transactions (submissions will be committed if valid), and anyone can participate in the consensus process. These trustless platforms are secured by mechanisms such as proof of work or proof of stake, a.k.a. cryptoeconomics. In other words, influence in the consensus process is proportional to the quantity of economic resources that entity can bring to bear.
- **Consortium**   Consensus is controlled by a preselected set of nodes and rules for achieving consensus. The right to read the blockchain can be open to the public, or it can also be restricted to a set of known participants—for example, 10 banks in a consortium that agree to the consensus rule that 7 of 10 banks must sign (approve) a block for it to be considered a valid representation of the truth.
- **Private**   Write permissions are kept centralized to a single organization or part of it. Read permissions may be public or restricted to a set of known participants.

In short, there are really two categories, *public* and *private*. The *consortium* is a derivative of the private blockchain with multiple identified and permissioned members/participants.

Here is a list of the advantages of a private blockchain:

- When read permission is enforced, a private blockchain provides privacy.
- A consortium or private entity can change the rules of a blockchain, allowing them to revert transactions, modify (fix) balances, etc. This functionality may be deemed necessary, although we must say these reasons look more like patches to fix defective functionality.
- The miners (or validators) are identified, defined, and known, so any risk of a 51 percent attack from colluding bad actors does not exist or can easily be identified and dealt with.
- Transactions are less expensive, since they only need to be verified by a limited set of trusted (and identified) nodes instead of by every node on the public network. There does not have to be any transaction fee. There may still be a requirement to run a validator node to participate in the network. This would be an expense, but would be less expensive to participants than a transaction fee on the public network. The validator node may also provide protection against a distributed denial-of-service (DDoS) attack.
- With fewer miners needed, consensus finality can be achieved much faster among a smaller group.

So, given the above, it is no surprise that financial institutions invariably choose private (or consortium) platforms for their blockchain applications. It is also a reason that private blockchains are also known as enterprise blockchains.

Private Blockchain Use Cases

The public blockchain has, in many cases by design, the following challenges to enterprise adoption, particularly those industries that are highly regulated:

- No privacy
- Anonymous processors
- Little to no governance
- Limited throughput with slow transaction confirmation (performance challenge)

In short, there are essentially two aspects to privacy itself: read permission and block generation (or write) permission. If the use case requires privacy, you will want to restrict read permission. If the use case requires trust spread across a limited and predetermined set of participants, you will want to restrict write permission. Both aspects individually or collectively may push you to a private (or consortium) blockchain platform.

Throughout this chapter we mention use cases for private blockchains. The following is a more complete collection of use cases:

- A permissioned interfinancial institution settlement layer for digital assets (currencies and securities)
- An intracompany ledger (balance sheet) containing private data without any single department being in authoritative control
- A permissioned platform for the issuance and maintenance of rewards, loyalty points, and gift cards

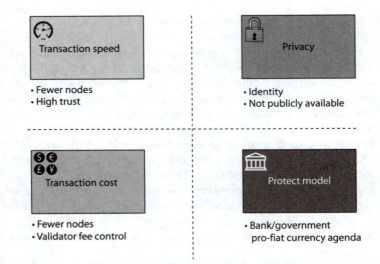

FIGURE 8-2   Requirements leading to private blockchains

- A tracking tool for private equity, debt, and other liquid agreements
- Database management, auditing, etc., internal to a single company
- Any use case that requires incredibly high numbers of transactions per second

Again, the considerations for choosing a private blockchain platform can be narrowed down to the requirements depicted in Figure 8-2.

Private Blockchain Technology

This section presents blockchain technology platforms that are applicable for the private and consortium spaces.

AlphaPoint Distributed Ledger Platform

AlphaPoint   Website: https://www.alphapoint.com/adlp.html

AlphaPoint Distributed Ledger Platform is a private, permissioned protocol that leverages blockchain, and it further allows firms complete control over their data. ADLP's key benefits are:

- **Secure architecture**   Multiple entities communicate and link via encrypted messages across secure networks.
- **Permissioned**   Parties can only access data that is explicitly shared with them.

The platform enables organizations to digitize, manage, and exchange financial instruments; deploy smart contracts along with automated workflows; and therefore reduce operational overhead.

Chain Core

Chain   Website: https://chain.com

Chain Core is a permissioned blockchain platform that is used to issue and/or transfer financial assets. Using it, financial institutions can launch and operate a blockchain network or connect to other networks in order to move assets around. The Chain protocol handles this by defining how assets are issued, transferred, and controlled. It allows a single entity (private) or a group of organizations (consortium) to operate a network, supports the coexistence of multiple types of assets (e.g., currencies, securities, derivatives, gift cards, and loyalty points), and has a degree of interoperability with other independent networks.

Corda

c·rda   Website: https://www.corda.net

Corda is an open-source platform that implements a distributed ledger made up of mutually distrusting nodes that records the state of deals and obligations between entities, which can be institutions or individuals. Unlike Ethereum, Corda's smart contracts are currently limited to the application of financial logic, and all nonfinancial applications are out of scope.

One of Corda's key features is pluggable consensus within the same network. This feature supports multiple consensus providers, and each can employ different algorithms. This type of distributed ledger has many applications focused around commerce, such as finance, trade, and supply chain tracking. Other key features are that this is a permissioned network, with access controlled by a doorman (TLS certificate provided to each node participant upon successful registration), and that all communication between nodes is point-to-point, instead of being sent to all nodes in a global broadcast.

Domus Tower

DOMUSTOWER   Website: http://domustower.com

Domus Tower has a vertical blockchain product that is solely designed to settle U.S. equities. The company's key selling point is that its technology can record a high rate of transactions in a scalable manner. The company's whitepaper begins with a statement that the product has been "benchmarked at ingesting over 1 million transactions per second on hardware costing less than $50 per hour on Amazon's Web Services with the potential to scale to greater than 10 million transactions per second."

It uses a double-entry approach for credits and debits, and data storage is contained in a Merkle directional acyclic graph (MerkleDAG), which ensures that the blockchain has not been altered or corrupted. All data transmitted to the blockchain is digitally signed and verified before it is written to a block. Authority is centralized under this model, and any node on the network that has write permission to a blockchain can write transactions to that chain.

The Elements Project

Website: https://elementsproject.org

Elements Core is an open-source, protocol-level technology developers can use to extend the functionality of Bitcoin to build new applications. Combinations of Elements (functionality) developed in this technical community can be brought together and fashioned into sidechains. It uses the periodic table and associated chemistry approaches to the naming and combining of functionality to build an application.

The current list of Elements are:

- **Ai (Asset Issuance)** Ability to issue confidential assets that represent any asset such as vouchers, coupons, currencies, deposits, bonds, shares, etc.
- **Ct (Confidential Transactions)** In a cryptographic way this keeps the amounts transferred visible only to participants in the transaction and those they designate, while still guaranteeing that no more coins can be spent than are available (double-spend).
- **Dp (Deterministic Pegs)** Allow cross-chain transactions to be constructed in a decentralized fashion, where tokens can be moved from one blockchain to another.
- **Op (New Opcodes)** Delivers new and re-enables some safe but disabled operation codes in Bitcoin (i.e., string concatenation, substrings, integer shifts, and some bitwise operations).
- **Rtl (Relative Time Lock)** Allows a transaction to be time-locked, preventing its use in a new transaction until a relative time change is achieved.
- **Sb (Signed Blocks)** Allows the creator of the block to verify their identity in the future.
- **Scv (Signature Covers Value)** Signature on a transaction can be invalidated if the inputs have been spent. Transaction can be validated fast by checking its signature.
- **Ss (Schnorr Signatures)** New way of constructing signatures for transactions.
- **Sw (Segregated Witness)** Reduces the required space for transactions in a block by a factor of 4.

Additionally, there are proposed Elements under development that are not yet ready for deployment on a public sidechain.

HydraChain

Website: https://github.com/HydraChain/hydrachain

HydraChain is 100 percent compatible with Ethereum; it extends the platform by adding support for creating permissioned distributed ledgers for private or consortium chain applications. All existing tools on the Ethereum platform can be reused. The essential difference is that HydraChain does not use proof-of-work for consensus, it relies on a registered and accountable set of validators, which propose and validate the order of transactions.

Hyperledger

Hyperledger is the umbrella project of open-source blockchains and supporting tools that was started in December 2015 by the Linux Foundation. The purpose of Hyperledger is to advance blockchain technology by identifying and then addressing important features that can transform the way business transactions are conducted on a distributed ledger.

The requirements for blockchains vary greatly across different use cases and industries, and Hyperledger is designed and implemented to be highly modular, with pluggable options to suit the differing industry requirements. The simplified project goals are:

- **Create framework and code base**   Users can then build and run robust, industry-specific business transactions.
- **Foster a community**   This will benefit the ecosystem for all.
- **Promote participation**   Includes end users, developers, and solution providers.
- **Neutral host**   Establish home for infrastructure, meetings, events, and collaborative discussions. Additionally, provide structure around the business and technical governance.

Hyperledger Frameworks

The Hyperledger initiative incubates and promotes a range of business blockchain technologies, including distributed ledger frameworks, smart contract engines, client libraries, graphical interfaces, utility libraries, and sample applications. The Hyperledger umbrella strategy encourages the reuse of common building blocks and enables rapid innovation of distributed ledger technology (DLT) components. Here are the frameworks for Hyperledger:

Hyperledger Fabric

Website: http://hyperledger.org

Intended as the foundation pillar for developing applications or solutions with a modular architecture, Fabric allows components such as consensus and membership services to be added in a plug-and-play fashion. Ledger data can be stored in multiple formats, consensus protocols can be switched in and out, and different identity verification methods are supported. There is support for channels, which are separate ledgers of transactions that are only made visible to specified groups of network participants.

Hyperledger Fabric Tutorial   Prior to running the tutorial, you will need to ensure that your computer has the following prerequisites installed:

- cURL (ensure your version handles redirects)
- Docker and Docker Compose
- Node.js runtime and NPM

The following listing contains the commands and the console output for setting up Hyperledger Fabric on a Mac. The first order of business is to set up Go in the Path:

```
$ echo $GOPATH

$ vi .bashrc
[create GOPATH variable and add it to your PATH]

$ source ~/.bashrc
$ echo $GOPATH
/Users/pallen/go
$ echo $PATH
/Users/pallen/.rvm/gems/ruby-2.2.1/bin
:/Users/pallen/.rvm/gems/ruby-2.2.1@global/bin
:/Users/pallen/.rvm/rubies/ruby-2.2.1/bin
:/usr/local/bin:/usr/bin:/bin:/usr/sbin:/sbin
:/usr/local/MacGPG2/bin:/Users/pallen/.rvm/bin
$ vi .bashrc
$ source ~/.bashrc
$ echo $PATH
/Users/pallen/.rvm/gems/ruby-2.2.1/bin
:/Users/pallen/.rvm/gems/ruby-2.2.1@global/bin
:/Users/pallen/.rvm/rubies/ruby-2.2.1/bin
:/usr/local/bin:/usr/bin:/bin:/usr/sbin:/sbin
:/usr/local/MacGPG2/bin:/Users/pallen/.rvm/bin:/Users/pallen/go/bin
```

Then upgrade Node Package Manager and install Node.js:

```
$ npm install npm@3.10.10 -g
(node:5955) fs: re-evaluating native module sources is not supported. If you
are using the graceful-fs module, please update it to a more recent version.
/usr/local/bin/npm -> /usr/local/lib/node_modules/npm/bin/npm-cli.js
- asap@2.0.3 node_modules/npm/node_modules/dezalgo/node_modules/asap
- lodash._arraycopy@3.0.0
...[output abbreviated]...
- tar@1.0.3 node_modules/npm/node_modules/node-gyp/node_modules/tar
- ansi@0.3.0 node_modules/npm/node_modules/npmlog/node_modules/ansi

...[output abbreviated]...
/usr/local/lib
└── npm@3.10.10
```

Create a working directory for where the clone of Hyperledger Fabric samples should go:

```
$ mkdir hl-fabric
$ cd hl-fabric/
```

Issue the clone command:

```
$ git clone https://github.com/hyperledger/fabric-samples.git
Cloning into 'fabric-samples'...
remote: Counting objects: 483, done.
remote: Compressing objects: 100% (24/24), done.
remote: Total 483 (delta 11), reused 25 (delta 8), pack-reused 450
Receiving objects: 100% (483/483), 155.54 KiB | 0 bytes/s, done.
Resolving deltas: 100% (138/138), done.
```

Install the platform-specific Hyperledger Fabric binaries:

```
$ curl -sSL https://goo.gl/iX9dek | bash
===> Downloading platform binaries

  % Total    % Received % Xferd  Average Speed   Time    Time     Time  Current
                                 Dload  Upload   Total   Spent    Left  Speed
100 22.4M  100 22.4M    0     0  4535k      0 0:00:05  0:00:05 --:--:-- 5222k
===> Pulling fabric Images
==> FABRIC IMAGE: peer

x86_64-1.0.0: Pulling from hyperledger/fabric-peer
aafe6b5e13de: Pull complete
...[output abbreviated]...
776cc74c9f73: Pull complete
Digest:

sha256:b7c1c2a6b356996c3dbe2b9554055cd2b63194cd7a492a83de2dbabf7f7e3c65
Status: Downloaded newer image for hyperledger/fabric-peer:x86_64-1.0.0
==> FABRIC IMAGE: orderer
```

```
x86_64-1.0.0: Pulling from hyperledger/fabric-orderer
aafe6b5e13de: Already exists
...[output abbreviated]...
12b8c0ba3585: Pull complete
Digest:

sha256:d0ea1f7e7ca04f0c4b7484f8835fd68e9bf13e6fcb700cf3a70f00a4059fc344
Status: Downloaded newer image for hyperledger/fabric-orderer:x86_64-1.0.0
==> FABRIC IMAGE: couchdb

x86_64-1.0.0: Pulling from hyperledger/fabric-couchdb
aafe6b5e13de: Already exists
...[output abbreviated]...
725164282bae: Pull complete
Digest:

sha256:e89b0f95f6ff674fd043795090dd65a11d727ec005d925545cf0b4fc48aa221d
Status: Downloaded newer image for hyperledger/fabric-couchdb:x86_64-1.0.0
==> FABRIC IMAGE: ccenv

x86_64-1.0.0: Pulling from hyperledger/fabric-ccenv
aafe6b5e13de: Already exists
...[output abbreviated]...
b505d76bd417: Pull complete
Digest:

sha256:eb2e87ea07e29a0b6b6e51e200efcc0cbaa571b8124c6b2dcc704da93bf39f24
Status: Downloaded newer image for hyperledger/fabric-ccenv:x86_64-1.0.0
==> FABRIC IMAGE: javaenv

x86_64-1.0.0: Pulling from hyperledger/fabric-javaenv
aafe6b5e13de: Already exists
...[output abbreviated]...
556833a5f7d4: Pull complete
Digest:

sha256:b19167b2caa9a6ac7c12457e7b50d7fbd1fb7f85ed49ad2fbabe8fdc5d3f4624
Status: Downloaded newer image for hyperledger/fabric-javaenv:x86_64-1.0.0
==> FABRIC IMAGE: kafka

x86_64-1.0.0: Pulling from hyperledger/fabric-kafka
aafe6b5e13de: Already exists
...[output abbreviated]...
3ca3fff5916e: Pull complete
Digest:
```

```
sha256:b396a45edf73520a7e8396ba8bd7bbf80fd55c3bfb8330745b3f09fdf8f1ef05
Status: Downloaded newer image for hyperledger/fabric-kafka:x86_64-1.0.0
==> FABRIC IMAGE: zookeeper


x86_64-1.0.0: Pulling from hyperledger/fabric-zookeeper
aafe6b5e13de: Already exists
...[output abbreviated]...
6de044b974eb: Pull complete
Digest:


sha256:3bf815ebef6850d56f73f42bc6c26006df05a8e659b7acb12c2431101770432f
Status: Downloaded newer image for hyperledger/fabric-zookeeper:x86_64-1.0.0
==> FABRIC IMAGE: tools


x86_64-1.0.0: Pulling from hyperledger/fabric-tools
aafe6b5e13de: Already exists
...[output abbreviated]...
75a35cd33119: Pull complete
Digest:


sha256:c107430c14344f4f37f0882f3eb8591520abd699a0b9da2b507f7527505612a7
Status: Downloaded newer image for hyperledger/fabric-tools:x86_64-1.0.0
===> Pulling fabric ca Image
==> FABRIC CA IMAGE


x86_64-1.0.0: Pulling from hyperledger/fabric-ca
aafe6b5e13de: Already exists
...[output abbreviated]...
7152da1670d2: Pull complete
Digest:


sha256:b7094644bcbf6c28948fcdd0c38ffe65f98889a57da0e1bf23bd18731ef44800
Status: Downloaded newer image for hyperledger/fabric-ca:x86_64-1.0.0


===> List out hyperledger docker images


hyperledger/fabric-tools      latest       0403fd1c72c7  3 weeks ago  1.32GB
hyperledger/fabric-tools      x86_64-1.0.0 0403fd1c72c7  3 weeks ago  1.32GB
hyperledger/fabric-couchdb    latest       2fbdbf3ab945  3 weeks ago  1.48GB
hyperledger/fabric-couchdb    x86_64-1.0.0 2fbdbf3ab945  3 weeks ago  1.48GB
hyperledger/fabric-kafka      latest       dbd3f94de4b5  3 weeks ago  1.3GB
hyperledger/fabric-kafka      x86_64-1.0.0 dbd3f94de4b5  3 weeks ago  1.3GB
hyperledger/fabric-zookeeper  latest       e545dbf1c6af  3 weeks ago  1.31GB
hyperledger/fabric-zookeeper  x86_64-1.0.0 e545dbf1c6af  3 weeks ago  1.31GB
hyperledger/fabric-orderer    latest       e317ca5638ba  3 weeks ago  179MB
```

```
hyperledger/fabric-orderer      x86_64-1.0.0    e317ca5638ba    3 weeks ago    179MB
hyperledger/fabric-peer         latest          6830dcd7b9b5    3 weeks ago    182MB
hyperledger/fabric-peer         x86_64-1.0.0    6830dcd7b9b5    3 weeks ago    182MB
hyperledger/fabric-javaenv      latest          8948126f0935    3 weeks ago    1.42GB
hyperledger/fabric-javaenv      x86_64-1.0.0    8948126f0935    3 weeks ago    1.42GB
hyperledger/fabric-ccenv        latest          7182c260a5ca    3 weeks ago    1.29GB
hyperledger/fabric-ccenv        x86_64-1.0.0    7182c260a5ca    3 weeks ago    1.29GB
hyperledger/fabric-ca           latest          a15c59ecda5b    3 weeks ago    238MB
hyperledger/fabric-ca           x86_64-1.0.0    a15c59ecda5b    3 weeks ago    238MB
```

There are four tutorials that come with Hyperledger Fabric. They are:

- **write_first_app**   Designed to show an application developer how to write their first application using the Node.js SDK.
- **build_network**   Oriented toward a network operator going through the process of establishing a blockchain network and deploying a simple application to test it out.
- **chaincode4ade**   Shows a developer how to write business logic agreed to by the members of the network.
- **chaincode4noah**   Demonstrates the administration of business logic by a network operator.

We will now step through the write_first_app tutorial, which again is designed to show the tasks involved and to provide the basis for writing a first application against the Hyperledger Fabric network. As with all other persistence layer–based (i.e., database or file system) applications that you've worked on before, this tutorial demonstrates the two common use cases of (1) reading from the chain and (2) writing to (or updating) the chain.

So, the first step is to navigate to the fabric directory and list its contents:

```
$ cd fabric-samples/fabcar
$ ls
creds    invoke.js    node_modules    package.json    query.js    startFabric.sh
```

Now start the Fabric network, which does the following:

- Starts a peer node, an ordering node, a Certificate Authority, and a CLI container
- Creates a channel and joins the peer node to the new channel
- Installs a smart contract onto the peer's file system and instantiates this contract on the channel by starting a chaincode (smart contract) container
- Calls the initLedger function on the smart contract to create 10 cars in the ledger

```
$ ./startFabric.sh

docker-compose -f docker-compose.yml down
Removing network net_basic
WARNING: Network net_basic not found.

docker-compose -f docker-compose.yml up -d ca.example.com orderer.example.com
```

```
peer0.org1.example.com couchdb
Creating network "net_basic" with the default driver
Creating orderer.example.com ...
Creating couchdb ...
Creating ca.example.com ...
Creating orderer.example.com
Creating ca.example.com
Creating orderer.example.com ... done
Creating ca.example.com ... done
Creating peer0.org1.example.com ... done

# wait for Hyperledger Fabric to start
# incase of errors when running later commands, issue

export FABRIC_START_TIMEOUT=<larger number>
export FABRIC_START_TIMEOUT=10
#echo ${FABRIC_START_TIMEOUT}
sleep ${FABRIC_START_TIMEOUT}

# Create the channel
docker exec -e "CORE_PEER_LOCALMSPID=Org1MSP" -e "CORE_PEER_MSPCONFIGPATH=/etc/hyperledger

/msp/users/Admin@org1.example.com/msp"

peer0.org1.example.com peer channel create

-o orderer.example.com:7050 -c mychannel

-f /etc/hyperledger/configtx/channel.tx
...[output abbreviated]...
2017-08-12 10:12:43.324 UTC [chaincodeCmd]

chaincodeInvokeOrQuery -> INFO 00a

Chaincode invoke successful. result: status:200
2017-08-12 10:12:43.325 UTC [main] main -> INFO 00b Exiting.....

Total execution time : 53 secs ...
```

Now view the processes that have been started:

```
$ docker ps
CONTAINER ID          IMAGE                                         {abbreviated...}
faf5b4d6dd3a          dev-peer0.org1.example.com-fabcar-1.0         {abbreviated...}
44c550584595          hyperledger/fabric-tools:x86_64-1.0.0         {abbreviated...}
ba112762ddd2          hyperledger/fabric-peer:x86_64-1.0.0          {abbreviated...}
be518bf52517          hyperledger/fabric-ca:x86_64-1.0.0            {abbreviated...}
b5ba01f09916          hyperledger/fabric-couchdb:x86_64-1.0.0       {abbreviated...}
19ce89d0baaa          hyperledger/fabric-orderer:x86_64-1.0.0       {abbreviated...}
```

Now install the SDK node modules so that the sample code will function:

```
$ npm install
Run the code to read from the blockchain:
$ node query.js
Create a client and set the wallet location
Set wallet path, and associate user  PeerAdmin  with application
Check user is enrolled, and set a query URL in the network
Make query
Assigning transaction_id:
dded6822d9a89d8d38967c115f0b9b39ce38ce81c446bbce4c79a4cdf3906440
returned from query
Query result count =  1
Response is  [
{"Key":"CAR0",  "Record":{"colour":"blue","make":"Toyota","model":"Prius",

"owner":"Tomoko"}},
{"Key":"CAR1",  "Record":{"colour":"red","make":"Ford","model":"Mustang",

"owner":"Brad"}},
{"Key":"CAR2",  "Record":{"colour":"green","make":"Hyundai","model":"Tucson",

"owner":"Jin Soo"}},
{"Key":"CAR3",  "Record":{"colour":"yellow","make":"Volkswagen","model":"Passat",

"owner":"Max"}},
{"Key":"CAR4",  "Record":{"colour":"black","make":"Tesla","model":"S",

"owner":"Adriana"}},
{"Key":"CAR5",  "Record":{"colour":"purple","make":"Peugeot","model":"205",

"owner":"Michel"}},
{"Key":"CAR6",  "Record":{"colour":"white","make":"Chery","model":"S22L",

"owner":"Aarav"}},
{"Key":"CAR7",  "Record":{"colour":"violet","make":"Fiat","model":"Punto",

"owner":"Pari"}},
{"Key":"CAR8",  "Record":{"colour":"indigo","make":"Tata","model":"Nano",

"owner":"Valeria"}},
{"Key":"CAR9",  "Record":{"colour":"brown","make":"Holden","model":"Barina",

"owner":"Shotaro"}}]
```

Let's take a look at the query.js code, in particular the highlighted sections that show how to connect to the chain and then issue a query:

```javascript
'use strict';
/*
* Copyright IBM Corp All Rights Reserved
*
* SPDX-License-Identifier: Apache-2.0
*/
/*
 * Hyperledger Fabric Sample Query Program
 */

var hfc = require('fabric-client');
var path = require('path');

var options = {
    wallet_path: path.join(__dirname, './creds'),
    user_id: 'PeerAdmin',
    channel_id: 'mychannel',
    chaincode_id: 'fabcar',
    network_url: 'grpc://localhost:7051',
};

var channel = {};
var client = null;

Promise.resolve().then(() => {
    console.log("Create a client and set the wallet location");
    client = new hfc();
    return hfc.newDefaultKeyValueStore({ path: options.wallet_path });
}).then((wallet) => {
    console.log("Set wallet path, and associate user ",
      options.user_id, " with application");
    client.setStateStore(wallet);
    return client.getUserContext(options.user_id, true);
}).then((user) => {
    console.log(
      "Check user is enrolled, and set a query URL in the network");
    if (user === undefined || user.isEnrolled() === false) {
        console.error("User not defined, or not enrolled - error");
    }
    channel = client.newChannel(options.channel_id);
    channel.addPeer(client.newPeer(options.network_url));
    return;
}).then(() => {
```

```
console.log("Make query");
var transaction_id = client.newTransactionID();
console.log("Assigning transaction_id: ",
    transaction_id._transaction_id);

    // queryCar - requires 1 argument, ex: args: ['CAR4'],
    // queryAllCars - requires no arguments , ex: args: [''],
    const request = {
        chaincodeId: options.chaincode_id,
        txId: transaction_id,
        fcn: 'queryAllCars',
        args: ['']
    };
    return channel.queryByChaincode(request);
}).then((query_responses) => {
    console.log("returned from query");
    if (!query_responses.length) {
        console.log("No payloads were returned from query");
    } else {
        console.log("Query result count = ", query_responses.length)
    }
    if (query_responses[0] instanceof Error) {
        console.error("error from query = ", query_responses[0]);
    }
    console.log("Response is ", query_responses[0].toString());
}).catch((err) => {
    console.error("Caught Error", err);
});
```

A slight adjustment to the query will let us read by a single key:

```
    // queryCar - requires 1 argument, ex: args: ['CAR4'],
    // queryAllCars - requires no arguments , ex: args: [''],
    const request = {
        chaincodeId: options.chaincode_id,
        txId: transaction_id,
        fcn: 'queryCar',
        args: ['CAR4']
    };
```

Submitting the adjusted query and showing the response:

```
$ node query2.js
Create a client and set the wallet location
Set wallet path, and associate user  PeerAdmin  with application
Check user is enrolled, and set a query URL in the network
Make query
```

```
Assigning transaction_id:
745d6cd549fc4206d7e99d35bb2c2821aa38a7c78d7f87a02f0c82e51b4b9c08
returned from query
Query result count =  1
Response is  {"colour":"black","make":"Tesla","model":"S","owner":"Adriana"}
```

Now we can move on to making some changes to the ledger. We will start off with the sample code that will add a new car to the chain. Here is the invoke.js code; again the section for inserting CAR10 is highlighted:

```javascript
'use strict';
/*
 * Copyright IBM Corp All Rights Reserved
 *
 * SPDX-License-Identifier: Apache-2.0
 */
/*
 * Chaincode Invoke
 */

var hfc = require('fabric-client');
var path = require('path');
var util = require('util');

var options = {
    wallet_path: path.join(__dirname, './creds'),
    user_id: 'PeerAdmin',
    channel_id: 'mychannel',
    chaincode_id: 'fabcar',
    peer_url: 'grpc://localhost:7051',
    event_url: 'grpc://localhost:7053',
    orderer_url: 'grpc://localhost:7050'
};

var channel = {};
var client = null;
var targets = [];
var tx_id = null;
Promise.resolve().then(() => {
    console.log("Create a client and set the wallet location");
    client = new hfc();
    return hfc.newDefaultKeyValueStore({ path: options.wallet_path });
}).then((wallet) => {
    console.log("Set wallet path, and associate user ",

        options.user_id, " with application");
```

```
        client.setStateStore(wallet);
        return client.getUserContext(options.user_id, true);
    }).then((user) => {
        console.log(

            "Check user is enrolled, and set a query URL in the network");
        if (user === undefined || user.isEnrolled() === false) {
            console.error("User not defined, or not enrolled - error");
        }
        channel = client.newChannel(options.channel_id);
        var peerObj = client.newPeer(options.peer_url);
        channel.addPeer(peerObj);
        channel.addOrderer(client.newOrderer(options.orderer_url));
        targets.push(peerObj);
        return;
    }).then(() => {
        tx_id = client.newTransactionID();
        console.log("Assigning transaction_id: ", tx_id._transaction_id);
        // createCar - requires 5 args, ex: args: ['CAR11', 'Honda',

        //  'Accord', 'Black', 'Tom'],
        // changeCarOwner - requires 2 args , ex: args: ['CAR10', 'Barry'],
        // send proposal to endorser
        var request = {
            targets: targets,
            chaincodeId: options.chaincode_id,
            fcn: 'createCar',
            args: ['CAR10', 'Chevy', 'Volt', 'Red', 'Nick'],
            chainId: options.channel_id,
            txId: tx_id
        };
        return channel.sendTransactionProposal(request);
    }).then((results) => {
        var proposalResponses = results[0];
        var proposal = results[1];
        var header = results[2];
        let isProposalGood = false;
        if (proposalResponses && proposalResponses[0].response &&
            proposalResponses[0].response.status === 200) {
            isProposalGood = true;
            console.log('transaction proposal was good');
        } else {
            console.error('transaction proposal was bad');
        }
        if (isProposalGood) {
            console.log(util.format(
```

```
'Successfully sent Proposal and received ProposalResponse: Status - %s,
 message - "%s", metadata - "%s", endorsement signature: %s',
 proposalResponses[0].response.status,
 proposalResponses[0].response.message,
 proposalResponses[0].response.payload,
 proposalResponses[0].endorsement.signature));
    var request = {
        proposalResponses: proposalResponses,
        proposal: proposal,
        header: header
    };
    // set the transaction listener and set a timeout of 30sec
    // if the transaction did not get committed within the timeout period,
    // fail the test
    var transactionID = tx_id.getTransactionID();
    var eventPromises = [];
    let eh = client.newEventHub();
    eh.setPeerAddr(options.event_url);
    eh.connect();

    let txPromise = new Promise((resolve, reject) => {
        let handle = setTimeout(() => {
            eh.disconnect();
            reject();
        }, 30000);

        eh.registerTxEvent(transactionID, (tx, code) => {
            clearTimeout(handle);
            eh.unregisterTxEvent(transactionID);
            eh.disconnect();

            if (code !== 'VALID') {
                console.error(
                    'The transaction was invalid, code = ' + code);
                reject();
            } else {
                console.log(
                    'The transaction has been committed on peer ' +
                    eh._ep._endpoint.addr);
                resolve();
            }
        });
    });
    eventPromises.push(txPromise);
    var sendPromise = channel.sendTransaction(request);
return Promise.all([sendPromise].concat(eventPromises)).then((results) => {
console.log(' event promise all complete and testing complete');
```

```
  return results[0];
  // the first returned value is from the 'sendPromise' which is from the
  // 'sendTransaction()' call
        }).catch((err) => {
            console.error(
 'Failed to send transaction and get notifications within the timeout period.'
            );
 return

});
```

When you execute the insert, here is the response:

```
$ node invoke.js
Create a client and set the wallet location
Set wallet path, and associate user  PeerAdmin  with application
Check user is enrolled, and set a query URL in the network
Assigning transaction_id:
4dd4ddc44307aa5fbe2caa1a003fe2ef40015bf8e5b978c28ca8dba528580a74
transaction proposal was good
Successfully sent Proposal and received ProposalResponse:

Status - 200, message - "OK", metadata - "", endorsement signature:

0D _�c��ȝAɥ�%�hī��j��9���w�'_ !$�(.�@���'4�V�*Q•.�O���
info: [EventHub.js]: _connect - options {}
The transaction has been committed on peer localhost:7053
 event promise all complete and testing complete
Successfully sent transaction to the orderer.
```

After adjusting the query.js code to read the new key (changed `'CAR4'` to `'CAR10'`) and executing:

```
$ node query.js
Create a client and set the wallet location
Set wallet path, and associate user  PeerAdmin  with application
Check user is enrolled, and set a query URL in the network
Make query
Assigning transaction_id:
13dd62ff7a655cffc24d8153d6fe3a7872f7d4d69764413722f68f123fa098de
returned from query
Query result count =  1
Response is  {"colour":"Red","make":"Chevy","model":"Volt","owner":"Nick"}
To perform an update, change the invoke.js so that it
calls the changeCarOwner function and switches the owner
from 'Nick' to 'Barry':
// createCar - requires 5 args, ex: args:
['CAR11', 'Honda', 'Accord', 'Black', 'Tom'],
```

```
// changeCarOwner - requires 2 args , ex: args: ['CAR10', 'Barry'],
// send proposal to endorser
var request = {
    targets: targets,
    chaincodeId: options.chaincode_id,
    fcn: 'changeCarOwner',
    args: ['CAR10', 'Barry'],
    chainId: options.channel_id,
    txId: tx_id
};
return channel.sendTransactionProposal(request);
```

Then execute the invoke.js code:

```
$ node invoke2.js
Create a client and set the wallet location
Set wallet path, and associate user  PeerAdmin  with application
Check user is enrolled, and set a query URL in the network
Assigning transaction_id:
694ee1db40f141ae7f2614520c8b9ea24342f1d3860f0bfa0227a3f64f06bef4
transaction proposal was good
Successfully sent Proposal and received ProposalResponse:
Status - 200, message - "OK", metadata - "", endorsement signature:
0D >;2cm2◆=d◆~◆◆#=◆5◆◆◆p•◆◆◆#(◆◆G jU"iz@d
info: [EventHub.js]: _connect - options {}
The transaction has been committed on peer localhost:7053
 event promise all complete and testing complete
Successfully sent transaction to the orderer.
```

Run query.js one more time to query CAR10; here is the response:

```
$ node query3.js
Create a client and set the wallet location
Set wallet path, and associate user  PeerAdmin  with application
Check user is enrolled, and set a query URL in the network
Make query
Assigning transaction_id:
b5dbf4f3a579599a520e38ac499597e4be1cc21bc15ba32a048b4b454cad4d1a
returned from query
Query result count =  1
Response is  {"colour":"Red","make":"Chevy","model":"Volt","owner":"Barry"}
```

Now we have stood up the blockchain, read from it, and written to it. The only thing left to do is to shut down the docker instance by issuing the following:

```
Pauls-Air:fabcar pallen$ cd ../basic-network/
Pauls-Air:basic-network pallen$ docker-compose down
Stopping cli ... done
Stopping peer0.org1.example.com ... done
```

```
Stopping ca.example.com ... done
Stopping couchdb ... done
Stopping orderer.example.com ... done
Removing cli ... done
Removing peer0.org1.example.com ... done
Removing ca.example.com ... done
Removing couchdb ... done
Removing orderer.example.com ... done
Removing network net_basic
```

This concludes the Hyperledger Fabric tutorial.

Hyperledger Iroha

Websites:
https://github.com/hyperledger/iroha
https://www.hyperledger.org/projects/iroha

Iroha was contributed to Hyperledger by the Japanese fintech company Soramitsu. It is a business blockchain framework designed to be simple and easy to incorporate into infrastructural projects requiring distributed ledger technology.

Some key features are:

- Creation and management of complex assets, including currencies, rights, serial numbers, patents, etc.
- Management and permission of user accounts (read and write), including business rules for transactions and queries

Iroha's goal is to provide the following encapsulated C++ components that other projects can use:

- Sumeragi consensus library (inspired by BChain, a chain-style Byzantine replication protocol that propagates transactions among the nodes with a chain topology)
- Ed25519 digital signature library
- SHA-3 hashing library
- Transaction serialization library
- P2P broadcast library
- API server library
- iOS, Android, and JavaScript libraries
- Blockchain explorer/data visualization suite

Hyperledger Sawtooth

Websites: https://github.com/hyperledger/sawtooth-core
https://www.hyperledger.org/projects/sawtooth

Hyperledger Sawtooth is a modular platform for building, deploying, and running distributed ledgers. Hyperledger Sawtooth includes a proprietary consensus algorithm, Proof of Elapsed Time (PoET), which targets large distributed validator populations with minimal resource consumption.

Hyperledger Tools

All platforms need tools and utilities, and blockchain is no different. The following are the current tools for the Hyperledger platform.

Hyperledger Cello

Cello

Websites: https://github.com/hyperledger/cello
https://www.hyperledger.org/projects/cello

Hyperledger Cello is a toolkit that aims to bring the on-demand "as-a-service" deployment model to the blockchain ecosystem. Its goal is to reduce the effort required for the setup, ongoing maintenance, and teardown of blockchains. Its highlights are:

- Instantly provision customizable blockchains, for example, Hyperledger Fabric
- Maintain a pool of executing blockchains on top of baremetals, VMs, Docker Swarm, and Kubernetes
- Administration dashboard that provides system status and allows adjustment to chain numbers or scale resources

Hyperledger Composer

Websites: https://github.com/hyperledger/composer
https://www.hyperledger.org/projects/composer

Hyperledger Composer is a collaboration tool for building blockchain business networks, accelerating the development of smart contracts and their deployment across a distributed ledger. See Figure 8-3 for sample screen captures of the tool. Hyperledger Composer is an extensive, open development collaboration toolset and framework to make developing blockchain applications easier. Its goal is to accelerate producing value by making it easier to

FIGURE 8-3 Hyperledger Composer

model a business network and then integrate a blockchain application with the existing/legacy business systems. It supports existing Hyperledger Fabric blockchains and supports pluggable consensus protocols that have been established by permissioned network members.

Hyperledger Explorer

Websites: https://www.hyperledger.org/projects/explorer
https://github.com/hyperledger/blockchain-explorer

Hyperledger Explorer, contributed by IBM, Intel, and DTCC, can view, invoke, deploy, or query blocks, transactions with associated data, network information (e.g., name, status), chain codes and transaction families, and other relevant information contained in the blockchain. See Figure 8-4 for sample screen capture of the tool.

FIGURE 8-4   **Hyperledger Explorer**

Interbit

Website: http://btl.co/interbit

Interbit is an enterprise-grade blockchain platform that enables applications to be built, managed, and run on a blockchain. Its key features are:

- **Privacy**   Ensures that data is only available to those who have permission to see and change it
- **Scalability**   Provides a platform that can scale to hundreds of thousands of transactions per second
- **Portability**   The first blockchain platform developed that is able to run full nodes on lightweight IoT devices

Monax

Website: https://monax.io

Monax is a permissionable smart contract machine. Released in December 2014, Monax provides a modular blockchain client with a permissioned smart contract interpreter built in part to the specification of the Ethereum Virtual Machine (EVM). In early 2017, blockchain startup Monax announced they were joining Hyperledger. It is the first code base with an EVM joining the consortium. Swift, an interbank transfer platform, has experimented with the Monax platform as part of its project to look at integrating blockchain into its payments platform. Let's walk through a Monax tutorial.

Monax Tutorial

One of the first things to be done for this tutorial is to establish the virtual environment; this can be either Docker or Vagrant. We will look at a Vagrant installation. The following assumes that you already have Vagrant installed and you have downloaded the associated monax.box file and the Monax workshop sources.zip file.

The first step is to register the Monax virtual machine:

```
$ vagrant box add monax monax.box
==> box: Box file was not detected as metadata. Adding it directly...
==> box: Adding box 'monax' (v0) for provider:
    box: Unpacking necessary files from: file:///Users/pallen/monax.box
==> box: Successfully added box 'monax' (v0) for 'virtualbox'!
```

Then change directory to the workshop material and initialize the vagrant instance:

```
$ cd workshop
$ vagrant init monax
A 'Vagrantfile' has been placed in this directory. You are now
ready to 'vagrant up' your first virtual environment! Please read
the comments in the Vagrantfile as well as documentation on
'vagrantup.com' for more information on using Vagrant.
```

Then start up the instance:

```
$ vagrant up
No usable default provider could be found for your system.

Vagrant relies on interactions with 3rd party systems, known as
"providers", to provide Vagrant with resources to run development
environments. Examples are VirtualBox, VMware, Hyper-V.

The easiest solution to this message is to install VirtualBox, which
is available for free on all major platforms.

If you believe you already have a provider available, make sure it
is properly installed and configured. You can see more details about
why a particular provider isn't working by forcing usage with
'vagrant up --provider=PROVIDER', which should give you a more specific
error message for that particular provider.
```

If you get the above error, it means you haven't installed VirtualBox. No big deal, just go ahead and download and install it and try starting up the instance again.

```
$ vagrant up
Bringing machine 'default' up with 'virtualbox' provider...
==> default: Importing base box 'monax'...
==> default: Matching MAC address for NAT networking...
==> default: Setting the name of the VM: workshop_default_1501867336806_8879
==> default: Clearing any previously set network interfaces...
==> default: Preparing network interfaces based on configuration...
    default: Adapter 1: nat
==> default: Forwarding ports...
    default: 22 (guest) => 2222 (host) (adapter 1)
==> default: Booting VM...
==> default: Waiting for machine to boot. This may take a few minutes...
    default: SSH address: 127.0.0.1:2222
    default: SSH username: vagrant
    default: SSH auth method: private key
==> default: Machine booted and ready!
==> default: Checking for guest additions in VM...
    default: The guest additions on this VM do not match the
    default: installed version of VirtualBox!
    default: In most cases this is fine, but in rare cases it can
    default: prevent things such as shared folders from working properly.
    default: If you see shared folder errors, please make sure the guest
    default: additions within the virtual machine match the version
    default: of VirtualBox you have installed on your host and reload
    default: your VM.
    default:
    default: Guest Additions Version: 4.3.36
    default: VirtualBox Version: 5.1
==> default: Mounting shared folders...
    default: /vagrant => /Users/pallen/workshop
```

The final part of the setup stage for the tutorial is to secure shell into it:

```
$ vagrant ssh

The programs included with the Debian GNU/Linux system are free software;
the exact distribution terms for each program are described in the
individual files in /usr/share/doc/*/copyright.

Debian GNU/Linux comes with ABSOLUTELY NO WARRANTY, to the extent
permitted by applicable law.
Last login: Thu Apr 27 19:05:28 2017 from 10.0.2.2
vagrant@contrib-jessie:~$
```

Note that the virtual machine login for the secure shell is `contrib-jessie`, the login of the person who originally created the virtual instance.

Make a Chain Configuration   With the Monax virtual machine setup completed, you can now begin the process of making a chain configuration. This process creates all of the necessary files for a private blockchain within the Monax platform. The following is the help text for the chain's make command:

```
vagrant@contrib-jessie:~$ monax chains make --help
Usage: monax chains make NAME [FLAG...]


create necessary files for your chain

Make is an opinionated gateway to the basic types of chains which most
Monax users will make most of the time. Make is also a command line
wizard in which you will let the marmots know how you would like your
genesis created.

Make can also be used with a variety of flags for fast chain making.

When using make with the --known flag the marmots will *not* create
keys for you and will instead assume that the keys exist somewhere.
When using make with the wizard (no flags) or when using with the
other flags then keys will be made along with the genesis.jsons and
priv_validator.jsons so that everything is ready to go for you to
[monax chains start].

Optionally chains make provides packages of outputted priv_
validator and genesis.json which you can email or send on your
slack to your coworkers. These packages can be tarballs or zip
files, and **they will contain the private keys** so please be
aware of that.

The make process will *not* start a chain for you. You will want to use
the [monax chains start NAME --init-dir ~/.monax/chains/NAME/ACCOUNT]
for that which will import all of the files which make creates into
containers and start your shiny new chain.

If you have any questions on [monax chains make], see the documentation here:
https://monax.io/docs

Examples:
----+----1----+----2----+----3----+----4----+----5----+----6----+----7----+---

$ monax chains make myChain --wizard -- will use the interactive
chain-making wizard and make your chain named myChain
$ monax chains make myChain -- will use the simplechain definition
file to make your chain named myChain (non-interactive);
use the [--chain-type] flag to specify chain types
$ monax chains make
```

```
myChain --account-types=Root:1,Developer:0,Validator:1,Participant:1
-- will use the flag to make your chain named myChain (non-interactive)
$ monax chains make myChain --known --validators
/path/to/validators.csv --accounts /path/to/accounts.csv -- will use the
csv file to make your chain named myChain (non-interactive)
(won't make keys)
$ monax chains make myChain --tar -- will create the chain and save
each of the "bundles" as tarballs which can be used by colleagues to
start their chains
```

```
Flags:
--account-types stringSlice    specify the kind and number of account
types. find these in ~/.monax/chains/account-types; incompatible with
chain-type
--accounts string              comma separated list of the accounts.csv
files you would like to utilize (requires --known flag)
--chain-type string            specify the type of chain to use. find
these in ~/.monax/chains/chain-types; incompatible with account-types
--known                        use csv for a set of known keys to
assemble genesis.json (requires both --accounts and --validators flags)
--output                       should monax-cm provide an output of its
job (default true)
--seeds-ip stringSlice         set a list of seeds (e.g.
IP:PORT,IP:PORT) for peers to join the chain
--tar                          instead of making directories in
~/.monax/chains, make tarballs; incompatible with and overrides zip
--unsafe                       require explicit confirmation to write
private keys from monax-keys to host during make in accounts.json
--validators string            comma separated list of the validators.csv
files you would like to utilize (requires --known flag)
-w, --wizard                   summon the interactive chain making wizard
--zip                          instead of making directories in
~/.monax/chains, make zip files
```

```
Global flags:
-d, --debug             debug level output
-m, --machine string    machine name for docker-machine that
is running VM (default "monax")
-v, --verbose           verbose output
```

In the following command, we make a chain configuration with one full node and three participants:

```
vagrant@contrib-jessie:~$ monax chains make myChain
--account-types=Full:1,Participant:3 --unsafe
```

Start the workshop chain:

```
vagrant@contrib-jessie:~$ monax chains start workshop
--init-dir /vagrant/chain-config/workshop_full_000/
```

Copy the user keys and import them into the development keys server:

```
vagrant@contrib-jessie:~$ cp -r /vagrant/chain-config/keys/*
~/.monax/keys/data/
vagrant@contrib-jessie:~$ monax keys import --all
```

Note that the import step may take a few minutes.

Tutorial: Phases   The next steps are the main deployment and test phases. It begins with Phase 1, which is a job that does the following:

- Deploys the course registry (a Solidity smart contract)
- Registers a participant
- Gets the number of participants registered
- Verifies that the number of course participants is 1

Here are the above steps expressed in the epm.yaml file:

```
jobs:


#####
# Deploy Course Registry
#####
- name: CourseRegistry
  job:
    deploy:
      contract: contracts/CourseRegistry.sol

- name: registerParticipant
  job:
    call:
      destination: $CourseRegistry
      function: registerParticipant
      data: ["Solidity101", $defaultAddr]

- name: getCourseSize
  job:
    query-contract:
      destination: $CourseRegistry
      function: getNumberOfParticipants
      data: ["Solidity101"]
```

```
- name: assertCourseSize
  job:
    assert:
      key: $getCourseSize
      relation: eq
      val: 1
```

To execute the above work and view the output for Phase 1:

```
vagrant@contrib-jessie:~$ cd /vagrant/phase1
vagrant@contrib-jessie:/vagrant/phase1$ monax pkgs do -c workshop
-a 4CDBDE25BBAB54751C25CEB9A33D551FC1FE13D5


*****Executing Job*****

Job Name                                        defaultAddr

*****Executing Job*****

Job Name                                        CourseRegistry
Saving ABI                                      abi/CourseRegistry
Deploying Contract                         name=CourseRegistry
                                           addr=7096D2C824949662E922866B7E26B934828B06C5


*****Executing Job*****

Job Name                                        registerParticipant

*****Executing Job*****

Job Name                                        getCourseSize
Return Value                                    1


*****Executing Job*****

Job Name                                        assertCourseSize
Assertion Succeeded                             1 == 1
```

The following listing shows the contents of the Course Registry smart contract being deployed (CourseRegistry.sol file):

```
pragma solidity ^0.4.4;

contract CourseRegistry {

    mapping (bytes32 => address[]) courseRegistry;

    function registerParticipant(bytes32 _course, address _participant) {
        courseRegistry[_course].push(_participant);
```

```
      }

      function getNumberOfParticipants(bytes32 _course) constant returns (uint) {
         return courseRegistry[_course].length;
      }

}
```

The next step in the tutorial, Phase 2, is to run a job that does the following:

- Deploys the course manager (another Solidity smart contract)
- Gets a handle on the course manager
- Registers a participant
- Gets the number of participants registered
- Verifies that the number of course participants is 1

Here are the above steps expressed in the epm.yaml file:

```
jobs:

- name: CourseManager
  job:
    deploy:
      contract: contracts/CourseManager.sol
      instance: all

- name: CourseRegistry
  job:
    query-contract:
      destination: $CourseManager
      function: getRegistry

- name: registerParticipant
  job:
    call:
      destination: $CourseRegistry
      abi: DefaultCourseRegistry
      function: registerParticipant
      data: ["Solidity101", $defaultAddr]

- name: getCourseSize
  job:
    query-contract:
      destination: $CourseRegistry
      abi: DefaultCourseRegistry
      function: getNumberOfParticipants
```

```
        data: ["Solidity101"]

- name: assertCourseSize
  job:
    assert:
      key: $getCourseSize
      relation: eq
      val: 1
```

To execute the above work and view the output:

```
vagrant@contrib-jessie:/vagrant/phase1$ cd /vagrant/phase2
vagrant@contrib-jessie:/vagrant/phase2$ monax pkgs do -c workshop
-a 4CDBDE25BBAB54751C25CEB9A33D551FC1FE13D5


*****Executing Job*****

Job Name                                    defaultAddr

*****Executing Job*****

Job Name                                    CourseManager
Saving ABI                                  abi/DefaultCourseRegistry
Deploying Contract                   name=DefaultCourseRegistry
                                     addr=7CE7F43206A40618852562CC6AC06F4506F5B5D3
Saving ABI                                  abi/CourseManager
Deploying Contract                   name=CourseManager
                                     addr=75FB775F6E92567AE4773696D1D1D3A32D8CBBCE


*****Executing Job*****

Job Name                                    CourseRegistry
Return Value                                FBC01ADB6D0A919A09BDC8E3686971066956AEF7

*****Executing Job*****


Job Name                                    registerParticipant

*****Executing Job*****

Job Name                                    getCourseSize
Return Value                                1

*****Executing Job*****


Job Name                                    assertCourseSize
Assertion Succeeded                         1 == 1
```

The following listing shows the contents of the course manager smart contract being deployed (CourseManager.sol file):

```solidity
pragma solidity ^0.4.4;

import "./CourseRegistry.sol";
import "./DefaultCourseRegistry.sol";

contract CourseManager {

   CourseRegistry registry = new DefaultCourseRegistry();

   function getRegistry() constant returns (address) {
      return registry;
   }

}
```

The following listing shows the contents of the course registry smart contract being deployed (CourseRegistry.sol file):

```solidity
pragma solidity ^0.4.4;

contract CourseRegistry {

   function registerParticipant(bytes32 _course, address _participant);

   function getNumberOfParticipants(bytes32 _course) constant returns (uint);

}
```

The following listing shows the contents of the default course registry smart contract being deployed (DefaultCourseRegistry.sol file):

```solidity
pragma solidity ^0.4.4;

import "./CourseRegistry.sol";

contract DefaultCourseRegistry is CourseRegistry {

   mapping (bytes32 => address[]) courseRegistry;

   function registerParticipant(bytes32 _course, address _participant) {
      courseRegistry[_course].push(_participant);
   }
```

```
function getNumberOfParticipants(bytes32 _course) constant returns (uint) {
    return courseRegistry[_course].length;
  }

}
```

Phase 3 is to run a job that does the following:

- Deploys the course manager (Solidity smart contract)
- Gets a handle on the course manager
- Registers a participant (that fails)
- Gets the number of participants registered
- Verifies that the number of course participants is 0
- Registers a participant (that succeeds)
- Gets the number of participants registered
- Verifies that the number of course participants is 1

Here are the above steps expressed in the epm.yaml file:

```
jobs:

- name: CourseManager
  job:
    deploy:
      contract: contracts/CourseManager.sol
      instance: all

- name: CourseRegistry
  job:
    query-contract:
      destination: $CourseManager
      function: getRegistry

- name: registerParticipantFail
  job:
    call:
      destination: $CourseRegistry
      abi: DefaultCourseRegistry
      function: registerParticipant
      data: ["Solidity101", $defaultAddr]

- name: getCourseSizeFail
  job:
    query-contract:
      destination: $CourseRegistry
      abi: DefaultCourseRegistry
```

```
        function: getNumberOfParticipants
        data: ["Solidity101"]

- name: assertCourseSizeFail
  job:
    assert:
      key: $getCourseSizeFail
      relation: eq
      val: 0

- name: registerParticipantSuccess
  job:
    call:
      destination: $CourseManager
      function: registerForCourse
      data: ["Solidity101", $defaultAddr]

- name: getCourseSizeSuccess
  job:
    query-contract:
      destination: $CourseRegistry
      abi: DefaultCourseRegistry
      function: getNumberOfParticipants
      data: ["Solidity101"]

- name: assertCourseSizeSuccess
  job:
    assert:
      key: $getCourseSizeSuccess
      relation: eq
      val: 1
```

To execute the above work and view the output:

```
vagrant@contrib-jessie:/vagrant/phase2$ cd /vagrant/phase3
vagrant@contrib-jessie:/vagrant/phase3$ monax pkgs do -c workshop
-a 4CDBDE25BBAB54751C25CEB9A33D551FC1FE13D5

*****Executing Job*****

Job Name                                    defaultAddr

*****Executing Job*****

Job Name                                    CourseManager
Saving ABI                                  abi/CourseManager
```

```
Deploying Contract                          name=CourseManager
                                            addr=BF5638B9B66DE74887F5D720E289E406D6A00759
Saving ABI                                       abi/DefaultCourseRegistry
Deploying Contract                          name=DefaultCourseRegistry
                                            addr=17731DD32E466D07340506F27C7FDA3DDE62E26E
Saving ABI                                       abi/Owned
Deploying Contract                          name=Owned
                                            addr=6CE22D71B99149E3627305D8BC780D79406E48C5


*****Executing Job*****

Job Name                                    CourseRegistry
Return Value                                A745CF88A10A49D6641A60CC2CFE061BE673544D

*****Executing Job*****

Job Name                                    registerParticipantFail

*****Executing Job*****

Job Name                                    getCourseSizeFail
Return Value                                0

*****Executing Job*****

Job Name                                    assertCourseSizeFail
Assertion Succeeded                         0 == 0

*****Executing Job*****

Job Name                                    registerParticipantSuccess

*****Executing Job*****

Job Name                                    getCourseSizeSuccess
Return Value                                1

*****Executing Job*****

Job Name                                    assertCourseSizeSuccess
Assertion Succeeded                         1 == 1
```

Phase 4 is a job that does the following:

- Deploys the courses library (Solidity smart contract)
- Deploys the course manager (link to the course library)
- Gets a handle on the course manager

- Adds a course (Solidity 101)
- Gets the number of courses available
- Verifies that the number of courses available is 1
- Registers a participant for the available course (Solidity 101)
- Gets the number of participants registered
- Verifies that the number of course participants is 1

Here are the above steps expressed in the epm.yaml file:

```
vagrant@contrib-jessie:/vagrant/phase4$ cat epm.yaml
jobs:

- name: CoursesLibrary
  job:
    deploy:
      contract: contracts/Courses.sol

- name: CourseManager
  job:
    deploy:
      contract: contracts/CourseManager.sol
      libraries: Courses:$CoursesLibrary
      instance: all

- name: CourseRegistry
  job:
    query-contract:
      destination: $CourseManager
      function: getRegistry

- name: addCourse
  job:
    call:
      destination: $CourseManager
      function: addCourse
      data: ["SOL101", "Solidity 101", 2017, 25]

- name: getNumberOfCourses
  job:
    query-contract:
      destination: $CourseRegistry
      abi: DefaultCourseRegistry
      function: getNumberOfCourses
```

```
- name: assertNumberOfCourses
  job:
    assert:
      key: $getNumberOfCourses
      relation: eq
      val: 1

- name: registerParticipant
  job:
    call:
      destination: $CourseManager
      function: registerForCourse
      data: ["SOL101", $defaultAddr]

- name: getCourseSize
  job:
    query-contract:
      destination: $CourseRegistry
      abi: DefaultCourseRegistry
      function: getNumberOfParticipants
      data: ["SOL101"]

- name: assertCourseSize
  job:
    assert:
      key: $getCourseSize
      relation: eq
      val: 1
```

To execute the above work and view the output:

```
vagrant@contrib-jessie:/vagrant/phase3$ cd /vagrant/phase4
vagrant@contrib-jessie:/vagrant/phase4$ monax pkgs do -c workshop
-a 4CDBDE25BBAB54751C25CEB9A33D551FC1FE13D5


*****Executing Job*****

Job Name                                    defaultAddr


*****Executing Job*****

Job Name                                    CoursesLibrary
Saving ABI                                  abi/Courses
Deploying Contract          name=Courses
                            addr=7AEFB4119B7742FE6023A13EFA821AED7426911B


*****Executing Job*****
```

```
Job Name                                    CourseManager
Saving ABI                                  abi/CourseManager
Deploying Contract           name=CourseManager
                             addr=9A10DA79DD5725F331FC9CC826BA34DA36312959

Saving ABI                                  abi/Courses
Deploying Contract           name=Courses
                             addr=BE382E4F2205BAF53076A2A9EEACE3BA9342FECB

Saving ABI                                  abi/DefaultCourseRegistry
Deploying Contract           name=DefaultCourseRegistry
                             addr=79ECE36DB8D0ED195C93CEB2A78132377B7F4B1C

Saving ABI                                  abi/Owned
Deploying Contract           name=Owned
                             addr=169DB815EAB132DC6B11FA8AC05E1808A9DC4D27


*****Executing Job*****

Job Name                                    CourseRegistry
Return Value                                C6F474E0188D8FF317F5B93D1B0B26B699AE97EF

*****Executing Job*****

Job Name                                    addCourse

*****Executing Job*****

Job Name                                    getNumberOfCourses
Return Value                                1

*****Executing Job*****

Job Name                                    assertNumberOfCourses
Assertion Succeeded                         1 == 1

*****Executing Job*****

Job Name                                    registerParticipant

*****Executing Job*****

Job Name                                    getCourseSize
Return Value                                1

*****Executing Job*****

Job Name                                    assertCourseSize
Assertion Succeeded                         1 == 1
```

That is the end of the tutorial. Now comes the teardown, which isn't documented. In order to tear down the whole virtual environment, you will first exit the secure shell, if you haven't already done so:

```
vagrant@contrib-jessie:/vagrant/phase4$ exit
logout
Connection to 127.0.0.1 closed.
```

Then you can start the teardown process as follows:

```
$ vagrant halt
==> default: Attempting graceful shutdown of VM..
$ vagrant destroy
    default: Are you sure you want to destroy the 'default' VM? [y/N] y
==> default: Destroying VM and associated drives...
$ vagrant box remove monax
Removing box 'monax' (v0) with provider 'virtualbox'...
$ rm Vagrantfile
```

The above tutorial is a brief introduction to the Monax offering. It demonstrated defining and starting up a chain, deploying smart contracts written in Solidity, and then calling functions on the smart contracts.

MultiChain

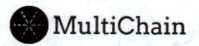

Websites:
https://www.multichain.com
https://github.com/MultiChain/multichain

MultiChain is an open-source platform for private chains based on Bitcoin's blockchain. Its key features are:

- **Managed permissions** Control over who can connect; send and receive transactions; create assets, streams, and blocks
- **Rapid deployment** Two steps to create a new blockchain and three to connect to an existing one
- **Unlimited assets** Tracked and verified at the network level
- **Data streams** Allow the creation of multiple key-value, time series, or identity databases on a blockchain

MultiChain provides maximal compatibility with the Bitcoin ecosystem, which includes the Bitcoin Core APIs/runtime parameters, the peer-to-peer protocol, and its transaction/block formats.

Openchain

Websites:
https://www.openchain.org
https://github.com/openchain

Openchain is an open-source distributed ledger platform for issuing and managing digital assets. The administrator of an Openchain instance defines the rules of the ledger, then the permissioned end users can exchange value on the ledger according to its rules. Each transaction on the ledger is digitally signed.

Openchain is a generic register of asset ownership. Some example use cases are:

- Securities, commodities, currencies
- Ownership titles (land, real estate, music or software licensing)
- Reward, gift, and loyalty cards

Quorum

Websites: https://github.com/jpmorganchase/quorum
https://www.jpmorgan.com/country/US/EN/Quorum

Quorum an open-source distributed ledger platform based on the official Go implementation of Ethereum. It is designed to support applications that require identity and (high-speed/throughput) performance of private transactions within a permissioned group of known participants. One of the design goals of Quorum is to reuse as much existing Ethereum technology as possible and to keep in sync with future versions of the public Ethereum code base.

Quorum also comes with Cakeshop, which is a graphical user interface for working with Quorum networks, smart contracts, and APIs. The Quorum consensus mechanism is based on majority voting, which results in faster blocktimes, transaction finality, and on-demand block creation.

Quorum uses cryptography to shield data from those who are not a party to the transaction. Quorum is a single shared blockchain and a combination of changes to Ethereum along with smart contracts to segment the private data. The Go-Ethereum code base changes are to the block proposal and block validation processes. For block validation, all nodes validate public transactions, and they also validate private transactions that they are party to when executing the contract code associated with the transactions.

Stellar

   Website: https://www.stellar.org

Stellar is an open-source, distributed payments infrastructure that connects banks, payment systems, and people. It enables the building of mobile wallets, banking tools, and smart devices. The servers in the chain communicate and sync with each other to ensure that transactions are valid and get applied to the ledger. Stellar uses its own form of consensus called Stellar Consensus Protocol (SCP). Its key properties are:

- Low latency.
- Digital signatures and hash families.
- Decentralized control where anyone is able to participate and no central authority dictates whose approval is required for consensus.
- Flexible trust. Users have the freedom to trust any combination of parties they see fit. For example, a small nonprofit may play a key role in keeping much larger institutions honest.

Symbiont Assembly

   Website: https://symbiont.io/technology/introducing-symbiont-assembly

Symbiont Assembly is an immutable (or "append-only") database that provides a single, global ledger whose transaction history is replicated out to all nodes in the network. It is a permissioned ledger, where each user signs their transactions so that their identity can be verified by all participants on the network.

Symbiont Assembly uses a proprietary Byzantine fault-tolerant consensus protocol called BFT-SMaRt, which was designed with simplicity and modularity in mind, and has improved performance over public blockchain consensus protocols.

Summary

There are many options for permissioned private blockchains, and the list is likely to grow. In many cases, government/industry regulation dictates that private control is needed. That being said, the freedom, neutrality, and openness that started Bitcoin on the public blockchain are things to keep in mind. The focus of decentralizing control and consensus on the public platform is clearly something to think about. There is a great deal of chatter and concern around privacy, identity, speed, and cost of the public blockchain solutions. It is important to note that by creating privately administered smart contracts on public blockchains, or cross-chain exchange layers that sit in between public and private blockchains, it is possible to deliver some degree of the properties of private blockchains on the public platforms. Time will tell if these types of capabilities and properties ever get built into the public blockchain.

9 Challenges

As blockchain evolves and new applications emerge, we the developers—and perhaps governance regulators and attorneys—will face a complex set of issues, as well as new dependencies. A key challenge associated with blockchain is a lack of awareness and technical skills needed to implement the technology, especially in sectors other than banking. A blockchain represents a large shift away from the traditional ways of developing digital technologies. It places trust and authority in a decentralized network rather than in a classic central institution. This loss of control makes business leaders hesitant. Blockchain is perhaps 80 percent business process change and 20 percent technology implementation. The speed and effectiveness with which blockchain networks currently execute peer-to-peer transactions comes at a high aggregate cost. As we have seen, this inefficiency arises because each node performs the same tasks as every other node on its own copy of the data. In this chapter, we will explore some possible alternatives. For the Bitcoin network, for example, which uses a proof-of-work approach in lieu of trusting participants in the network, total running costs associated with validating and sharing transactions is $600 million in 2017 and rising. Blockchains are a productivity paradox. Therefore, decisions about implementing blockchain applications need to be carefully considered and analyzed before implementation. The law and regulations they spawn have always struggled to keep up with advances in technology. Indeed, technologies like the Bitcoin blockchain bypass regulation completely to solve inefficiencies in conventional intermediated payment networks. That said, there are still strong arguments for blockchain applications to work within the laws and regulatory structures, not outside of them, but this means that lawyers and business leaders need to understand the technology and its impact on the businesses and consumers in their sector.

While no technology is completely secure, no one has managed as yet to compromise the encryption and decentralized architecture of a blockchain. For security and privacy, identities created within a blockchain are unique and offer a high level of assurance that the party is who they claim to be. We must consider how privacy and security can drive and inform the design. Public acceptance of blockchain applications will likely mean proactively framing the discussion of privacy around concepts of value, security, and trust. We will explore these challenges and other issues in this chapter.

All software systems as they evolve from proof of concept prototypes to virtual necessity naturally face technical challenges. Blockchains as distributed systems not only face technical challenges but, as we have seen, a host of governance challenges as well. We will explore challenges around governance, including the Bitcoin rift and the Ethereum fork. On the technical side, there are challenges such as "51 percent attacks", and the all too familiar denial-of-service attacks we see in the cybersecurity news each day. Some new wave challenges include the growing use of smart contracts, and the reliability thereof, as well as the perennial scaling problems which all popular technology faces.

Blockchain Governance Challenges

Governance challenges encompass the philosophical, economic, and social issues that come from those already supporting a given blockchain or cryptocurrency, but disagree on how to move the technology forward. These are challenges that will consistently arise and be different every time. They all revolve around how to upgrade the code to deal with some issue but cannot agree on how to do so. In other words, it's an issue of how to achieve consensus on the *community level*, of how protocol upgrades are managed. In a decentralized environment, you can't force anyone to upgrade, but this has presented a number of problems, including:

- Bitcoin blocksize debate
- Ethereum DAO fork
- Ethereum moving to proof-of-stake

Bitcoin Blocksize Debate

The Bitcoin blocksize debate has been a long-standing, growing rift in the Bitcoin space. It revolves around the 1MB limitation on blocksize that is hardcoded in the code (see https://github.com/bitcoin/bitcoin/blob/master/src/consensus/consensus.h):

```
static const unsigned int MAX_BLOCK_BASE_SIZE = 1000000;
```

The limitation was originally put there by Satoshi Nakamoto to prevent denial-of-service attacks. The fear was that without this limitation some miners could create blocks so large that smaller miners would not be able to process and keep up, in effect cutting them off from participating in the network. When Satoshi first put the limitation in place, it was with the understanding that it will be removed when the network is ready. But even after the capabilities of the network have improved due to hardware advances, the 1 MB limit has remained.

The problem with having such a limit is simply that there are only so many transactions that can fit into a 1MB block (roughly 2,000). Since there is a new block only every 10 minutes, this translates into three or four transactions per second. Obviously, this is untenable for a global system where, for comparison, Visa handles 20,000 transactions per second.

The blocksize issue first arose in 2013 with Jeff Garzik saying the blocksize needed to be increased. Gavin Andresen and Mike Hearn decided to weigh in in 2015 when they felt the issue needed to be taken seriously. Hearn wrote a blog post entitled "The Capacity Cliff," urging the Bitcoin community to increase the blocksize immediately. He argued that once blocks reached capacity and people's transactions were not processed they would lose faith in Bitcoin's functionality, and there would be a downward spiral in Bitcoin's market value. Hearn sold all his bitcoins at the time. Andresen argued that by March 2016 Bitcoin blocks would be full. He was accurate with his prediction. Hearn's doomsday scenario did not come to pass, however.

Instead of the issue working its way closer to a resolution, it has instead drifted in the opposite direction, toward heated technical debates, arguments over the use and nature of Bitcoin, and name calling and infighting. The core developers felt that changing the blocksize would disadvantage small miners and lead to further miner centralization. They also felt a "fee market" is healthy for Bitcoin. They felt that there needs to be competition to get into a block in order to eliminate transaction spam and increase the transaction fees in general. They argued that a small (less than 10 cents) transaction fee is too small for a network that needs to store that transaction forever.

The community split itself into proponents of big blocks and proponents of small blocks. Each side accused the other of trying to destroy Bitcoin. On Reddit there was an r/btc spinoff from r/bitcoin, where r/btc accused r/bitcoin of censoring posts that were in favor of any size increase. There is indeed a lot of evidence backing up the claim of censorship. r/bitcoin in turn accused r/btc of just bashing anyone who wanted to keep the status quo. There were endless blog posts and articles from both sides, with everyone from Brian Armstrong, CEO of Coinbase, to Vitalik Buterin weighing in.

The effects of full blocks meant that transaction fees had to rise, and by late 2017 it was typical to pay $2 to $5 on a transaction when only a couple years back Bitcoin was heralded as being nearly free to use. Figure 9-1 shows the rise of transaction costs in 2017, in terms of satoshis (i.e., 0.00000001 bitcoin) per byte. In addition, instead of transactions confirming in the first block, it would often take several blocks to get a confirmation, turning what used to be

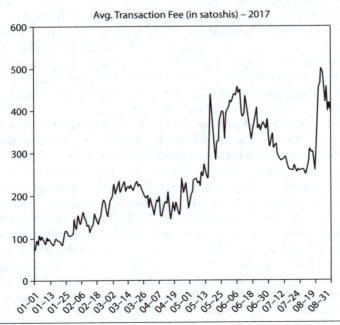

FIGURE 9-1   Average transaction costs January–September 2017, in terms of satoshis per byte

a 10-minute wait into 30 minutes. Many transactions would not confirm at all and get stuck in the mempool. Eventually these transactions would drop out and a user could resend it with a higher fee, but nevertheless the ever-increasing number of transactions in the mempool does not bode well.

These issues led many bitcoiners to argue for "forking" Bitcoin—releasing a version of Bitcoin that can create 2MB blocks, known as Bitcoin Classic, and a version that removes the hardcoded limit altogether, known as Bitcoin Unlimited. In early summer 2017, a new version known as Bitcoin Cash was proposed, which would raise the blocksize to 8MB. On August 1, it had enough support to go into effect, and Bitcoin Cash was born. The Bitcoin network split into two.

The Bitcoin blocksize issue is disconcerting because even a relatively minor change could not get enough support to prevent a fork. If the Bitcoin community cannot agree on a small code change, how is there any hope for implementing significant improvements to the protocol needed for scaling and sidechains? We may be headed toward a world of many Bitcoin blockchains, each one born out of a modification that couldn't get universal support.

The Ethereum DAO Fork

Before July 2016 there was only one Ethereum (ETH). Then the Ethereum network forked. Most of the community, around 90 percent, were behind the Ethereum Foundation, which had made just one change to the code: it undoes all transactions from one DAO transaction, the one that moved $60 million worth of ether from the DAO contract into a hacker's personal contract. While most of the community was behind this change, there was some strong opposition too—not because people wanted the hacker to get away with it, only that it's the lesser of two evils. The bigger evil was reneging on the promise of blockchains— indeed, the claim made on ethereum.org: "unstoppable code." Blockchain promised code that cannot be changed and transactions that cannot be rolled back. If this transaction were rolled back, how could anyone have faith that their transaction wouldn't suffer a similar fate? Of course, the fear is somewhat unjustified because you're only at risk of having a transaction rolled back if the majority of the Ethereum community unites to undo a transaction, and this is only likely in the event of something monumental like the DAO hack. In any case, there were some strong holdouts who did not want to upgrade.

On July 20, 2016, at block number 1920000 the new version of Ethereum went into effect. It was a success—at least it was immediately heralded as one by most of the community. There was very little hash power on the non-upgraded chain, and within the first two days it seemed the old chain would die out completely—there would be no miners left creating blocks on that chain. But then something surprising happened. The chain started getting more hash power and more vocal proponents. Then the largest Ethereum exchange—Poloniex—listed these "old chain" tokens, dubbed Ethereum Classic (ETC). This was a watershed moment opening up ETC to traders and speculators, some crediting Poloniex for propping the coin up, if not criticizing them for adding it for their own self-interests. Ethereum Classic has continued to maintain a solid following and has been among the top coins by market cap ever since.

This all illustrates the challenge for public tokens: how to get the whole community in agreement on changing the code in some way. If at every change it spawns a sister chain, then the value proposition of cryptocurrencies is watered down.

Ethereum's Move to PoS and Scaling Challenges

In continuation with the above, Ethereum faces more governance issues in its near future. Ethereum has always proposed to move to a proof-of-stake (PoS) mining algorithm. And while miners knew from day one that such a change will be implemented at some point, they now have a lot vested in proof-of-work mining equipment. It may not be in their best interests to go along with the transition to proof-of-stake. Indeed there is already such talk among a small percentage of Ethereum miners to maintain the consensus algorithm as is. Senior Ethereum developer Vlad Zamfir has also argued for reducing the mining rewards before the move to PoS, in light of the high price of ether. However good the arguments are, if they don't satisfy the vast majority of miners, then any change will result in yet another version of Ethereum.

Perhaps more challenging will be Ethereum's architecture changes to allow sharding—Ethereum's scaling proposal. The changes will likely be quite significant—and risky. It's hard to imagine there not being vocal opposition to implementing changes that can potentially introduce a bug to wipe out all of Ethereum's market value.

In the early days of Bitcoin, it was also thought that it will undergo major changes to allow for scaling. Today, those dreams are squashed with the recognition that it would be too difficult to change Bitcoin now. However, unlike Ethereum, Bitcoin's core function has always been as a "store of value." Ethereum, on the other hand, has been championed as a world computer. A world computer must be able to handle more than a couple dozen transactions per second. It's an existential threat that Ethereum uniquely faces.

Blockchain Technical Challenges

Blockchains face some unique challenges as a piece of software. There's very little room for error in blockchain code, especially public blockchains. If there are billions of dollars of cryptocurrency riding on the soundness of the platform, a bug can cost literally billions and potentially be fatal altogether. The DAO hack has already demonstrated this: a subtle bug resulted in the loss of tens of millions of dollars, not to mention hurting confidence in the overall system. So blockchain code must be compared to software that flies a plane, or that monitors an oil drill.

Technical challenges come in two main varieties: security challenges and usability challenges. We will explore the following:

- Security challenges: the core code, denial-of-service attacks, smart contracts
- Usability challenges: scaling

Bugs in the Core Code

In Bitcoin's history it's had two issues with its core code that could have been potentially disastrous. On August 8, 2010, Bitcoin developer Jeff Garzik announced on bitcointalk.org, "The 'value out' in this block is quite strange," referring to a block that had somehow contained 92 billion BTC, which is precisely 91,979,000,000 more bitcoins than are ever supposed to exist. Block number 74638 exploited an integer overflow to make a negative total transaction. Ultimately the blockchain needed to be rolled back to before the introduction of these bitcoins.

Then in 2012 there was an update to Bitcoin core that had an unintentional side effect. In the new version, 0.8, it was using an updated version of MongoDB (the backend DB of Bitcoin). This version was incompatible with 0.7 and caused blocks produced on the older version to not be recognized by 0.8. The blockchain forked. After a frantic few hours on the bitcointalk message board, it was decided that all those who did upgrade would roll back to the 0.7 version and abandon their chain. Thankfully, these miners—who were actually the more conscientious ones, following along with upgrades—were willing to take a hit and lose their mining rewards for the good of the network. Nevertheless, this was another demonstration of side effects arising in subtle ways.

Denial-of-Service Attacks

Ethereum also faced a problem that isn't so much a bug but more of a miscalibration, which allowed for denial-of-service (DoS) attacks to be carried out against the network. We normally think of denial-of-service attacks as an adversary overwhelming a website or service with so many requests that the service cannot respond to legitimate users, effectively taking the service offline. Figure 9-2 shows this scenario.

In Ethereum this happened slightly differently. In Ethereum the user needs to pay for operations on the network. So you'd think this would block any denial-of-service attacks by the fact that it costs money to execute. But that assumes the cost to execute operations

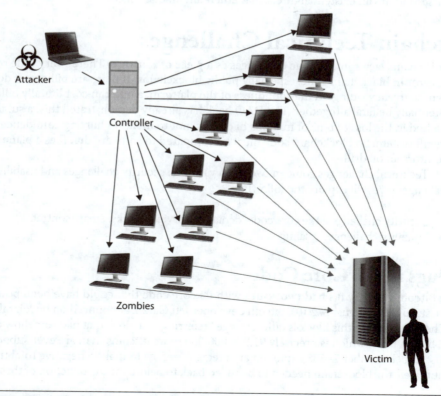

FIGURE 9-2   Denial-of-service attack

is commensurate with the processing overhead needed to run them; this was not the case. Each operation type in the EVM has a price associated with it. And as it happened some of the operations were mispriced, not reflecting the computational overhead needed to fulfill them. An attacker unleashed a smart contract and invoked it repeatedly to perform memory-intensive work, dramatically slowing down the Ethereum network. In fact it would have brought the network to a standstill if not for an alternative, less popular, client called Parity, which was able to process those transactions far more efficiently and keep up with the demand. The more popular Geth client became useless. The Geth developers quickly rolled out an improvement, but a full fix was only possible with a hard fork to put in appropriate pricing. Unfortunately, even with the fork there was still an operation—suicide—invoked when the contract was killed that took up too many resources, and another fork needed to be rolled out for that.

In short, there was a period of two months where there were repeated attacks on the Ethereum blockchain that resulted in some form of denial-of-service attacks and demonstrated that these networks must be vigilant and resilient against them.

Security in Smart Contracts

Perhaps the most important security concern in blockchain is the security of the smart contracts, because while the core blockchain is heavily vetted and tested, smart contracts are often rushed out the door. While the blockchains can be rolled back in a catastrophic attack, a smart contract generally cannot.

The DAO Hack

The DAO hack is the most dramatic example of what happens with poor smart contract design. The DAO contract had $150 million worth of ether when a hacker began to drain it. The hacker successfully moved $60 million worth to an intermediate holding contact where they were in sole control. The hack happened because the DAO allowed the user to withdraw their funds repeatedly, known as a reinjection vulnerability. The hole was in that when ether was withdrawn, it was sent to the withdrawer (the hacker in this case) and only *then* updated the withdrawer's balance to 0. Figure 9-3 shows the general structure of the DAO, where users can invoke the "Split DAO" operation and request payout of their funds from the parent DAO to the child DAO. The hacker figured out a way to request a payout again and again before their balance was updated.

Here are the problematic lines of code in the `splitDAO()` function where the user can withdraw their ether and move it into their own DAO:

```
withdrawRewardFor(msg.sender); // The receiver gets paid out here
totalSupply -= balances[msg.sender];
// only now is the receiver's balance updated --
balances[msg.sender] = 0;
// PROBLEM BELOW: This should have been done first before payout
paidOut[msg.sender] = 0;
return true;
```

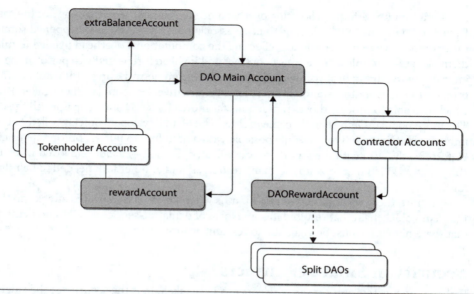

FIGURE 9-3 The normal movement of funds in the DAO, including the Split DAO function

The DAO contract wasn't the only one to suffer from the reinjection vulnerability. MakerDAO, which stored millions of dollars in its decentralized exchange platform, also had this bug but luckily the developers were able to drain the funds themselves using the vulnerability before a hacker got to the funds.

Other Smart Contract Bugs

Many other projects suffered from bugs in their smart contracts. Ethereum Name Service (ENS) is a well-respected project led by Nick Johnson at the Ethereum Foundation. ENS is a system to associate user-friendly names with Ethereum addresses, whether user addresses or contracts, just as DNS associates domain names with IP addresses. Instead of referring to a long hexadecimal address you can refer to companyname.eth. ENS is a contract that acts as a registry, mapping names to addresses. It has a very fair system to reserve such names. In order to claim one, you must first open an auction for your name, which gives anyone three days to bid on the name. After the bidding period, there are two days where everyone can reveal their bids, with the highest bidder winning the name and being refunded whatever money they paid above the next highest bidder. In other words, the winning bidder only pays the amount of the second highest bid. Figure 9-4 illustrates the bidding flow. When bids are placed they are encrypted, masking the actual bid until the reveal period, when bids are uncovered. It's an elegant system.

A few hours after the ENS contract went live, a bug was found that allowed someone to keep bidding during the reveal period, overbidding any revealed bids. This flaw was especially damaging because it didn't depend on special circumstances as the DAO hack did. It was

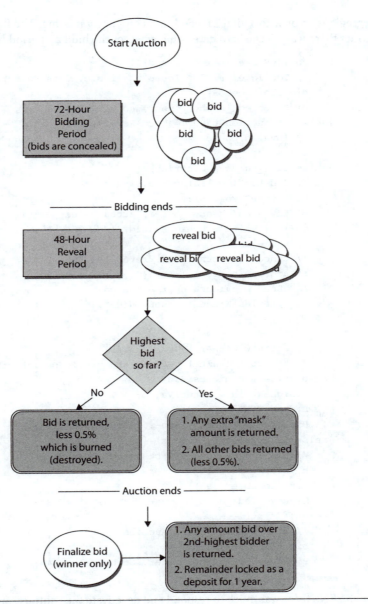

FIGURE 9-4 The stages of an ENS bid

an egregious error with a vital `if` condition completely missing. The flaw was that in the contract there was no check to determine whether the bidding period had closed.

```
if(auctionState == Mode.Owned) {
    // Too late! Bidder loses their bid. Gets 0.5% back.
    bid.closeDeed(5);
    BidRevealed(_hash, _owner, actualValue, 1
} else if(auctionState != Mode.Reveal) {
    // Invalid phase
    throw;
} else if (_value < minPrice) {
    // Bid too low, refund 99.5%
    bid.closeDeed(995);
    BidRevealed(_hash, _owner, actualValue, 0);
} else if (_value > h.highestBid) {
    // new winner
    // cancel the other bid, refund 99.5%
    if(address(h.deed) != 0) {
        Deed previousWinner = h.deed;
        previousWinner.closeDeed(995);
    }

    // set new winner
    // the cost (value) becomes the previous highestBid
    h.value = h.highestBid;
    h.highestBid = actualValue;
    h.deed = bid;
    BidRevealed(_hash, _owner, actualValue, 2);
} else if (_value > h.value) {
    // not winner, but affects second place
    h.value = actualValue;
    bid.closeDeed(995);
    BidRevealed(_hash, _owner, actualValue, 3);
} else {
    // bid doesn't affect auction
    bid.closeDeed(995);
    BidRevealed(_hash, _owner, actualValue, 4);
}
```

The ENS team was quick to respond and deactivate the contract, promising a fix would be released that same evening. They blamed the bug on a last-minute refactor that introduced it—a bad oversight but quickly addressed. The fix was to change an above check to

```
else if (_value < minPrice || bid.creationDate() > h.registrationDate - revealPeriod)
```

It looked like all was well and back on track, but a second bug was reported a few hours later. The contract could be tricked into making someone the highest bidder even if they put in a very low bid. It came down to using a wrong but similarly named variable in one of the if conditions. The variable _value was the wrong reference and should have referred to actualValue:

```
else if (_value > h.highestBid) {
    // new winner
    // cancel the other bid, refund 99.5%
    if(address(h.deed) != 0) {
        Deed previousWinner = h.deed;
        previousWinner.closeDeed(995);
}
```

In detail, a user enters a bid into the auction. They may pay ether here, but there is no enforced relationship between the amount of ether they pay and the value declared when defining the bid. The value of the deed will be defined by the amount paid, and the deed will own that amount, but this may not be the value the user declared when defining the bid.

When unsealBid is called, they must identify the bid with its declared value _value, which may differ from the value of the Deed that represents it. The function will compute a quantity actualValue, which will be the minimum of the value paid and the value declared. So, if the user underpaid, actualValue will be the value that they've actually paid.

However, when checking to see if they've won the auction (or if they have at least the minimum price), the declared value _value is used rather than actualValue to decide if the bidder won. If the declared value is sufficiently high, they eject the previous winner of the auction. The winning bid gets set to actualValue, which may be lower than the user's declared value, and lower than the prior winning bid. So someone could win auctions by declaring very high values but underfunding them (and unsealing their bids late in the reveal period, since their low actually paid value becomes an easily displaceable highestBid).

Two embarrassing bugs on the very first day—not a good start for ENS. The team said they were going to take a time-out and postpone the release until a complete audit could be carried out. Why wasn't it fully vetted before?

The ENS incident is a good example of a high-profile project by a high-profile team failing to meet the standards required for a blockchain program. If they couldn't release solid code, what hope is there for amateur teams or engineers at large to create smart contracts that are safe and execute as intended?

The DAO and other smart contract bugs have convinced many in the community that there must be a better approach if this technology is to work. Hoping that everyone becomes a more vigilant coder is not enough. We will continue to see bugs. The alternative is to change the very nature of how smart contracts are written to make it difficult for bugs to appear in the first place—to use a formally verifiable language or formal verification tools, a feature of functional languages.

In functional code, the output value of a function depends only on the arguments that are passed to the function, so calling a function f twice with the same value for an argument x will produce the same result $f(x)$ each time. This is in contrast to procedures depending on local or global state, which may produce different results at different times when called with the same arguments but different program state. Eliminating side effects—i.e., changes in state that do not depend on the function inputs—can make it much easier to understand and predict the behavior of a program, which is one of the key motivations for the development of functional programming.

Vitalik Buterin has talked at length about the need for such techniques, and it's considered one of Ethereum's existential needs. The problem is that not only does it require a lot of resources to develop such a language or tool, but it's far more difficult to learn and program in such languages. Engineers will need to be retrained, and the pool of such engineers will likely be smaller.

Scaling

For public blockchains, the biggest challenge is scalability. The Bitcoin network can process 4 to 7 transactions per second, the Ethereum network around 15. This is minuscule for a global platform. What use is a public blockchain if it cannot actually serve a global audience? If Bitcoin or Ethereum were to have as many users as Visa or Instagram today, the network would grind to a halt.

When you think about it, if every transaction, every computation, is performed by every node in the network, then the processing capability of the entire network is limited by the processing capability of a single node. If the solution is to have super-powerful nodes that have massive memory, CPU, and bandwidth resources, the network is not very decentralized. Only the powerful will have powerful computers.

In reality, it's overkill to have everyone do everything. And in order to allow blockchains to scale to the level of Visa, we must find a way around this design paradigm. The solution must take some form of not having everyone process everything. There are many solutions in the works, but none have been yet implemented. Here's an overview of what we know.

Don't Do Everything on the Blockchain

One solution is to build an intermediate layer or many intermediate layers. These are called second-layer solutions, and they go by the names Lightning Network (for Bitcoin) and Raiden Network (for Ethereum). Users can create state channels that allow them to make many transactions that effectively count as one transaction. After some period of time, perhaps a week, the channel is closed and the total balances for each party are updated on the blockchain.

However, even state channels only go so far. You still need to open a channel between every two parties. If you have too many users, the blockchain won't be able to accommodate state channels for all of them.

Don't Record Every Transaction on Every Node

Ultimately the only way to get around the scaling problem is to eliminate the needless redundancy of recording everything everywhere. In a sense, this is in practice already with transactions happening upon multiple blockchains. The existence of the Litecoin and Ethereum blockchains takes some of the load off the Bitcoin chain. It's almost as if there were Bitcoin[1], Bitcoin[2], etc. Of course, the problem with such solutions is that there isn't direct interoperability between all these chains. However, this has led to research into network-of-blockchain solutions, including Cosmos, Polkadot, and many others. The idea is that there is an external (decentralized) system that is listening for transactions or operations on one blockchain and relaying them to another blockchain.

However, multiple blockchains or even interconnectivity among multiple blockchains is not true scalability. What you want is that as your network grows and gives you more security, the transaction throughput grows accordingly. While having multiple blockchains does grow transaction throughput, it comes at a cost: the security of the entire system is only as strong as the weakest blockchain.

Sharding

We can view shards as mostly independent blockchains that are designed to communicate well with each other. Validators are assigned some shards to keep track of, which may vary hour by hour, and users maintain a light client to all the shards. If the number of shards is $S = O(c)$, where c is the number of transactions a shard can support, then this approach can support up to $O(c^2)$ transactions. However, with more complex shard-of-shard schemes, the maximum number can be increased exponentially to $O(exp(c))$.

Since each shard now only has $O(n/c)$ of nodes working for it, where n is the total number of nodes across all shards, the question is, can we still leverage the $O(n)$ strength of the entire network for each shard? Indeed we can. If the mechanism for determining the state and history of each shard is done intelligently, we can leverage the strength of the entire network as if they were all working on one unified blockchain.

The easier scenario to deal with is when applications for the most part live entirely on one shard—either they don't have many users, or there aren't many interactions between them. When an interaction is needed with another shard, then cross-shard communication via receipts can be used to pass information securely. Note that we don't restrict which shard a user or application has to use—everyone is free to use whatever shard they please.

When cross-shard communication is needed, shard X generates a receipt of some activity happening on it. Shard Y will consume that receipt, do some action because of it, and possibly pass back to X some acknowledgment that the task was completed. Generalizing this pattern is not difficult and can be built in to a high-level programming language. Figure 9-5 illustrates this concept.

However, the process cross-shard communication will have weaker functionality than mechanisms for intra-shard communication, and some operations that we do on current non-scalable blockchains will only be doable within one shard.

Also, communicating between shards in an asynchronous way is not always easy. Consider the following example described by crypto-veteran Andrew Miller. Suppose a user wants to purchase a plane ticket and reserve a hotel room, but wants both reservations to go through or both fail. They don't want to be stuck with one without the other. In the case where both systems are on the same shard, the procedure is easy—if both reservations don't complete, revert everything. But in the case where the systems are on different shards, then in an asynchronous system there's an extra requirement. Each system must allow for a temporary hold on a reservation. This will allow the user to confirm one booking and then the other. There is a faster, more efficient way with synchronous cross-shard transactions, but designing such a system is not trivial. If an application is larger than what can be supported on one shard, it will need to live on multiple shards and would in general require transactions to be processed serially across chains.

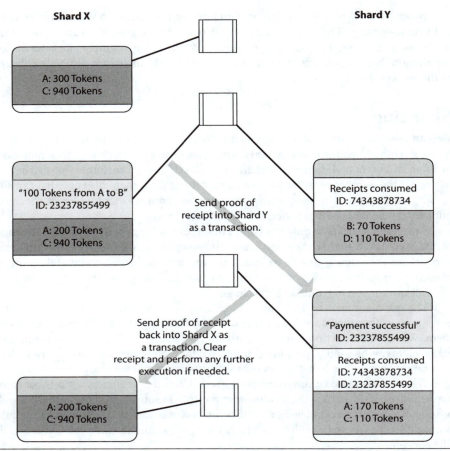

FIGURE 9-5 Shard X generates a receipt to be consumed by Shard Y.

According to Amdahl's law, in any process that has non-parallelizable components, those components quickly become the bottleneck in a system that can otherwise be parallelized. Since Ethereum is in general a computation system, we can easily come up with non-parallelizable programs. For instance, imagine a contract that keeps track of a value x and sets $sha3(x, tx\_data)$ upon receiving a transaction. No sharding solution can give performance better than $O(c)$. So even though over time shared blockchains will get better and better at handling more diverse and involved applications, they will still fall short from single-blockchain architectures in some ways.

Security via Random Sampling

How do we coordinate all nodes to achieve the security of all of them working together? The answer is random sampling. Each validator is assigned randomly to a shard and can be reassigned every few hours or less. From the shard's assigned set of validators (say, 150), one will be chosen from the pool to create a block. Even though far fewer nodes are verifying and creating blocks on each shard at any point in time, it's almost as if all the nodes are doing so, statistically speaking. If we assume an honest two-thirds supermajority on all the nodes, then there is a 99.999 percent probability that two-thirds of a random sample of 150 will be honest. The probability can be brought very close to 100 percent if we assume an even higher honest supermajority.

Summary

While blockchains are heralded as being a technological breakthrough that will solve many problems, it's clear that they face a large number of unique challenges. These challenges are not insurmountable, but they will still require a lot of work to develop infrastructure and safety mechanisms to overcome them.

10 Sample Application: Blockchain and Betting

In this chapter, we're going to take a look at a practical application of blockchain technologies by creating a sports betting distributed application (dapp) from scratch. We will:

- Set up a full development environment
- Write and explain in detail the Ethereum Solidity code to perform the betting application functionality

Our dapp will be modeled off PeerBet, an open-source peer-to-peer sports betting platform. If you'd like to view a working version of the code we are about to implement, the PeerBet main code repository can be found at https://github.com/k26dr/peerbet and a working implementation can found at peerbet.co. A branch has been set up for the simplified version used in the book and can be found at https://github.com/k26dr/peerbet/tree/for-book.

What Is a Dapp?

Dapp is the name given to a distributed application or smart contract that is deployed on a blockchain like Ethereum. As opposed to a standard web application, a distributed application has no central server for storing data or performing computations. Instead, all computation and data storage are handled by transactions on a blockchain network. The transactions are executed by every node in the blockchain peer-to-peer network, and the data is stored by every node in the network. Because of this, dapps are much harder to censor and take down than a centralized system, making them ideal for use cases where central servers could be compromised either by the law or by attackers.

Not all blockchains are capable of hosting dapps. The Bitcoin blockchain, for example, is not designed to handle the sort of general purpose computation required to host a proper dapp. In fact, the majority of blockchains cannot handle dapps. This is because most blockchains have been designed for a specific use case, such as Bitcoin for financial transactions.

In order to support dapps, a blockchain must be able to encode transactions in a Turing complete programming language. There exists a formal definition of Turing completeness that is mathematically rigorous, but for our purposes it will suffice to define a Turing complete language as one that supports loops and conditionals. JavaScript and Python are both examples of Turing complete languages, while SQL and XML are not. Bitcoin has a custom scripting language it uses for clearing transactions, but it was intentionally designed without loops and conditionals to avoid the complications associated with Turing completeness on a blockchain. The more features the scripting language has, the greater its "attack surface"—that is, it is more vulnerable to security flaws and hacks.

There are currently two major blockchains that feature Turing complete transaction languages: Hyperledger and Ethereum. Hyperledger is a permissioned private blockchain (for more on the difference between public and private blockchains, see Chapter 8, "Private Blockchain Use Cases").

The largest Turing complete public blockchain by market cap is Ethereum, and that is what we will be using to host our dapp. Ethereum uses a minimalist smart contract programming language named Solidity for developing contracts. The Solidity compiler converts Solidity code to Ethereum Virtual Machine (EVM) bytecode. The EVM bytecode is what actually gets stored and executed on the blockchain, but we will be doing all our development in Solidity. There are other languages supported by the EVM, such as Serpent and LLL (Low-level Lisp-like Language), but Solidity is the most popular.

Introduction to Lotteries, Betting, and Gambling on the Blockchain

Sports betting applications already exist on the Internet in various forms. In Europe and Asia, legal betting houses such as Bet365 and Bovada offer online sports books with house odds. So what's the advantage of a blockchain for betting?

The majority of blockchain applications are solutions looking for a problem. Today a blockchain is an expensive, inefficient, and slow way of performing computation and storage. This will change as the technology matures. Cloud servers and storage offer magnitudes more computation and storage for a fraction of the cost. In exchange, however, a blockchain offers certain specific advantages and features. An application that does not sufficiently benefit from or is hindered by these advantages should be implemented using traditional server technologies instead.

Before deciding to develop your application on the blockchain, run through the following lists and make sure your application is a good fit for the technology.

Advantages:

- Anonymous, cryptographically secure authentication
- Fast, frictionless, anonymous, low fee payments
- Uncensorable network with 100 percent uptime
- Publically verifiable and guaranteed code transaction execution
- Immutable data storage

Disadvantages:

- Limited, expensive storage
- Limited, expensive computation
- Slow network
- Limited transaction rate
- Contract code deployment cannot exceed the block gas limit (~1000 loc)

Other features that could go either way:

- Transaction fees are paid by users, not contract owners.
- All data is public.

A clear example of a class of applications that would be a poor fit for a blockchain are social media applications. Here's a list of requirements and features for a typical social media application:

- Scale to millions of users
- Scale to thousands of requests per second
- Large codebases
- Big data storage for generating advertising insights
- Users expect the service to be free
- Users want to control their data

If you go through each of these requirements, each of them contradicts one of the principles of blockchain development listed above.

Let's take a look now at betting applications. Here are some features required for a betting application:

- Frequent payment processing
- Handle bets from multiple countries with different currencies
- Avoid antigambling laws in certain countries
- Maintain an even balance of money on both sides of a bet
- Option to bet anonymously
- Provide verifiable and consistent bet execution
- Provide competitive odds and fees

These requirements are much better suited to a blockchain solution. One of the biggest pain points for online betting has been moving money around through wires and bank transfers. Users must wait three to five business days to deposit or withdraw money from their bank accounts and must trust the betting site with their banking information. The sites in turn must secure this information, take appropriate security measures to protect their sites from hacking, and stay in compliance with a series of financial regulations in the various countries in which they operate. Additionally, transacting in different countries requires supporting a variety of different currencies and banks, all of which contribute to the complexity of the operation.

Additionally, many bettors like to preserve their anonymity and rely on the sites to safeguard identifying information. Unfortunately, hackers regularly manage to gain access to this data and can use it to extort clients who don't want their gambling debts to become public.

Using a blockchain solution allows bettors to bet anonymously, transfer money across borders easily for international betting sites, and have a guarantee that their bet will be paid out in a timely fashion.

So let's begin writing our peer-to-peer blockchain betting dapp!

Setting Up a Development Environment

Before getting started, we will need to download the necessary tools. This section will cover the installation process for Windows, OS X, and Debian-based Linux systems.

In order to set up a proper development environment, we will need the following tools installed on our machines:

- Mist browser
- The Go Ethereum command line client (geth)
- NodeJS + NPM
- Google Chrome browser
- MetaMask Chrome extension
- Solidity compiler

Geth comes bundled with the Mist browser, and both can be installed by downloading the latest release and following the installation instructions at https://github.com/ethereum/mist/releases.

NodeJS and NPM can be installed by following the instructions on the official NodeJS download page, https://nodejs.org/en/download/. If you are running OS X or Linux, you can also use a package manager for the installation.

```
# OS X
brew install node


# Linux
sudo apt-get install nodejs
```

MetaMask currently only supports Chrome, so you will have to download the Google Chrome browser (https://www.google.com/chrome/).

Once Chrome is installed, open it and navigate to the MetaMask home page, https://metamask.io/, to download the Chrome extension/plugin.

The Solidity compiler is distributed as an NPM package. To install it globally:

```
npm install -g solc
```

Syncing an Ethereum Node

Before we can get started with development, we will need a full, synced Ethereum node running on our computer. As opposed to a light client, a full node contains a full copy of the current

Ethereum state tree (the blockchain database) so that we can run transactions against it. Run the following command in order to do so:

```
geth
```

Geth will automatically connect to the main Ethereum network (mainnet), locate peers, and begin downloading a copy of the blockchain onto our local node. The syncing process can take several hours, and it is usually best to leave it on overnight and check back in the morning by which time it should be complete. Once the node is synced, we can begin development on our dapp.

Creating and Configuring a Private Development Chain

Create a folder for our betting dapp. All of our project code will go in this folder.

To be able to test our code locally, we need to run a private blockchain on our own computer. This will allow us to deploy, interact with, and iterate on our contract without polluting the main Ethereum network or constantly having to pay transaction fees.

The command to properly set up a private testnet is a bit verbose, so we are going to create a file to hold the command for us. Open up a file called geth.sh and insert the following code into it. This line of code is intended for a Linux machine. OS X users should replace all instances of ~/.ethereum with /Library/Ethereum and Windows users should replace it with %APPDATA%/Ethereum.

```
geth --dev --datadir ~/.ethereum/privatenet --ipcpath ~/.ethereum/geth.ipc
--networkid 45 --rpc --rpcapi web3,net,eth,personal --rpccorsdomain "*" --mine
console
```

- **--dev**   This convenience option bootstraps a new private chain, creates a genesis block for the chain, and sets a series of debugging flags.
- **--datadir**   This allows us to specify a custom directory to store chain data. The default directory is being used for the mainnet, so we specify an alternate path to store our private chain.
- **--ipcpath**   By default, geth stores its interprocess communication (IPC) file at the directory specified by `--datadir`. The Mist browser, however, can only communicate with an IPC file located at `~/.ethereum/geth.ipc`, so we must specify this as our IPC path.
- **--networkid**   The network ID flag is used to identify to peers which network (mainnet, Ropsten testnet, Morden testnet, etc.) our chain is synced to. Since we are running a private network, we specify a random unused network ID so that peers do not connect to us.
- **--rpc**   This flag turns on RPC (Remote Procedure Call) mode, which allows light clients and other nodes to access our node via the JSON RPC API. This flag is required so that web3.js and our front ends can access our node.
- **--rpcapi**   By default, RPC mode enables the web3, net, and eth modules. In order to be able to access our node's accounts and private keys to sign transactions, we will enable the personal module as well.

- **`--rpccorsdomain`**   Web browsers using the JSON RPC API are restricted by the standard browser same-origin policy. In order to allow browsers to access our API, we will set our CORS domain to the broadest possible setting `"*"` (allow all access).
- **`--mine`**   Mine our own network, so that transactions are processed and blocks created. Normally, miners would handle this process, but we will have to do it ourselves for our private chain. The `--dev` option by default sets a network mining difficulty that can be reasonably mined by a single CPU.
- **`console`**   This will open the geth console, which allows us to interact directly with our node and private chain using JavaScript commands.

Once the script has been created and saved to geth.sh, we can execute the file directly to run our private chain. Ensure the file is executable, then run it:

```
chmod +x geth.sh # make file executable
./geth.sh # run file
```

You should now see a series of log output indicating that the private chain is running and being mined.

Creating a Killable Contract

Before we begin developing our full contract, we are going to develop a small test contract to ensure that our development chain is working and can deploy and debug contracts.

All of our contracts will be written in Solidity, a smart contract language that compiles into Ethereum Virtual Machine (EVM) bytecode. We will only have a single .sol file for this project, named bet.sol.

To prevent blockchain bloat and allow removal of old contracts from the blockchain, most contracts include a `kill` function that allows the contract to be removed from the blockchain by the owner.

The code for a simple killable contract looks as follows:

```
contract Bet {
    address owner;

    function Bet() {
        owner = msg.sender;
    }

    function kill() {
        if (msg.sender != owner) throw;
        selfdestruct(owner);
    }
}
```

Let's review this contract line by line:

```
contract Bet {
```

The contract keyword creates a contract that goes by the succeeding name. The contract name will be required in later steps and we will be referring back to it.

```
address owner;
```

This creates a variable named `owner` of type `address` and allocates space for it in the contract storage.

Every contract has storage and memory space allocated to it. Storage variables are stored on the blockchain and changes to it propagate across the network. Memory variables are temporary variables created during a function execution and destroyed at the end of the function. They do not get stored onto the blockchain. We will see examples of memory variables later in the chapter.

All variables declared in the global scope outside of a function are declared as storage variables.

`address` is a data type unique to Solidity. It is a 20-byte field that is designed specifically to hold Ethereum wallet and contract addresses.

```
function Bet() {
```

In the Bet contract, the `Bet` function is a special type of function called a constructor function (similarly, in a Bid contract, the name of the constructor function would be `Bid`). The constructor function is executed immediately upon deployment of the contract onto the blockchain, and usually contains setup logic and variable initializations for the contract.

```
owner = msg.sender;
```

Solidity defines a series of built-in convenience functions and values. One of these is `msg.sender`, which is an `address` variable containing the value of the wallet or contract address that initiated the current function call. Since the constructor function is executed when the contract is deployed, `msg.sender` is the deployer of the contract.

```
function kill() {
```

This defines a public function (we will discuss private functions later) named `kill` that can be called with no arguments.

```
if (msg.sender != owner) throw;
```

By convention, only the owner of a contract is allowed to destroy it. If anybody else attempts to destroy the contract, this line will throw an error. The `throw` command consumes all the gas passed to the function to deter abuse.

Sometimes you will want to gracefully exit a function without forcing a user to lose all the gas they provided. This will be covered later.

```
selfdestruct(owner);
```

The `selfdestruct` function is built into Solidity. Calling it from within a contract deletes the contract and any data stored in the contract storage, then sends any ether contained at that contract address to the provided address. In this case, there should be no ether contained at the address, but in case someone accidentally sends ether to the contract address, we can send that money to the owner.

Compiling the Contract

The Ethereum blockchain can only store and execute EVM bytecode, so in order to deploy or execute our Solidity code, we have to first convert it into EVM bytecode by using the Solidity compiler. To compile, run:

```
solc --bin --abi --optimize -o bin peerbet.sol
```

The options we invoked do the following:

- `--bin`: Include a bytecode file in the output. This will be the bytecode we deploy to the blockchain.
- `--abi`: Output a JSON file that describes the ABI interface for the contract. web3.js uses this to make interacting with our deployed contract easy.
- `--optimize`: Run optimizations to minimize the data footprint of the contract. This is important because deploying the contract requires gas proportional to the size of the bytecode output. As our contract gets larger, an unoptimized output can exceed the block gas limit and make our contract undeployable.
- `-o`: Specify an output directory for our bytecode and ABI files (bin/).
- `peerbet.sol`: The contract file we wish to compile.

Any errors present in our contract file will prevent compilation and be displayed in the output. Correct any errors that you see and recompile. If everything was copied properly from the previous section, your code should compile.

The compiler should output two files into the `bin` directory:

```
Bet.bin: The bytecode output
bet.sol:Bet.abi: The ABI JSON
```

Deploying a Contract

Now that we've written a simple killable test contract, let's deploy it to our private chain and try interacting with it. Deploying a contract to an Ethereum chain can be a complex operation, so we will be writing a small script to take care of it for us. The script is going to require the web3.js library, so let's go ahead and install that before we get started.

```
npm init --yes # creates a package.json file
npm install web3@0.18.2 --save
```

Here's what our basic deploy script will look like. Our script assumes that we've already compiled our bytecode and ABI to the bin/ directory.

```
var Web3 = require('web3');
var fs = require('fs');
var exec = require('child_process').execSync;

var web3 = new Web3();
web3.setProvider(new web3.providers.HttpProvider('http://localhost:8545'));
```

```
var walletAddress = web3.eth.accounts[0];
web3.personal.unlockAccount(walletAddress, process.argv[2]);

exec(`solc --bin --abi --optimize -o bin peerbet.sol`);

var abi = fs.readFileSync('bin/peerbet.sol:PeerBet.abi');
var PeerBet = web3.eth.contract(abi);

var compiled = '0x' + fs.readFileSync("bin/PeerBet.bin");
var peerbet = PeerBet.new({
    from: walletAddress,
    data: compiled,
    gas: 40e5,
    gasPrice: 20e9
}, function (e, contract){
    if (e) console.log(e);
    if (typeof contract.address !== 'undefined') {
        console.log('Contract mined! address: ' + contract.address +
            ' transactionHash: ' + contract.transactionHash);

        fs.writeFileSync("contract_address", contract.address);
    }
});
```

There's a lot going on here, so let's break it down.

```
var Web3 = require('web3');
var fs = require('fs');
var exec = require('child_process').execSync;
```

This opening block requires the necessary libraries. The fs and child_process libraries are built into Node.

```
var web3 = new Web3();
web3.setProvider(new web3.providers.HttpProvider('http://localhost:8545'));
```

The web3.js library needs a provider that exposes the Ethereum JSON RPC API. By this point, we should have a private chain synced and running on our command line. This block connects to that node and will fail if the node is not running.

```
var walletAddress = web3.eth.accounts[0];
web3.personal.unlockAccount(walletAddress, process.argv[2]);
```

All Ethereum transactions, including contract deployments, must originate from a wallet address. This block accesses our account address, then unlocks the account so it can be used for the deployment transaction. Earlier when we created our private chain, we made sure the RPC API option contained the `personal` module. If we hadn't done so, we would not have been able to access the accounts on this node from our script.

The second argument to the `unlockAccount` function is the password. Since you may wish to store this code on GitHub or some other public hosting service, the script is designed to take the password in as a command line argument. DO NOT under any circumstances include your password in a source file. While this password cannot be used maliciously on a private chain, later on we will be using this same code on the mainnet. A node with an exposed `personal` rpc module exposes all the public keys associated with that node. The only thing stopping a hacker from using your private key to sign a transaction and stealing all your ether is your password, so protect it accordingly!

```
exec(`solc --bin --abi --optimize -o bin peerbet.sol`);
```

Usually we want to compile and deploy our script at the same time, so as a convenience we can include the compilation step as a child process. This line is not necessary. You can compile and deploy separately if you prefer.

```
var abi = fs.readFileSync('bin/peerbet.sol:PeerBet.abi');
var PeerBet = web3.eth.contract(abi);
```

web3's contract object allows for easy deployment and contract interaction. To set up this object, we read in the ABI and pass it to the contract constructor.

```
var compiled = '0x' + fs.readFileSync("bin/PeerBet.bin");
```

Read in the contract hex (remember, hex is just an alternate representation for binary) bytecode. A quirk of web3.js is that it requires all hex strings to be prefixed with `'0x'`, so we have done so.

```
var peerbet = PeerBet.new({
    from: walletAddress,
    data: compiled,
    gas: 40e5,
    gasPrice: 20e9
}
```

The `.new` function on a contract object deploys the contract. The first arguments are the transaction (`tx`) options, and the second argument is a callback.

The wallet address specified in the `from` field must be an unlocked wallet, and you must have access to the private key for that wallet. Attempting to use a public key whose private key is not stored in the local node will fail.

The data for a contract creation transaction is the bytecode for the contract.

We have set a very high gas limit for now, but the actual gas consumed should be much lower (< 5e5). Any gas not used will be refunded, while transactions without enough gas will throw an OutOfGasError, so it is better to aim too high than too low. Gas limits are typically specified in increments of 100,000 (1e5). The block gas limit is currently set at 47e5 gas/block, so always make sure your gas limit is below this number or your transaction will fail.

The default gas price in Ethereum is 20e9. Gas prices are typically measured in units of gigawei (1e9 wei, 1e-9 ether). On the privatenet, this number is meaningless. On the mainnet, it is real money, so you will have to pay attention to this number. Transactions will clear with gas prices as low as 1 Gwei, but the clearing times will be slow. Miners will prioritize the transactions with the highest gas prices for their blocks.

```
...
}, function (e, contract){
    if (e) console.log(e);
    if (typeof contract.address !== 'undefined') {
        console.log('Contract mined! address: ' + contract.address +
            ' transactionHash: ' + contract.transactionHash);

        fs.writeFileSync("contract_address", contract.address);
    }
});
```

This is the callback portion of the deployment function. This callback is executed when the miner attempts to mine the transaction. It uses the standard Node (error, data) argument format. If there is an error, we log it. If there is no error, the contract address should be set, and the second `if` statement should execute. For the user's benefit, we will log that the contract has been mined, then write the contract address to a file, so we can use it later to load the contract into web3.

If you've understood everything above, it is now time to deploy the contract. Save the file as deploy.js, then in your command line run:

```
node deploy.js [password]
```

Make sure to replace `[password]` with the password to your wallet key. The contract may take up to a minute to deploy. Once it is deployed, the log output will indicate that the contract has been mined.

Congratulations! You have deployed the contract to a private dev net. Now let's put together a script for interacting with the contract.

Contract Debugging and Interaction

Similar to how we set up a deploy script, we are now going to set up a debugging script. In order to have a live debugging environment, we are going to use the NPM package locus. Let's install locus:

```
npm install locus --save
```

Once that is installed, we are ready to write our script. Here's the full script:

```
var Web3 = require('web3');
var web3 = new Web3();
var fs = require('fs');

// Connect to local node, same as in deploy script
web3.setProvider(new web3.providers.HttpProvider('http://localhost:8545'));
```

```
var abi = JSON.parse(fs.readFileSync("bin/peerbet.sol:PeerBet.abi", "ascii"));
var contractAddress = fs.readFileSync("contract_address", "ascii");
var contract = web3.eth.contract(abi).at(contractAddress);

// Unlock wallet, same as in deploy script
var walletAddress = web3.eth.accounts[0];
web3.personal.unlockAccount(walletAddress, process.argv[2]);

eval(require('locus'));
```

There are only two new blocks in this script, so let's break those down.

```
var abi = JSON.parse(fs.readFileSync("bin/peerbet.sol:PeerBet.abi", "ascii"));
var contractAddress = fs.readFileSync("contract_address", "ascii");
var contract = web3.eth.contract(abi).at(contractAddress);
```

The web3 existing contract constructor requires an ABI and contract address. This block loads those in from the file system, and creates the contract object.

```
eval(require('locus'))
```

This creates an active debugging environment similar to the node console but with all of our loaded variables.

Execute the script to view the debugging environment:

```
node debug.js [password]
```

You should see a debugging prompt that looks like this:

```
 => 69: eval(require('locus'));
    70:

  ʃ:
```

Solidity automatically creates getter functions for public storage variables. Type `contract.owner()` into the debugging prompt and it should return the address of your contract.

We can interact directly with the contract now. Let's try to use the `kill` function we defined earlier.

```
tx = contract.kill({ from: walletAddress, gas: 40e5 })
```

You may get back an error saying `Error: authentication needed: password or unlock`. This is because the password on your wallet key has expired. Use the following to unlock your account.

```
var pwd = '...' // replace this with your password
web3.personal.unlockAccount(walletAddress, pwd)
```

All transactions follow this same format. List the arguments to the function followed by a `tx` options object. The `kill` function takes no arguments, so the only argument here is the `tx` options object.

When using a web3 contract object, `from` is the only required `tx` option. `data` is created by the library (it would be complex to create on our own), `gasPrice` defaults to 20e9, and `gas` defaults to 0.9e5. The default `gas` value is usually too low to execute a contract transaction, so it is generally specified explicitly.

When a contract transaction is sent, it returns immediately with a transaction id, but the transaction doesn't execute until it is actually mined. Type `tx` into the debugger to view the transaction id. To see if the transaction has been mined, use:

```
web3.eth.getTransactionReceipt(tx)
```

If the function returns `null`, that means it has not been mined yet. If it has been mined, you will see a transaction receipt object in the console.

Just because you see a receipt does not mean the function executed properly. Transactions that throw errors or run out of gas will still display receipts. It is up to you to verify that the state changes you requested were made.

In this case, the Solidity `selfdestruct` function deletes all the contract data by setting their values to 0. Check the value of `contract.owner` in the debugger. If you get back `0x`, the contract has been successfully killed.

Now that we have successfully deployed and killed a simple contract, it is time to build out a full betting contract.

Defining Data Structures

Before we can start coding our contract, we need to define the necessary data structures. Figure 10-1 shows a rough flowchart of what we want our data relations to look like.

Solidity uses structs to group related pieces of data. Solidity structs are similar to C structs. They contain a name and a series of member definitions.

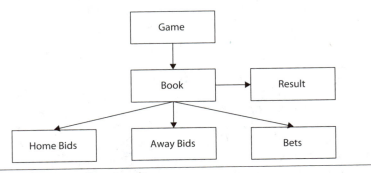

FIGURE 10-1   **Flow of contract functionality**

Let's define our data structures using Solidity structs now so that we can use them in our application.

```
struct Game {
    uint id;
    address creator;
    string home;
    string away;
    uint16 category;
    uint64 locktime;
    GameStatus status;
    Book book;
    GameResult result;
}
```

Our Game struct stores some information about the game, a mapping of books (in case we want to add additional books later), and a GameResult. The locktime is equivalent to the game's start time. Bets placed after the locktime will be rejected.

GameStatus is a Solidity enum, which functions very similarly to a C enum. We will go into more depth on enums later in this section and list the enum definitions for our application.

```
struct GameResult {
    int home;
    int away;
    uint timestamp; // when the game was scored
}
```

The GameResult struct stores a score for each team and a timestamp.

```
struct Book {
    Bid[] overBids;
    Bid[] underBids;
    Bet[] bets;
}
```

The Book struct is modeled after a proper Vegas book, containing over bids, under bids, and bets. The full PeerBet application contains Spread, Money Line, and Over/Under books, but for our sample application we will only be building an Over/Under book.

The overBids and underBids arrays will actually be sorted stacks to allow for efficient bid matching. Unlike C structs, Solidity structs cannot be recursive, so they can't be used to define recursive data structures like linked lists or stacks. Instead, Solidity allows for dynamic-length arrays, so we must use those instead.

Since bids and bets require us to track multiple pieces of information, we will define structs for them as well.

```
struct Bid {
    address bidder;
    uint amount; /* in wei */
    bool over; /* true=over, false=under */
```

```
    int32 line;
}

struct Bet {
    address over;
    address under;
    uint amount; /* in wei */
    int32 line;
    BetStatus status;
}
```

Since bids are unmatched, they only contain one address field. Matched bets have two parties, one on each side of the bet, so the struct contains an address field for each.

Those are all the structs we will be using in our application. In addition to structs, we would like to define a few enumerations (enum) as well to make our code easier to read. Enumerations in Solidity are similar to enumerations in C in that they are never necessary and can always be replaced with integer values but are convenient for readability.

Enumerables

Here are the enums we will be using in our application:

```
enum GameStatus { Open, Locked, Scored, Verified }
enum BetStatus { Open, Paid }
```

Games are Open when bets are being taken, Locked after the locktime has passed, Scored when the game has been scored, and Verified when bets have been paid out.

Bets are Open when the result is undetermined, and Paid when the result has been determined and the participants' balances have been updated.

Storage Variables

Storage variables must be explicitly defined in the global scope in a Solidity contract. Storage variables use space in the Ethereum state tree, and can be expensive to create, so minimizing the total size of a contract's storage variables is important.

Here are the storage variables we will be creating:

```
address public owner;
Game[] games;
mapping(address => uint) public balances;
```

owner has been covered in the simple killable contract we wrote earlier.

games is a dynamic-length array of Game structs. It will be responsible for the majority of the storage space and is our primary storage variable. Custom structs cannot be made public, so games will remain private. As a reminder, Solidity automatically creates getter ABI functions for public variables but not private ones.

`balances` is a public mapping that stores user balances. A user is allowed to withdraw the value of their balance from the contract whenever they want. Mappings in Solidity can be tricky because there is no way to determine the keys of a mapping without storing them in a separate array. So given an address, we can determine the address's balance, but given the amount of ether held in the contract, we cannot determine what the allocation of balances between addresses is.

Events

Solidity events are used to log transaction activity to the blockchain. Event logs are much cheaper to create than new entries in the state tree, so it is a great way to store read-only data. Logs are not accessible from within a contract (only variables are) but can be read by external client libraries such as web3.js.

Ethereum transactions are asynchronous and usually do not mine for 15–30 seconds after they have been broadcast to the network. Because of this, transactions cannot return values. The only way a transaction can create an output is by modifying the state or adding an event log. Client libraries usually parse the logs to determine the output of a transaction.

A Solidity event is a schema for logs. Logs are automatically indexed by contract address and event type for efficient querying. In addition, Solidity events allow you to define three custom indexed fields. Only indexed fields can be queried when parsing logs. Currently, indexed string fields cannot be parsed for a value, so it is best practice to avoid creating string indexes. Here are the logs we will be using in our contract:

```
event GameCreated(uint indexed id, address indexed creator, string home,
    string away, uint16 indexed category, uint64 locktime);
event BidPlaced(uint indexed game_id, address bidder, uint amount,
    bool over, int32 line);
event BetPlaced(uint indexed game_id, address indexed user, bool over,
    uint amount, int32 line);
event GameScored(uint indexed game_id, int homeScore, int awayScore,
    uint timestamp);
event Withdrawal(address indexed user, uint amount, uint timestamp);
```

There is an event associated with each of the major state modifications that can occur in our contract. Together, they provide a history of the actions taken by the contract on the blockchain.

Functions

Before we dive into the code, let's create a list of the functions we will be defining in our application. Functions, like variables, can be either public or private. Public functions can be accessed by other contracts and client libraries (like web3.js) and are listed as part of the ABI. Private functions are only accessible by other functions in the same contract.

In addition, there are constant functions which read from but do not modify the blockchain. Public constant functions return immediately with their result, do not send a transaction to the network, and do not consume any gas when called.

Here are the public non-constant ABI functions we will be defining:

```
createGame(string home, string away, uint16 category, uint64 locktime)
bid(uint game_id, bool over, int32 line) payable
setGameResult(uint game_id, int homeScore, int awayScore)
withdraw()
```

A payable function is one that can accept a non-zero `value` in the `tx` options object. Here are the public constant functions we will be defining:

```
getActiveGames constant returns (uint[])
getOpenBids(uint game_id) constant returns (bytes)
```

Constant functions return a value whose type must be specified with the syntax above. In addition, we will be defining some private functions for our own internal use:

```
getGameById(uint game_id) constant private returns (Game storage)
matchExistingBids(Bid bid, uint game_id) private
addBidToStack(Bid bid, Bid[] storage stack, bool reverse) private
cancelOpenBids(Book storage book) private
payBets(uint game_id) private
```

Note	By default, variables in a function definition are presumed to be memory variables. To specify that the variable is a pointer to an existing storage variable in the state tree, it must be explicitly stated as above with `Bid[] storage stack` and `Game storage`.

Let's step through each of the functions and explain the code as we go:

Creating a Game

```
function createGame (string home, string away, uint16 category, uint64 locktime)
returns (int) {
    uint id = counter;
    counter++;

    games.length += 1;
    Game game = games[games.length - 1];

    game.id = id;
    game.creator = msg.sender;
    game.home = home;
    game.away = away;
    game.category = category;

    game.locktime = locktime;
    game.status = GameStatus.Open;
```

```
    GameCreated(id, game.creator, home, away, category, locktime);
    return -1;
}
```

The function definition specifies that the function returns an int even though we've mentioned that non-constant public functions don't return a value because they don't execute until the block is mined. The reason we include a return value anyway is for debugging purposes. There are three ways we can invoke a public function.

```
# sends a transaction to the network
contract.createGame.sendTransaction(...)
# To create a game we need to pass in all the information about the game (home,
# away, category, locktime).

# runs the function locally, does not send a transaction to the network
# commonly referred to as "calling" the function
contract.createGame.call(...)

# performs the default action:
#    sendTransaction for non-constant functions
#    call for constant functions
contract.createGame(...)
```

When we call a non-constant function, it returns with a value just like a constant function. It runs the exact sequence of steps the miner would run in a transaction but doesn't update the state tree or broadcast the transaction, so it's great for debugging. A call that throws an error returns with the zero/null value of the return type. So for an int return type, an error will return 0. By convention, we will be returning -1 in all our functions to indicate that the function executed with no errors, and use the positive integers to indicate an error code.

Creating a game requires us to pass in the game parameters (home, away, category, locktime). The locktime is in seconds since the UNIX epoch.

We start by creating an id from the global counter then incrementing the global counter so that our id remains unique. We then extend the games array length by 1 to accommodate our new game, get a reference to the game we just created, and fill in the appropriate properties on the new game object.

Once the game has been created, we emit a GameCreated event to log the state modification we just made and return -1 to indicate that there were no errors.

Bidding

```
function bid(uint game_id, bool over, int32 line) payable returns (int) {
    Game game = getGameById(game_id);
    Bid memory bid = Bid(msg.sender, msg.value, over, line);

    // validate inputs: game status, gametime
    if (game.status != GameStatus.Open)
        return 1;
```

```
    if (now > game.locktime) {
        game.status = GameStatus.Locked;
        cancelOpenBids(game.book);
        return 2;
    }

    Bid memory remainingBid = matchExistingBids(bid, game_id);

    // Use leftover funds to place open bids (maker)
    if (bid.amount > 0) {
        Bid[] bidStack = over ? game.book.overBids : game.book.underBids;
        if (over)
            addBidToStack(remainingBid, bidStack, true);
        else
            addBidToStack(remainingBid, bidStack, false);
        BidPlaced(game_id, msg.sender, remainingBid.amount, over, line);
    }

    return -1;
}
```

To place a bid, the client must provide the game_id for the game they wish to bid on, which side of the bet they are taking (over or under), and the line limit at which they would like to place the bet. Bids will be matched at or below the limit for over bids and at or above the line for under bids.

The function is payable so clients can send a value with the transaction. For this function, that value will be interpreted as the bid amount. The value sent to a payable Solidity function is available in the built-in msg.value variable.

This function is more complex than the createGame function, so let's step through and explain it in parts:

```
Game game = getGameById(game_id);
Bid memory bid = Bid(msg.sender, msg.value, over, line);
```

This portion grabs the desired game from storage and creates a temporary Bid in memory. msg.sender contains the address of the wallet/contract that signed and sent the transaction, while msg.value is a uint variable that contains the value of the ether sent to the function in units of wei (1e-18 ether).

Struct variables by default are initialized as storage pointers, but struct constructors always return a pointer to memory. Without specifying Bid memory, the variable assignment will throw a compiler error saying the types of the value and variable do not match.

getGameById is a helper function we will use to get a pointer to a specific game. Here's the code for the getGameById function:

```
function getGameById(uint game_id) constant private returns (Game storage) {
    bool game_exists = false;
    for (uint i = 0; i < games.length; i++) {
```

```
            if (games[i].id == game_id) {
                Game game = games[i];
                game_exists = true;
                break;
            }
        }
        if (!game_exists)
            throw;
        return game;
}
```

We have defined the function as both private and constant. It is constant because it does not modify the state. It must be defined as private as well because public functions are not allowed to return custom structs. The return type must be specified as `Game storage` because function definitions default to memory as the variable location and the game we wish to point to is contained in storage in the state tree.

The function loops through the games array and checks for a matching game id. It maintains a flag that is set to true if a matching game exists in the array. If the game exists, it returns a storage pointer to the game.

If the game does not exist, it throws an error. The `throw` keyword ends the execution of both the current function and the current transaction. Any changes made during the current transaction are rolled back and all the gas provided to the transaction is consumed and given to the miner.

```
// validate inputs: game status, gametime
if (game.status != GameStatus.Open)
    return 1;
if (now > game.locktime) {
    game.status = GameStatus.Locked;
    cancelOpenBids(game.book);
    return 2;
}
```

The game status must be open to accept a bet. Additionally, a game may still have its status set as open when it is past the locktime. In that case, we lock the game and cancel all open bids. Both of these validations return error codes.

now is a built-in variable set to the value of the UNIX timestamp of the current block being mined. This will not be the same as the time the transaction was sent.

cancelOpenBids is a private helper function that cancels and refunds unmatched bids in a book. Here is the code for the function:

```
function cancelOpenBids(Book storage book) private returns (int) {
    for (uint i=0; i < book.overBids.length; i++) {
        Bid bid = book.overBids[i];
        balances[bid.bidder] += bid.amount;
    }
    delete book.overBids;
```

```
for (i=0; i < book.underBids.length; i++) {
    bid = book.underBids[i];
    balances[bid.bidder] += bid.amount;
}
delete book.underBids;

return -1;
}
```

It is important that the parameter to this function be a storage pointer. If it were a memory pointer, we would be deleting items in local memory instead of on the state tree.

We start by looping through the over bids and refunding the bids by adding the amount of the bid to the bidder's balance. We do not need to worry about initializing the keys.

A key in a Solidity mapping is converted to a 32-byte address that points to a location in the Ethereum state tree, which has a Patricia trie as the underlying data structure. The 32-byte address is generated by computing the keccak256 hash of a series of values, including the contract address, variable address, and mapping key. If the 32-byte address does not exist in the Patricia trie, its value is assumed to be the null value for the type. Since `balances` is of type `mapping(address => uint)`, all addresses can be assumed to be set initially to the null value for `uint`, 0.

Once the open bids have been refunded, the overBids array is deleted. The `delete` keyword sets a variable back to its null value by removing it from the state tree. The null value for a dynamic array is an array of length 0, so overBids is now an array of length 0.

The same actions are then performed on the underBids array.

```
Bid memory remainingBid = matchExistingBids(bid, game_id);
```

Once a bid is validated, the first step in processing it is to match it against existing bids. Here's the code for the `matchExistingBids` helper function:

```
function matchExistingBids(Bid bid, uint game_id) private returns (Bid) {
    Game game = getGameById(game_id);
    Bid[] matchStack = bid.over ?  game.book.underBids : game.book.overBids;

    int i = int(matchStack.length) - 1;
    while (i >= 0 && bid.amount > 0) {
        uint j = uint(i);
        if (matchStack[j].amount == 0) { // matched bids
            i--;
            continue;
        }
        if (bid.over && bid.line < matchStack[j].line
            || !bid.over && bid.line > matchStack[j].line)
            break;

        uint betAmount;
        if (bid.amount < matchStack[j].amount)
            betAmount = bid.amount;
```

```
        else
            betAmount = matchStack[j].amount;
        bid.amount -= betAmount;
        matchStack[j].amount -= betAmount;

        Bet memory bet = Bet(
            bid.over ? bid.bidder : matchStack[j].bidder,
            bid.over ? matchStack[j].bidder : bid.bidder,
            betAmount,
            matchStack[j].line,
            BetStatus.Open
        );
        game.book.bets.push(bet);
        BetPlaced(game_id, bid.bidder, bid.over, betAmount, matchStack[j].line);
        BetPlaced(game_id, matchStack[j].bidder, !bid.over,
                betAmount, matchStack[j].line);
        i--;
    }
    return bid;
}
```

This is a long function that goes through the stack for the opposing side of the bid, matches and deletes as many bids as it can, and logs every bet it places. It then returns a bid with the remaining unmatched amount so it can be added to the proper stack later.

Let's break this function down as well:

```
Game game = getGameById(game_id);
Bid[] matchStack = bid.over ? game.book.underBids : game.book.overBids;
```

We start by getting a storage pointer to the game and determining which stack we will be matching against. Over bids will match the under stack, and under bids will match the over stack.

```
int i = int(matchStack.length) - 1;
while (i >= 0 && bid.amount > 0) {
    uint j = uint(i);
```

We are going to assume that the array is ordered into a stack already, with the best outstanding bid (highest bid for over stack, lowest bid for under stack) at the bottom of the stack. See Figure 10-2 for the stack arrangements. We start looping from the bottom of the stack by setting the iterator variable, i. We want to keep looping until the iterator is out of bounds, which in this case will be when it's negative. In order to do this, we have to use an int instead of a uint because uint exhibits undefined behavior when it goes negative and will never express a value less than zero. However, array index accessing requires a uint, so we create a uint version of the iterator, j, once we enter the loop and have verified that the iterator is not negative.

```
if (matchStack[j].amount == 0) { // matched bids
    i--;
    continue;
}
```

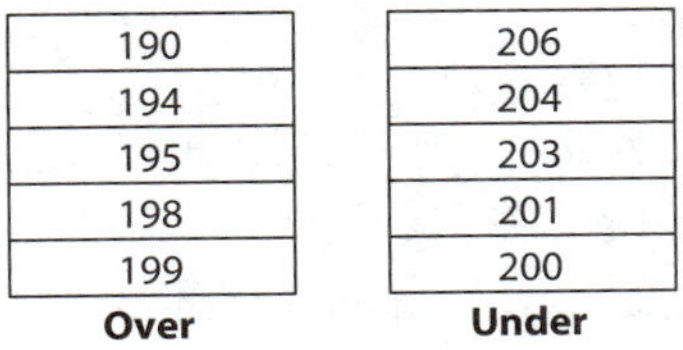

Over		Under
190		206
194		204
195		203
198		201
199		200

FIGURE 10-2   Bid stack structure

Next, we validate the stack bid by checking if the bid has already been matched. Matched bids will have an amount of 0. In most languages, we would rid ourselves of matched bids by deleting them from the stack. Unfortunately, our stacks are arrays instead of linked lists because Solidity doesn't allow recursive data structures, so deleting an item requires many rewrites and would be an expensive operation. In order to minimize gas costs, we will be leaving matched bids in the stack and overwriting them whenever possible when inserting new bids.

```
if (bid.over && bid.line < matchStack[j].line
    || !bid.over && bid.line > matchStack[j].line)
    break;
```

The break conditions for the stack are as follows:

For an over bid, if the bid line is less than the underline pointed to by the stack iterator, break out of the loop. Because the under stack is sorted so that lines get higher as you move up the stack, once you encounter one under line that is too high to match, all lines above it will be too high to match as well.

For an under bid, it is the opposite. If the bid line is greater than the over line pointed to by the stack iterator, break out of the loop. All lines above it will be too low to match as well.

```
uint betAmount;
if (bid.amount < matchStack[j].amount)
    betAmount = bid.amount;
else
    betAmount = matchStack[j].amount;
bid.amount -= betAmount;
matchStack[j].amount -= betAmount;
```

If it has been determined that the break condition is not satisfied, we have ourselves a valid bet that can be matched. The bet amount is going to be the lower of the stack bet amount and the bid amount. The bet amount is subtracted from both the stack bid and the current bid. If the current bid amount is lower than the stack bid, the bid amount will be 0 after subtraction and the loop condition will fail to satisfy on the next iteration. If the stack bid is lower, the remaining bid will be greater than 0 and the loop will continue.

```
Bet memory bet = Bet(
    bid.over ? bid.bidder : matchStack[j].bidder,
    bid.over ? matchStack[j].bidder : bid.bidder,
    betAmount,
    matchStack[j].line,
    BetStatus.Open
);
```

```
game.book.bets.push(bet);
BetPlaced(game_id, bid.bidder, bid.over, betAmount, matchStack[j].line);
BetPlaced(game_id, matchStack[j].bidder, !bid.over,
        betAmount, matchStack[j].line);
```

Once a bet has been placed, it has to be added to the stack and logged with the appropriate event. To make it easier to parse the logs by user, the BetPlaced event is called twice, once for each user.

```
    i--;
}
return bid;
```

Decrement the iterator variable, and continue the loop. When the loop is complete, return the remaining bid so it can be added to the appropriate bid stack.

Once bid matching is complete, we return back to the original bid function and add the bids to the stack.

```
// Use leftover funds to place open bids (maker)
if (remainingBid.amount > 0) {
    Bid[] bidStack = over ? game.book.overBids : game.book.underBids;
    if (over)
        addBidToStack(remainingBid, bidStack, true);
    else
        addBidToStack(remainingBid, bidStack, false);
    BidPlaced(game_id, msg.sender, remainingBid.amount, over, line);
}
```

If the remaining bid amount is 0, this code block doesn't execute. If it isn't, the bid gets added to the stack. Over and under bids get added differently. The third argument indicates the order in which the stack will be sorted: highest line at the bottom for over and lowest line at the bottom for under. Once the bid has been placed we emit an event, logging the action to the chain.

Let's look into the addBidToStack helper function to see how that works:

```
function addBidToStack(Bid bid, Bid[] storage stack, bool reverse) private
    returns (int) {
    if (stack.length == 0) {
        stack.push(bid);
        return -1;
    }

    // determine position of new bid in stack
    uint insertIndex = stack.length;
    if (reverse) {
        while (insertIndex > 0 && bid.line <= stack[insertIndex-1].line)
            insertIndex--;
    }
```

```
    else {
        while (insertIndex > 0 && bid.line >= stack[insertIndex-1].line)
            insertIndex--;
    }

    // try to find deleted slot to fill
    if (insertIndex > 0 && stack[insertIndex - 1].amount == 0) {
        stack[insertIndex - 1] = bid;
        return -1;
    }
    uint shiftEndIndex = insertIndex;
    while (shiftEndIndex < stack.length && stack[shiftEndIndex].amount > 0) {
        shiftEndIndex++;
    }

    // shift bids down (up to deleted index if one exists)
    if (shiftEndIndex == stack.length)
        stack.length += 1;
    for (uint i = shiftEndIndex; i > insertIndex; i--) {
        stack[i] = stack[i-1];
    }

    stack[insertIndex] = bid;

    return -1;
}
```

This is probably the most complicated function in the whole contract because it requires us to maintain a stack that can be sorted in both directions, add items to that stack, and replace bids that have been already matched instead of extending the stack length whenever possible.

We mentioned earlier that adding a bid by extending the stack length or deleting an item from the stack is a very expensive operation. Space must be allocated or destroyed for the item in the state tree, then every item in the stack below the insertion/deletion index must be rewritten, so a significant amount of state must be modified with each resize. Normally, using a linked list would make these operations less expensive, but Solidity does not permit recursive data structures so that option is not available to us.

In order to avoid performing an expensive deletion operation, we left bids with 0 amount remaining in the stack during bid matching. Now we will perform the second part of the optimization by rewriting 0 amount bids whenever possible instead of extending the array. Let's step through how:

```
function addBidToStack(Bid bid, Bid[] storage stack, bool reverse) private
    returns (int) {
```

We need to specify the bid to be inserted, the stack into which it should be inserted, and whether the stack is going sorted in normal or reverse order. For our purposes, normal order will be when the lowest bid is at the bottom and reverse order will be when the highest bid is at the bottom.

```
if (stack.length == 0) {
    stack.push(bid);
    return -1;
}
```

This is the trivial case. If there are no items in the stack, there's no need to go through the sorting or rewriting process, just append the item to the stack and return out.

```
// determine position of new bid in stack
uint insertIndex = stack.length;
if (reverse) {
    while (insertIndex > 0 && bid.line <= stack[insertIndex-1].line)
        insertIndex--;
}
else {
    while (insertIndex > 0 && bid.line >= stack[insertIndex-1].line)
        insertIndex--;
}
```

Before inserting the item into the sorted stack, we need to determine the index at which the insertion should occur. For a reverse stack, we start at the bottom and go up the stack while the bid line is less than the stack line. For a normal stack, we start at the bottom and go up the stack while the bid line is greater than the stack line.

```
// try to find deleted slot to fill
if (insertIndex > 0 && stack[insertIndex - 1].amount == 0) {
    stack[insertIndex - 1] = bid;
    return -1;
}
uint shiftEndIndex = insertIndex;
while (shiftEndIndex < stack.length && stack[shiftEndIndex].amount > 0) {
    shiftEndIndex++;
}
```

Ordinarily, we would shift down all the items below the insert index to make room for the new item in the sorted stack, but because creating additional storage is an expensive operation, we will attempt to find an empty bid (bid.amount == 0) and overwrite that instead.

The first check is to see if the slot above the insert index is an empty bid. If it is, nothing needs to be shifted, we can overwrite that bid with the new bid, and return out of the function. Next, we go down the stack starting at the insert index, and attempt to find the first empty bid. When we do, we exit the loop. If there are no empty bids, we will exit the loop once we hit the end of the stack.

```
// shift bids down (up to deleted index if one exists)
if (shiftEndIndex == stack.length)
    stack.length += 1;
```

```
for (uint i = shiftEndIndex; i > insertIndex; i--) {
    stack[i] = stack[i-1];
}
```

```
stack[insertIndex] = bid;
```

If there were no empty bids in the stack below the insert index, we have to extend the stack length by 1. Starting from right above the shift index and up to the insert index, we will shift all bids down by 1 slot. This will overwrite the bid at the shift index and open up a slot at the insert index, where we then insert the current bid.

Scoring Games and Payouts

Once a game has started and betting has closed, the game result can be set by the creator of the game using the `setGameResult` function:

```
function setGameResult(uint game_id, int homeScore, int awayScore)
    returns (int) {
    Game game = getGameById(game_id);
    if (game.locktime > now) return 1;
    if (game.status == GameStatus.Scored) return 2;

    cancelOpenBids(game.book);

    game.result.home = homeScore;
    game.result.away = awayScore;
    game.result.timestamp = now;
    game.status = GameStatus.Scored;
    payBets(game_id);

    GameScored(game_id, homeScore, awayScore, now);

    return -1;
}
```

This function sets the home and away scores for a specified game. The first part of this function performs a series of validations. The game must be past its locktime and not have been scored yet. Failing either of these validations returns an error code.

All open bids on the book are canceled. The `cancelOpenBids` helper function was explained in the bidding section. The scores for the home and away teams are updated in storage, the game status is updated, bets are paid out, and an event is logged indicating that the game has been scored.

The `payBets` helper function looks like this:

```
function payBets(uint game_id) private returns (int) {
    Game game = getGameById(game_id);
    Bet[] bets = game.book.bets;
```

```
    int totalPoints = game.result.home + game.result.away;
    for (uint i=0; i < bets.length; i++) {
        Bet bet = bets[i];
        if (bet.status == BetStatus.Paid)
            continue;
        if (totalPoints > bet.line)
            balances[bet.over] += bet.amount * 2;
        else if (totalPoints < bet.line)
            balances[bet.under] += bet.amount * 2;
        else {
            balances[bet.under] += bet.amount;
            balances[bet.over] += bet.amount;
        }
        bet.status = BetStatus.Paid;
    }

    return -1;
}
```

This function first uses the game result to calculate the total points scored. It then loops through each of the bets. If the bet has already been paid out, it skips the bet and moves to the next one. This should never be the case, but to prevent a future version of the code from invoking this function twice for the same game, it has been included. If the calculated point total is greater than the bet line, double the bet amount is added to the address of the over bet. If the calculated point total is less than the bet line, double the bet amount is added to the address of the under bet. If the point total and bet line are the same, both sides of the bet are refunded the bet amount. Once the bet has been paid out, the bet status is marked as paid.

Withdrawing

Once a bet has been resolved and the user balances have been updated, the winning users will want to withdraw their money. The withdraw function allows them to do so.

```
function withdraw() returns (int) {
    var balance = balances[msg.sender];
    balances[msg.sender] = 0;
    if (!msg.sender.send(balance)) {
        balances[msg.sender] = balance;
        return 1;
    }
    Withdrawal(msg.sender, balance, now);
    return -1;
}
```

To withdraw, we retrieve the balance of the user from the balances mapping and store it into a temporary variable. Then we zero out the user's balance and send the ether to their wallet. If the send fails, we refund the amount to their balance and return an error code. If the send succeeds, we log the event.

The order of logic in this function is *very* important. The infamous DAO hack was caused by an unidentified bug in this exact withdraw implementation. It seems a bit inefficient to zero out the balance of the user, then refund it later if the send fails. The reason for doing this is that the entity calling the `withdraw` function can be a contract. Contracts can define a fallback function that executes as the default action when no matching ABI function can be found. If the attacker's contract defines a payable fallback function that runs another withdrawal on our contract and the balance has not been zeroed, it can run withdrawals over and over again until our contract's balance has been drained. This was how the DAO attacker was able to drain all the funds from the DAO contract.

Reading Games

We need a way for the front end to read active games from the blockchain. Doing so is a two-step process because we can't directly return a custom struct in a public ABI function. Instead, what we will do is get a list of active game IDs from the contract, then parse the logs for the game details.

Here is the contract ABI function for the first step of the process. The second step will be covered in the front-end section.

```
function getActiveGames () constant returns (uint[]) {
    uint[] memory game_ids = new uint[](games.length);
    for (uint i=0; i < games.length; i++) {
        game_ids[i] = (games[i].id);
    }
    return game_ids;
}
```

The function creates an empty memory array of game IDs initialized to the length of the games array. A memory array is used instead of a storage array because it is a constant function, meaning it can't modify storage. We loop through the games and add each id to the memory array, then return the array.

Reading Bids

The order book changes with each placed bid, so we need a way of getting a current snapshot of the order book. Unfortunately, the logs aren't going to be of much use to us here because placed bids can be matched and deleted, so a logged bid may not exist anymore. To get a current view of the book, we have to return bids directly from the contract. Unfortunately, as mentioned earlier, we can't return custom structs directly in the ABI. So instead we're going to run a hack job and return a byte array containing the information, then parse the byte array back into a bid array on the front end.

Here's the contract function to encode the bids into a byte array.

```
function getOpenBids(uint game_id) constant returns (bytes) {
    Game game = getGameById(game_id);
    uint nBids = game.book.overBids.length + game.book.underBids.length;
    bytes memory s = new bytes(57 * nBids);
    uint k = 0;
```

```
    for (uint i=0; i < nBids; i++) {
        if (i < game.book.overBids.length)
            Bid bid = game.book.overBids[i];
        else
            bid = game.book.underBids[i - game.book.overBids.length];
        bytes20 bidder = bytes20(bid.bidder);
        bytes32 amount = bytes32(bid.amount);
        byte home = bid.over ? byte(1) : byte(0);
        bytes4 line = bytes4(bid.line);

        for (uint j=0; j < 20; j++) { s[k] = bidder[j]; k++; }
        for (j=0; j < 32; j++) { s[k] = amount[j]; k++; }
        s[k] = home; k++;
        for (j=0; j < 4; j++) { s[k] = line[j]; k++; }


    }

    return s;
}
```

Let's break this code down since it gets complicated in places.

```
Game game = getGameById(game_id);
uint nBids = game.book.overBids.length + game.book.underBids.length;
bytes memory s = new bytes(57 * nBids);
uint k = 0;
```

The function is constant to indicate that it does not modify storage. First, we grab a storage pointer to the game. Then we count the total number of bids in the book and use that to allocate a byte array in memory. bytes is the data type for a dynamically sized byte array. An iterator variable, k, is initialized as well. This iterator variable will point to the current index in the byte array that is being written. Every time a byte is written to the byte array, we will increment the iterator.

```
for (uint i=0; i < nBids; i++) {
    if (i < game.book.overBids.length)
        Bid bid = game.book.overBids[i];
    else
        bid = game.book.underBids[i - game.book.overBids.length];
```

Loop through all the bids, and determine whether the current bid is in the over or under stack.

```
    bytes20 bidder = bytes20(bid.bidder);
    bytes32 amount = bytes32(bid.amount);
    byte home = bid.over ? byte(1) : byte(0);
    bytes4 line = bytes4(bid.line);
```

TABLE 10-1 **Bid Byte Structure**

- 1-20	bidder	address
- 21-52	unsigned int	bid amount in wei
- 53	boolean bit	1 for over, 0 for under
- 54-57	two's complement integer	bid line

```
        for (uint j=0; j < 20; j++) { s[k] = bidder[j]; k++; }
        for (j=0; j < 32; j++) { s[k] = amount[j]; k++; }
        s[k] = home; k++;
        for (j=0; j < 4; j++) { s[k] = line[j]; k++; }
    }

return s;
```

Convert each bid property into its byte representation. The bytesxx data types are defined for all values up to 32 (bytes2, bytes3, etc.) and for a single `byte`. Next, loop through each byte representation and add them to the main byte array, byte by byte.

Once all the bids have been encoded and concatenated, we return the byte array. We will cover how to parse the byte array into a JavaScript object on the front end later. For now it will suffice to define a data dictionary for the bid byte structure by byte index (see Table 10-1).

Summary

In this chapter, we have introduced the development life cycle of a full-function betting application built on Ethereum. The focus was primarily on coding with Solidity. In the next chapter, we will deploy the contract and develop a simple front end to run the application.

11 Deploying the Sample Application: Blockchain and Betting

Deploying Full Contract

In Chapter 10, we introduced the development steps for writing a smart contract. Now that the contract is fully written, let's deploy it to our test chain, and interact with it.

```
node deploy.js ethereum && node debug.js ethereum
```

Fix any errors that pop up during compilation, then run the deployment again if necessary. If everything worked properly, you should see the interactive prompt pop up. Let's run a couple of test functions to make sure our contract is working.

```
locktime = parseInt(new Date().getTime() / 1000) + 3600;
tx = contract.createGame("Golden State", "Cleveland", 1, locktime,
    { from: walletAddress, gas: 5e5 })
```

The first line creates a UNIX timestamp 1 hour (3600s) in the future. The JavaScript Date type uses milliseconds after the UNIX epoch instead of seconds after the UNIX epoch like most other languages, so a conversion is required. The third parameter is the category, with 1 referring to NBA for our purposes. Executing the createGame function will return a transaction id that can be used to check whether the transaction has been mined.

At any point, you can run:

```
web3.eth.getTransactionReceipt(tx);
```

to see if the transaction has been mined. If it hasn't, it will return null. If it has, it will return a receipt object.

Once the transaction has cleared, you should be able to read the newly created game from the contract.

```
// there should be one active game now with id=1
// getActiveGames is a constant function, so a _call_ is executed and returns
// immediately with a result
contract.getActiveGames()

// to get more details about the game we can parse the logs for GameCreated
// events. Helper functions for accessing events are available on the contract
// object as well. By default, fromBlock is the latest block, so that
// parameter has to be set manually
contract.GameCreated({}, { fromBlock: 1 }).get(console.log)
```

You should be able to view a single game in the output of both those statements.

Deploying to the Mainnet

Deploying to the mainnet is very similar to deploying to our private chain. Repeat all the exact steps above with two exceptions.

First, exit the geth process running our private chain by navigating to that tab and typing CTRL-C. Then run the Ethereum mainnet with the command:

```
| geth --rpc --rpcapi web3,eth,net,personal
```

If you haven't synced a full geth node in the past, this process will take up to a day. If you have, it should only take a few minutes to sync up fully. In order to deploy to the mainnet, you will have to create a wallet address and obtain ether from an exchange. This process is covered in earlier chapters.

Once the node is synced and caught up to the main chain, run the `deploy` command from the previous section. You should see confirmation of your deployment in the output. You can now run the test scripts from the previous section to confirm that the contract deployed.

Seeding Data

Manually seeding our contract with data every time we deploy is a tedious and slow process, so we're going to write a script to seed data for us.

Here's what our seeds.js file is going to look like:

```
var Web3 = require('web3');
var web3 = new Web3();
var fs = require('fs');

web3.setProvider(new web3.providers.HttpProvider('http://localhost:8545'));
```

```javascript
// Load ABI, contract address, contract
var abi = JSON.parse(fs.readFileSync("bin/peerbet.sol:PeerBet.abi", "ascii"));
var contractAddress = fs.readFileSync("contract_address", "ascii");
var contract = web3.eth.contract(abi).at(contractAddress);
var walletAddress = web3.eth.accounts[0];
web3.personal.unlockAccount(walletAddress, process.argv[2]);

// Create a series of locktimes
var thirty_secs = parseInt(new Date().getTime() / 1000) + 30;
var three_days = parseInt(new Date().getTime() / 1000) + 3*3600*24;
var three_hours = parseInt(new Date().getTime() / 1000) + 3*3600;
var three_minutes = parseInt(new Date().getTime() / 1000) + 3*60;

// Seed games
var games = [
    ["Cleveland", "Indiana", 1, thirty_secs],
    ["San Antonio", "Memphis", 1, three_hours],
    ["Boston", "Chicago", 1, three_minutes],
    ["Los Angeles Clippers", "Utah", 1, three_days],
    ["Golden State", "Portland", 1, three_hours],
    ["Oklahoma City", "Houston", 1, three_minutes]
]
games.forEach(function (game) {
    contract.createGame.sendTransaction(...game, {
        from: walletAddress,
        gas: 200000
    });
});

for (var i=0; i < 100; i++) {
    var random_index = Math.floor(Math.random() * 6) + 1; // 1-6
    var random_amount = Math.floor(Math.random() * 100 * 1e15); // 1-100 mETH
    var over = Math.random() > 0.5; // true or false
    var random_line = Math.floor(Math.random() * 50) + 175; // 175-225
    contract.bid(random_index, over, random_line,
        { from: walletAddress, value: random_amount , gas: 500000 });
}
```

Let's break this down by section:

```javascript
var Web3 = require('web3');
var web3 = new Web3();
var fs = require('fs');

web3.setProvider(new web3.providers.HttpProvider('http://localhost:8545'));
```

These are the standard includes and provider setup logic we've seen before.

```
// Load ABI, contract address, contract
var abi = JSON.parse(fs.readFileSync("bin/peerbet.sol:PeerBet.abi", "ascii"));
var contractAddress = fs.readFileSync("contract_address", "ascii");
var contract = web3.eth.contract(abi).at(contractAddress);
var walletAddress = web3.eth.accounts[0];
web3.personal.unlockAccount(walletAddress, process.argv[2]);
```

We load the ABI and contract address from their appropriate files and use it to create a contract object. We then access our default wallet and unlock it with our wallet password, which will be passed into the script as the first command line argument.

```
// Create a series of locktimes
var thirty_secs = parseInt(new Date().getTime() / 1000) + 30;
var three_days = parseInt(new Date().getTime() / 1000) + 3*3600*24;
var three_hours = parseInt(new Date().getTime() / 1000) + 3*3600;
var three_minutes = parseInt(new Date().getTime() / 1000) + 3*60;
```

To mix it up, we define four different locktimes to use in our games logic.

```
var games = [
    ["Cleveland", "Indiana", 1, thirty_secs],
    ["San Antonio", "Memphis", 1, three_hours],
    ["Boston", "Chicago", 1, three_minutes],
    ["Los Angeles Clippers", "Utah", 1, three_days],
    ["Golden State", "Portland", 1, three_hours],
    ["Oklahoma City", "Houston", 1, three_minutes]
]
games.forEach(function (game) {
    contract.createGame(...game, { from: walletAddress, gas: 200000 });
});
```

We create six games here by defining an array of game property arrays, looping through the array, then using the JavaScript spread operator, . . ., to pass the parameters into the createGame contract function. This should create six National Basketball Association (NBA) games (category = 1) with different locktimes and teams.

```
for (var i=0; i < 100; i++) {
    var random_game = Math.floor(Math.random() * 6) + 1; // 1-6
    var random_amount = Math.floor(Math.random() * 100 * 1e15); // 1-100 mETH
    var over = Math.random() > 0.5; // true or false
    var random_line = Math.floor(Math.random() * 50) + 175; // 175-225
    contract.bid(random_game, over, random_line,
        { from: walletAddress, value: random_amount , gas: 500000 });
}
```

Run a loop 100 times and seed 100 bids into the contract. Each bid will go to a random game, with a random amount, at a random line, to a random side of the bet.

Save this file to seeds.js, then run our full deploy-seed-debug dev flow with:

```
node deploy.js [password] && node debug.js [password] node seeds.js [password]
```

As always, replace `[password]` with your wallet password. Wait about 1 minute for all the transactions to clear. You can monitor the status of the transactions in the terminal tab running the private chain.

In the debug console, examine the order book for a game:

```
contract.getOpenBids(2)
```

Since `getOpenBids` is a constant function, it should return immediately with a hex string that looks like this:

'0xe506a922a5ae5a9855307f996cedb97f2ac0bec50000000000000000000000000000000000000000
0000000000157eeb788dd3d9e01000000b3e506a922a5ae5a9855307f996cedb97f2ac0bec50000000
000000000000000000000000000000000000000000000000000052f7616f19157001000000b7e506a922a5ae5a9
855307f996cedb97f2ac0bec5000000000000000000000000000000000000000000000000000000000d00dadb
b6c5af601000000bde506a922a5ae5a9855307f996cedb97f2ac0bec500000000000000000000000000
00000000000000000000000002b17fd14e5387a01000000bee506a922a5ae5a9855307f996cedb97f2
ac0bec5000000000000000000000000000000000000000000000000000012e79a7fbe22d4400000000e0e
506a922a5ae5a9855307f996cedb97f2ac0bec5000000000000000000000000000000000000000000000000
00000014a27bcf218dfa400000000e0e506a922a5ae5a9855307f996cedb97f2ac0bec500000000000
0000000000000000000000000000000000043ca9129f8d63000000000dbe506a922a5ae5a98553
07f996cedb97f2ac0bec50000000000000000000000000000000000000000000000000000108a2dc8a22b
74100000000d5e506a922a5ae5a9855307f996cedb97f2ac0bec5000000000000000000000000000000
000000000000000000000000000000000cee506a922a5ae5a9855307f996cedb97f2ac0b
ec5000000000000000000000000000000000000000000000000000000000000000cb'

This is the unparsed byte array created for us by the contract function. To view the book, we have to parse the byte array back into a bid array. Exit the debugger, then include these functions in debug.js:

```
function parseBid(hex) {
    return {
        bidder: '0x' + hex.slice(0,40),
        amount: parseInt(hex.slice(40,104), 16),
        over: parseInt(hex.slice(104,106)) == 1,
        line: ~~parseInt(hex.slice(106), 16)
    }
}

function parseBids(hex) {
    hex = hex.slice(2); // to get rid of the '0x'
    var bids = []
    for (var i=0; i < hex.length; i += 114)
        bids.push(parseBid(hex.slice(i, i+114)));

    return bids;
}
```

The `parseBid` function takes a 114-character hex string and converts it into a bid object using the data dictionary we defined earlier in the chapter. The `parseBids` function strips away the leading `0x`, splits the long hex into 114-character hex strings, and turns the parsed bids into an array. Why 114 (57 * 2) characters instead of 57, which is the length of the bid representation in bytes? Because it takes two hex characters to encode a byte, so twice the number of characters are required.

Enter back into the debugger:

```
node debug.js ethereum
```

```
// In the debug console
parseBids(contract.getOpenBids(2))
```

Now your parsed result should look something like this:

```
[ { bidder: '0xe506a922a5ae5a9855307f996cedb97f2ac0bec5',
    amount: 96808389054381470,
    over: true,
    line: 179 },
  { bidder: '0xe506a922a5ae5a9855307f996cedb97f2ac0bec5',
    amount: 23352945938077040,
    over: true,
    line: 183 },
  { bidder: '0xe506a922a5ae5a9855307f996cedb97f2ac0bec5',
    amount: 58561834980760310,
    over: true,
    line: 189 },
  { bidder: '0xe506a922a5ae5a9855307f996cedb97f2ac0bec5',
    amount: 12129799743289466,
    over: true,
    line: 190 },
  { bidder: '0xe506a922a5ae5a9855307f996cedb97f2ac0bec5',
    amount: 85139205359021380,
    over: false,
    line: 224 },
  { bidder: '0xe506a922a5ae5a9855307f996cedb97f2ac0bec5',
    amount: 92930434783567780,
    over: false,
    line: 224 },
  { bidder: '0xe506a922a5ae5a9855307f996cedb97f2ac0bec5',
    amount: 19081548262856240,
    over: false,
    line: 219 },
  { bidder: '0xe506a922a5ae5a9855307f996cedb97f2ac0bec5',
    amount: 74488461945648960,
    over: false,
    line: 213 },
```

```
{ bidder: '0xe506a922a5ae5a9855307f996cedb97f2ac0bec5',
  amount: 0,
  over: false,
  line: 206 },
{ bidder: '0xe506a922a5ae5a9855307f996cedb97f2ac0bec5',
  amount: 0,
  over: false,
  line: 203 } ]
```

The over bids show up first, with the highest line at the bottom, then the under bids are at the bottom half, with the lowest line at the bottom. The amounts for some of the bids will be 0, indicating that they have been matched but have not yet been overwritten by a new bid.

There should be placed bets as well. We can check for those by searching the logs for `BetPlaced` events in the debug console.

```
contract.BetPlaced({}, { fromBlock: 1 }).get(console.log)
```

Front-End User Interface

All public contract functions expose an ABI that can be accessed through the web3.js library. If you wish to run a betting server without a user interface, your work is complete, and the contract is ready to use. However, most sites will require a front-end interface, so we will build out a simple one for our betting contract.

Since the focus of this book is on blockchains and not web interfaces, we will not be building a full-fledged web UI. It is assumed that the reader has a basic understanding of HTML, JavaScript, and jQuery, but no CSS or styling will be used. The purpose of our front end will be to demonstrate how to use the web3.js library with an Ethereum contract, and we will not build out further functionality beyond that. With that, let's get started!

Pages in the User Interface

Our front end is going to have three pages with the following functionality:

- View list of games (index.html)
- View book for a single game (bet.html)
- Withdraw winnings (withdraw.html)

Displaying Games

Our home page, index.html, is going to display a table with all of our active games. In addition there is a link to the withdraw page we will be building later. Here's the HTML for the page:

```
<html>
<body>

    <nav>
        <a href="withdraw.html">Withdraw</a>
    </nav>
```

```
<h1>Games</h1>
<table id="games-table">
    <thead>
        <tr>
            <th>Home</th>
            <th>Away</th>
            <th>Score</th>
            <th>Category</th>
            <th>Date</th>
            <th>Time</th>
            <th></th>
        </tr>
    </thead>
    <tbody></tbody>
</table>


<!-- jQuery CDN -->
  <script src="https://code.jquery.com/jquery-3.1.1.js"
        integrity="sha256-16cdPddA6VdVInumRGo6IbivbERE8p7CQR3HzTBuELA="
        crossorigin="anonymous"></script>


<!-- Our JavaScript file -->
<script src="main.js"></script>
</body>

</html>
```

As you can see, there's a link to the withdraw page above the header, followed by the header and games table. The games table contains a series of descriptive columns about each game. The column with no title is where the links to the game's betting page will go.

There are two JavaScript files included on the page: the jQuery CDN and our main.js file. The jQuery CDN and the MetaMask Chrome extension (which injects the web3.js library) are the only dependencies for the front end.

Let's take a look at the custom JavaScript required in the main.js file piece by piece. We will be using the main.js file for all three of our HTML pages, so there will be some overlapping code that will be explained as we go.

This first batch of code loads up some file dependencies and prepares the page for execution. It is common to all three of our pages.

```
// Load ABI and contract address
var abiPromise = $.get("bin/peerbet.sol:PeerBet.abi");
var contractAddressPromise = $.get("contract_address");

// Wait for MetaMask to inject web3
var web3Promise = new Promise(function (resolve, reject) {
    var interval = setInterval(function () {
```

```
    if (typeof web3 !== 'undefined') {
        resolve(web3);
        clearInterval(interval);
    }
}, 50);
});
```

The first two lines use jQuery's AJAX functionality to load up the two pieces of data we will need to create our web3 `Contract` object, the ABI and contract address, and defining promises for both AJAX calls.

For those unfamiliar with the concept, promises are a construct that allows for asynchronous code execution. Similar to threads, promises begin execution of a function, then return without waiting for the block of code to finish executing. Instead, the promise resolves when the code is finished executing, and bindings are provided that allow code to execute after a promise resolves instead of immediately when the function returns. Promises are outside the scope of this book but are an integral part of writing good front-end JavaScript code, so please familiarize yourself with the concept before attempting to build a front end for your contract.

As we mentioned earlier, the MetaMask Chrome extension and Chrome browser are requirements for the application. The MetaMask extension injects the web3.js library into our application, so we don't have to require it ourselves. However, the injection occurs asynchronously, so any code that uses the library (in our case, the entire application) must wait until the injection completes in order to execute. The second block of code handles the asynchronous behavior, by defining a promise that resolves when web3 has been injected. It does so by checking for the existence of the library every 50ms until the library is found.

```
var contract;
$.when(contractAddressPromise, abiPromise, web3Promise)
    .always(function (contractAddress, abiJSON) {
    var contractAddress = contractAddress[0];
    var abi = JSON.parse(abiJSON[0]);
    contract = web3.eth.contract(abi).at(contractAddress);
    switch (window.location.pathname) {
        case '/bet.html':
            betsPage();
            break;
        case '/withdraw.html':
            withdrawPage();
            break;
        default:
            gamesPage();
    }
});
```

Once web3 is available and the required files have loaded, we can create the `Contract` object. `$.when` is similar to the built-in `Promise.all` function, and allows us to wait for a series of promises to return before executing a block of code. Once we have a `Contract` object, our code branches into three different tracks using a `switch` statement, one for each of the three pages. The default track is the games page, which is the track we will be exploring in this section.

```
function gamesPage () {
    getGames().then(function (games) {
        games.forEach(addGameToTable);
    });
}
```

The games page gets a list of games and adds them to the games table. Both of those functionalities are handled in helper functions.

Let's take a look at the `getGames` helper:

```
function getGames () {
    var activeGamesPromise = new Promise((resolve, reject) => {
        contract.getActiveGames.call(function (err, game_ids) {
            if (err) reject(err);
            else resolve(game_ids);
        });
    });

    var gamesPromise = new Promise((resolve, reject) => {
        activeGamesPromise.then(game_ids => {
            contract.GameCreated({ id: game_ids }, { fromBlock: 1 })
                .get(function (err, logs) {
                    var games = logs.map(log => log.args);
                    resolve(games);
                });
        });
    });

    var scoresPromise = new Promise((resolve, reject) => {
        activeGamesPromise.then(game_ids => {
            contract.GameScored({ game_id: game_ids }, { fromBlock: 1 })
                .get((err, logs) => {
                    var scores = logs.map(log => log.args);
                    resolve(scores);
                });
        });
    });

    return new Promise((resolve, reject) => {
        $.when(gamesPromise, scoresPromise).then((games, scores) => {
            var scoresObj = {}
            scores.forEach(score => scoresObj[score.game_id] = score);
            games.forEach(game => {
                if (scoresObj[game.id]) {
                    game.result = {
```

```
                            home: scoresObj[game.id].homeScore,
                            away: scoresObj[game.id].awayScore,
                            timestamp: parseInt(scoresObj[game.id].timestamp)
                        }
                    }
                    else
                        game.result = { home: '-', away: '-' }
                });
                resolve(games);
            });
        });
    }
```

The first block runs a call to the `getActiveGames` function, which returns an array of game ids. Those game ids are then resolved through a promise, so they can be available asynchronously to the remainder of the function. Those game ids are then used to access two separate event logs, the GameCreated event and the GameScored event. This occurs in the second and third logs. The results of both those log accesses are resolved through individual promises, then the two are combined in the final block. The game scores are merged with the game information object and the combined object is resolved through the returned promise.

If the scores are not defined because the game has not yet been scored, the home and away scores will be represented by a single `'-'`. This way, when we display the scores later with a `'-'` separating the home and away scores, an unscored game will show `'---'`.

Once we have the games, we add them to our table through another helper function, `addGameToTable`:

```
function addGameToTable (game) {
    var category = 'NBA';
    var gametime = new Date(parseInt(game.locktime) * 1000);
    var date = gametime.toString().slice(0,10);
    var time = gametime.toTimeString().slice(0,5);


    var row = `<tr class="game">
        <td>${game.home}</td>
        <td>${game.away}</td>
        <td>${game.result.home} - ${game.result.away}</td>
            <td>${category}</td>
        <td>${date}</td>
        <td>${time}</td>
        <td class="bets-cell">
            <a href="bet.html?id=${game.id}">Bet</a>
        </td>
    </tr>`;
    $(`#games-table tbody`).append(row);
}
```

This function is very simple. It takes the game object, turns it into an HTML table row, then inserts it into the table.

That's all the code for the games page. The simplest way to run the server is in the command line for the folder:

```
python2 -m SimpleHTTPServer
```

Python 2 is preinstalled on OS X and Linux, but on Windows you may have to download the package from https://www.python.org/downloads/.

Make sure your geth private net is running in a terminal tab. Then set your MetaMask extension to connect to the private net by clicking the fox icon in the upper-left corner. Select the item in the drop-down labeled Localhost 8545 (see Figure 11-1).

If everything has been set up properly, you should see a page that looks like Figure 11-2. Congratulations, you've got yourself an ugly but functional games page!

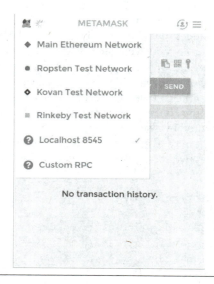

FIGURE 11-1   MetaMask

Home	Away	Score	Category	Date	Time	
Cleveland	Indiana	100 - 98	NBA	Tue Jun 13	18:55	Bet
San Antonio	Memphis	- - -	NBA	Tue Jun 13	21:54	Bet
Boston	Chicago	- - -	NBA	Tue Jun 13	18:57	Bet
Los Angeles Clippers	Utah	- - -	NBA	Fri Jun 16	18:54	Bet
Golden State	Portland	- - -	NBA	Tue Jun 13	21:54	Bet
Oklahoma City	Houston	- - -	NBA	Tue Jun 13	18:57	Bet

Withdraw

Games

FIGURE 11-2   Betting application page 1

Bet Page Markup

We're going to be creating a separate page to display the order book and place bets. We saw earlier that our main thread split into three different tracks, one for each page.

```
switch (window.location.pathname) {
    case '/bet.html':
        betsPage(); // <------ betting track
        break;
    case '/withdraw.html':
        withdrawPage();
        break;
    default:
        gamesPage();
}
```

We will now be pursuing the betting track and explaining the markup and code associated with the page. To start, here's the basic HTML outline we will be following. There will be other functionalities available on this page as well, and we will add them to this HTML base as we go.

```
<html>
<body>

    <script src="https://code.jquery.com/jquery-3.1.1.js"
        integrity="sha256-16cdPddA6VdVInumRGo6IbivbERE8p7CQR3HzTBuELA="
            crossorigin="anonymous"></script>
    <script src="main.js"></script>
</body>

</html>
```

This is the same frame as for the games page. From here, we will add bet page–specific functionality. First, we want to display some basic game information:

```
<h1>
    <span class="home">---</span> vs <span class="away">---</span>
</h1>

<div>Gametime: <span class="locktime"></span></div>

<div id="score-row">
    Final Score:
    <span class="game-score">
        <span class="home-score"></span> -
        <span class="away-score"></span>
    </span>
</div>
```

There are display locations for the home team, away team, game time, and score. These will be filled in by our JavaScript on page load. As before, we will not be styling the page.

Next, we need sections for placing our over and under bets.

```
<div id="bet-placements">
    <h3>Bet Over</h3>

    <label>Line</label>
    <input id="over-line" type="number">

    <label>Amount (ETH)</label>
    <input id="over-amount" type="number">

    <button id="place-bet-over">Place Bet</button>

    <hr>

    <h3>Bet Under</h3>

    <label>Line</label>
    <input id="under-line" type="number">

    <label>Amount (ETH)</label>
    <input id="under-amount" type="number">

    <button id="place-bet-under">Place Bet</button>
</div>
```

This displays two identical sections, one for placing an over bet and one for placing an under bet. Each section has two inputs, one for the line and one for the bet amount, and a button for placing the bet.

In addition to bet placement, this page will display the order book and a section for setting the game score. Let's first look at the HTML for displaying open bids.

```
<hr>

<h3>Open Over Bids</h3>
<table id="over-bids-table">
    <thead>
        <tr>
            <th>Line</th>
            <th class="currency">Amount (ETH)</th>
        <tr>
    </thead>
    <tbody></tbody>
</table>

<hr>
```

```html
<h3>Open Under Bids</h3>
<table id="under-bids-table">
    <thead>
        <tr>
            <th>Line</th>
            <th class="currency">Amount (ETH)</th>
        <tr>
    </thead>
    <tbody></tbody>
</table>

<hr>
```

This sets up two tables, one for over bids and one for under bids. Both tables contain columns for the bet line and the bet amount. The table body and table header are given separate sections because later on we will be inserting rows directly into the body without touching the header. The `<hr>` tag separates the section with a horizontal divider.

We will also be displaying bets that have already been matched and placed into the book.

```html
<h3>Latest Bets</h3>
<table id="bets-table">
    <thead>
        <tr>
            <th>Line</th>
            <th class="currency">Amount (ETH)</th>
        <tr>
    </thead>
    <tbody></tbody>
</table>

<hr>
```

This table is very similar to the bids table and contains the same columns. The only difference will be in the data we add to the table.

Finally, we want a small form that we can use to score the game when betting has closed and the game is complete.

```html
<h3>Score Game</h3>

<label class="home"></label>
<input id="home-score-input" type="number">

<label class="away"></label>
<input id="away-score-input" type="number">

<button id="score-btn">Score Game</button>
```

The form has inputs for the home and away scores, and a button that can be used to submit the score.

That will be all for the HTML. The actual displayed data will come from web3, and we will use JavaScript to print the data onto the page.

Displaying Game Information

To display information about a single game, we will be reusing the `getGames` function we defined earlier, and defining a new helper function to grab the game we want:

```
function getGame(id) {
    return getGames().then(function (games) {
        var game = games.find(g => g.id == id);
        return game;
    })
}
```

This function gets the list of the games then finds the desired game. Returning an item within a `.then` callback will cause that promise to resolve with the returned value. So this function returns a promise that resolves with the desired game.

Using this function, we can display the game information on our page:

```
function betsPage() {
    var id = parseInt(window.location.search.split('=')[1]);
    getGame(id).then(function (game) {
        $('.home').html(game.home);
        $('.away').html(game.away);

        // Display gametime
        var locktime = new Date(game.locktime * 1000);
        $('.locktime').html(locktime.toString());

        // Display scores
        var homeScore = parseInt(game.result.home);
        var awayScore = parseInt(game.result.away);
        $('.home-score').html(homeScore);
        $('.away-score').html(awayScore);
    });

    ...

}
```

The home and away team names are displayed from the game object. Then the locktime is converted from a UNIX timestamp to a JavaScript Date and displayed. The scores will not be defined if the game has not been scored yet. In this case, the score will display `'---'` because the home and away scores will both be set to a single `'-'` by the `getGames` helper.

Displaying Open Bids

Earlier, we defined `parseBids` and `parseBid` helper functions in our debug.js file to parse the byte array returned by the contract's `getOpenBids` ABI function. We will be reusing those functions here. The code is reproduced below without explanation. Please refer to the "Seeding Data" section earlier in the chapter for the code explanation.

```
function parseBid(hex) {
    return {
        bidder: '0x' + hex.slice(0,40),
        amount: parseInt(hex.slice(40,104), 16),
        over: parseInt(hex.slice(104,106)) == 1,
        line: ~~parseInt(hex.slice(106), 16)
    }
}

function parseBids(hex) {
    if (hex.slice(0,2) == '0x')
        hex = hex.slice(2);
    var bids = []
    for (var i=0; i < hex.length; i += 114)
        bids.push(parseBid(hex.slice(i, i+114)));

    return bids;
}
```

In addition, we will define a `getOpenBids` helper function to make the web3 call to the contract, parse the returned byte array, and resolve it all through a promise.

```
function getOpenBids(game_id) {
    return new Promise(function (resolve, reject) {
        contract.getOpenBids(game_id, function (err, hex) {
            var bids = parseBids(hex);
            bids = bids.filter(bid => bid.amount > 0);
            bids.forEach(bid => bid.amount = parseFloat(bid.amount / 1e18));
            resolve(bids);
        });
    });
}
```

The `getOpenBids` contract ABI function is a constant function, so web3 executes a call that returns immediately. As always, the first argument in the callback is the error (null if no error) and the returned byte array is the second argument in the form of a hex string (`"0xf43..."`). The hex string is parsed into a byte array, empty bids with an amount of 0 are removed, and the bid amount is converted from wei to ether. The resulting array is then resolved through the returned promise.

Finally, we will define a helper function that adds the bids to the table:

```
function addBidToTable (table, bid) {
    var row = `<tr class="bid">
        <td>${bid.line}</td>
        <td class="currency">${bid.amount}</td>
    </tr>`;
    $(table + " tbody").prepend(row);
}
```

This function takes a table selector (e.g., "#over-bids-table") and adds a row to the body of the table with the given bid's information.

Putting these helper functions together, we can retrieve bids and display them on our page:

```
function betsPage() {
    ...

    getOpenBids(id).then(function (bids) {
        bids.filter(bid => bid.over)
            .forEach(bid => addBidToTable("#over-bids-table", bid));
        bids.filter(bid => !bid.over)
            .forEach(bid => addBidToTable("#under-bids-table", bid));
    });

    ...
}
```

The bids are filtered twice, once to get the over bids and display them on the over bids table, and then again to get the under bids and display them on the under bids table.

Displaying Bets

We would like to display existing matched bets in addition to the open bids. In order to do so, we will define a couple more helper functions to get the bets and add them to the bets table.

First, let's define the helper to retrieve bets from the blockchain logs.

```
function getBets(game_id) {
    return new Promise(function (resolve, reject) {
        contract.BetPlaced({ game_id: game_id }, { fromBlock: 1 })
        .get(function (err, logs) {
            var bets = logs.map(log => log.args);
            bets.forEach(bet =>
            bet.amount = parseFloat(bet.amount / 1e18));
            resolve(bets);
        });
    });
}
```

The bets are stored in the logs with an index on the game_id field. We can take advantage of that and parse the logs only for bets with our game id. The first object passed to a web3 contract event getter is an object of index-value pairs for the search. The second object is a config object. As stated earlier, the only config we need to specify is the `fromBlock` field. The other default values will suffice. Once we get the logs, we extract just the event data from them through the `args` property and resolve the data through the returned promise.

We will also require a simple helper to add our bet information to the bets table.

```
function addBetToTable(bet) {
    var row = `<tr class="bet">
        <td>${bet.line}</td>
        <td class="currency">${bet.amount}</td>
    </tr>`;
    $("#bets-table tbody").prepend(row);
}
```

This function takes the bet information, creates a table row with it, then adds the row to the bets table body.

Using these helpers, we can now retrieve bets and display them on our page.

```
function betsPage() {

    . . .

    getBets(id).then(function (bets) {
        bets.filter(bet => bet.over).forEach(addBetToTable);
    });


    . . .

}
```

For every two-sided bet that occurs in the contract, two separate logs are produced, one for the over side and one for the under side. If we displayed all of the bet logs, each bet would be displayed twice, so we filter out just the over bets and display those. The side chosen is irrelevant; we could just as well filter out the under bets and display those. The result would be the same.

Placing Bids/Bets

When placing a bet, the user will fill in the line and amount for their chosen side and click the corresponding Place Bet button. Our JavaScript code will be responsible for translating that click into a real bid placement on our deployed contract.

We will have to define a helper function that gets the current user's wallet address in order to do this.

```
function getWalletAddress () {
 return new Promise(function (resolve, reject) {
  // MetaMask
  if (web3 && web3.eth.accounts[0]) {
   var walletAddress = web3.eth.accounts[0];
  }
```

```
// Mist
else if (typeof mist !== 'undefined') {
 mist.requestAccount(function (err, accounts) {
  if (err) reject(err);
  else
   var walletAddress = accounts[accounts.length - 1];
  })
 }
 resolve(walletAddress);
})
}
```

Getting the user's wallet address is different based on whether we are using MetaMask or the Mist browser. While we haven't been testing our dapp with the Mist browser up to this point, this function is the only one that has different implementations for the different browsers, so we will include it in the interest of interoperability.

MetaMask exposes the wallet addresses as an array at web3.eth.accounts. The first address will be the one that user has currently selected for use.

The Mist browser requires you to request account permission before unlocking the address. A pop-up, shown in Figure 11-3, will be presented to the user asking them to authorize the application before the address can be used.

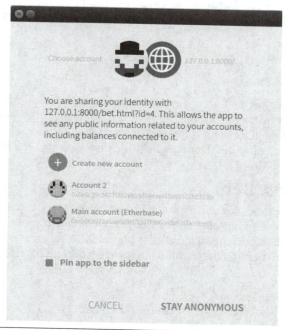

FIGURE 11-3 Mist browser request for account permission

This function abstracts away the browser-level differences and returns a promise that resolves with the wallet address regardless of which browser is being used.

```
function betPage() {
    ...

    $("#place-bet-over, #place-bet-under").click(function (e) {
        getWalletAddress().then(function (walletAddress) {
            var over = e.target.id == "place-bet-over";
            var side = over ? "over" : "under";
            var line = parseFloat($(`#${side}-line`).val());
            var amount = parseFloat($(`#${side}-amount`).val()) * 1e18;

            contract.bid(id, over, line,
                { from: walletAddress, value: amount , gas: 5e5 },
                function (err, tx) {
                    // callback code would go here
                });
        });
    });

    ...

}
```

Within the `betPage` function, we will register an event listener that listens for both the over and under bet placement simultaneously. The listener first retrieves the wallet address asynchronously. It then uses the id of the event target (the clicked button) to determine whether the over or under button was clicked and grabs the corresponding line and amount from the inputs. The user enters their bet amount in ether, but the contract expects the bet amount to be in wei, so we multiply by 1e18 to convert the ether amount to wei.

Once all the bid parameters are parsed and determined, we call the contract's bid ABI function with the parameters. The callback is left empty, but any postprocessing code (such as UI adjustments) could go there.

Let's test this functionality by attempting to place a bet with Chrome and MetaMask. You should at this point be looking at a page that looks like Figure 11-4. You may have to wait a few seconds after the page loads for the game information to populate.

Enter a line of 200 and a bet amount of 0.1 into the over inputs and place your bet. MetaMask should display a confirmation pop-up asking you to verify the transaction; see Figure 11-5.

If the gas field is empty, enter in a value of 20 Gwei. This is the default gas price on Ethereum. Click Accept, then open up your geth tab. You should see a log output similar to this indicating the transaction was sent:

```
INFO [06-16|19:24:56] Submitted transaction
fullhash=0x786637b84ee07b4853bd3341dded3fd0b879f44b6ca2c5ed5649dc06ea2c7f87
recipient=0xe5ee3208beaa162d952d8f7f627c2df450d87837
```

Wait a minute or so to ensure that the transaction gets mined. Now reload the page. You should see your bet in the bets section if it was matched, or in the open bids section if it wasn't.

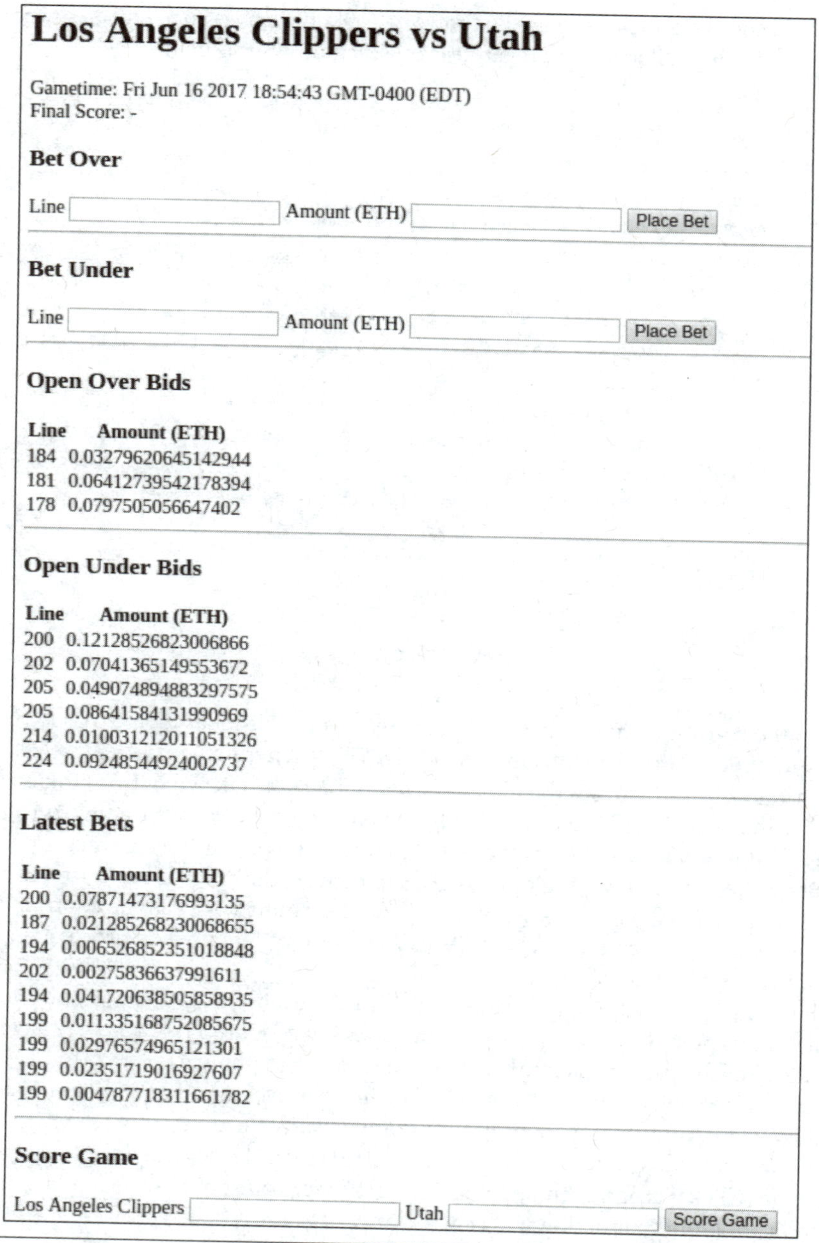

Los Angeles Clippers vs Utah

Gametime: Fri Jun 16 2017 18:54:43 GMT-0400 (EDT)
Final Score: -

Bet Over

Line [_____] Amount (ETH) [_____] [Place Bet]

Bet Under

Line [_____] Amount (ETH) [_____] [Place Bet]

Open Over Bids

Line	Amount (ETH)
184	0.03279620645142944
181	0.06412739542178394
178	0.0797505056647402

Open Under Bids

Line	Amount (ETH)
200	0.12128526823006866
202	0.07041365149553672
205	0.0490748948883297575
205	0.08641584131990969
214	0.010031212011051326
224	0.09248544924002737

Latest Bets

Line	Amount (ETH)
200	0.07871473176993135
187	0.021285268230068655
194	0.006526852351018848
202	0.00275836637991611
194	0.041720638505858935
199	0.011335168752085675
199	0.02976574965121301
199	0.02351719016927607
199	0.004787718311661782

Score Game

Los Angeles Clippers [_____] Utah [_____] [Score Game]

FIGURE 11-4   Placing a bet

FIGURE 11-5   MetaMask confirmation pop-up

Scoring Games

When a game is complete, we want to be able to score it and pay out bets to the winners. To do so, we have already created a form for score inputs. The JavaScript to handle the score submission looks like this:

```
$("#score-btn").click(function () {
    var homeScore = parseInt($("#home-score-input").val());
    var awayScore = parseInt($("#away-score-input").val());
    getWalletAddress().then(function (walletAddress) {
        contract.setGameResult(id, homeScore, awayScore,
            { from: walletAddress, gas: 500000 },
            function (err, tx) {
                // callback code goes here
            });
    });
});
```

We get the home and away scores from the inputs, use the id from the parent function, get the wallet address, and send a transaction to the contract's `setGameResult` ABI function. The callback is again left blank, but can be filled in with code in the future.

To test game scoring, go back to the games page, then navigate over to a game that has passed its locktime. Remember, scoring a game before it has locked will throw an error and no state changes will occur. The Cleveland-Indiana game will be a good one since it was set to lock 30 seconds after the contract was deployed.

Enter home and away scores into the inputs (e.g., 100 and 98), then submit the score. A MetaMask pop-up should appear again. Set the gas price if necessary, then click Accept. Wait again for a minute, then reload the page. At the top, the final score should now be updated to the score you entered.

Withdrawing Money

The winning side of the bet needs some way of accessing the money that belongs to them in the contract. The withdrawal ABI function allows a user to withdraw the balance of their account.

We will be building a withdraw page to allow users to withdraw their ether. Here is the basic HTML:

```html
<html>
<body>
    <nav>
        <a href="/">Games</a>
    </nav>

    <h3>Withdraw</h1>

    <table class="table">
        <tr>
            <td>My Address</td>
            <td id="address"></td>
        </tr>
        <tr>
            <td>My Balance</td>
            <td>
                <span id="balance"></span> ETH
                <button id="withdraw">Withdraw</button>
            </td>
        </tr>
    </table>

    <script src="https://code.jquery.com/jquery-3.1.1.js"
    integrity="sha256-16cdPddA6VdVInumRGo6IbivbERE8p7CQR3HzTBuELA="
    crossorigin="anonymous"></script>
    <script src="main.js"></script>
</body>

</html>
```

Outside of the standard html, body, and script tags, there is a link to the games page, a table with rows for a user's address and balance, and a button to allow a user to withdraw their money. The address and balance will be injected via JavaScript.

This time we will be following the `withdraw` track in our `switch` statement:

```
switch (window.location.pathname) {
    case '/bet.html':
        betsPage();
        break;
    case '/withdraw.html': // <--- The withdraw track
        withdrawPage();
        break;
    default:
        gamesPage();
}
```

Our `withdrawPage` function starts by querying for the user's balance.

```
function withdrawPage () {
    getWalletAddress().then(function (walletAddress) {
        $("#address").html(walletAddress);
        contract.balances(walletAddress, function (err, balance) {
            balance = parseInt(balance) / 1e18;
            $("#balance").html(balance);
        });
    });
    
    . . .
```

We get the wallet address, display it on the page, then use it to call the `balances` ABI function. The `balances` function isn't explicitly stated in the contract, but Solidity automatically creates getters for public state variables so it's available. Because it's a mapping, the default getter requires the key to be passed in. We pass in the wallet address as the key, get the balance of the user back, and display it on the page.

If the user has a non-zero balance, they can withdraw it by clicking the Withdraw button. Here's the event listener code:

```
$("#withdraw").click(function (e) {
    getWalletAddress().then(function (walletAddress) {
        contract.withdraw({ from: walletAddress, gas: 50000 },
            function (err, tx) {
                // callback code goes here
            });
    });
});
```

When the user clicks the Withdraw button, we get their wallet address, then use the `withdraw` ABI function to withdraw the user's balance.

You can test this out by redeploying the contract, placing multiple bets on one of the games that expires in three minutes, then scoring the game once it locks. Once you score the game you should see a non-zero balance on the withdraw page. Withdraw your money (accept the MetaMask pop-up when it appears), and check your balance on MetaMask. If everything works, it should go up!

Deploying to AWS

In order for your application to be available publicly on the Internet, you will have to deploy the application to a server. For our purposes, we will be using Amazon S3 static website hosting to host our front end.

For the full application to work, you must first deploy your smart contract to the Ethereum Main Net using the steps outlined in "Deploying to the Mainnet" earlier in the chapter. If you deployed the contract earlier, then replace the contents of the `contract_address` file with the address of the mainnet contract. Otherwise, the front end will attempt to access the address of the latest test contract deployed instead of the mainnet contract that you want to access.

First, if you don't have an account with AWS, you will have to create one at https://aws.amazon.com. Once you have created an account, navigate over to the S3 console. S3 is a cheap storage service for static files. We will be using its static web server functionality.

Create a new bucket in the console, and give it a name. In the setup dialog, in the Set Permissions > Manage Public Permissions section, select the "Grant public read access to this bucket" option. This will allow the outside world to access our files.

Once you've created the bucket, click on the bucket in the main S3 console and upload the following files to the bucket:

- bin/peerbet.sol:PeerBet.abi
- contract_address
- index.html
- withdraw.html
- bet.html
- main.js

These are the files that are required to run just the front end of our site. The back-end smart contract should already be deployed to the Ethereum Main Net, so the back-end and test files will not be required on the static host.

Next, go to the Properties section and click on Static Website Hosting and enable it by selecting "Use this bucket to host a website." Use index.html for the Index Page, then save the settings. Your static website is now enabled.

To view the site, click back on the Static Website Hosting section and go to the URL provided in the settings. For the site to work, MetaMask must be connected to the main network, so go to the MetaMask network settings and select the Ethereum Main Net. Once you have done so, the website should be visible and connected.

Summary

If you have read, understood, and tried some of the code in this chapter you can now write new scripts to deploy and test your own contracts. You can create a contract, and you can create a front end to interact with the contract.

Index

A

ABI (application binary interface)
    deploying sample betting application, 267–268,
        272–274, 284–290
    fast-track application tutorial, 136–137, 141
    public functions listed on, 93–94
    sample betting application, 240, 242, 244, 247–248
access, smart property and, 42–44
accessor functions, Solidity, 137
accounts, Ethereum, 105–110
`addBetToTable` helper function, 283
`addBidToTable` helper function, 282
`addGameToTable` helper function, 275
ADP (Automatic Data Processing), 7
AlphaPoint Distributed Ledger Platform, private
    blockchain, 176–177
Amdahl's law, 230
American Revolution, Byzantine Generals Problem,
    10–11
ANJ (Aragon Network Jurisdiction), DAO, 97–99
architecture
    INFURA, 120–122
    Web 3.0 technology stack, 72–73
    Whisper layered, 71
Arizona Electronic Transactions Act (AETA), 86–88
ARPANET, 1970s, 55–56
Asor, Ohad, 68–69
asset management settlement use case, 38–39
asset ownership, Openchain, 214
automated testing, smart contracts, 171
Automatic Data Processing (ADP), 7
AWS (Amazon Web Services), deploying application
    to, 290

B

b-money (Wei Dai), 15
BaaS (Blockchain-as-a-Service), cloud platform, 13
bandwidth, Web 2.0, 57

Base58 encoded hash, IPFS objects as, 61
Berners-Lee, Tim, 57–58
best practices. *See* Ethereum application best practices
bets. *See* sample betting application; sample betting
    application deployment
BFT-SMaRt consensus protocol, Symbiont Assembly
    private blockchain, 215
BGL (block gas limit), 156–157, 235, 240, 242
BGP (Byzantine Generals Problem), 8–11
bids. *See* sample betting application; sample betting
    application deployment
Bitcoin (BTC)
    blocksize and SegWit, 18–19
    blocksize governance challenges, 218–220
    bugs in core code, 221–222
    Byzantine fault tolerance and, 10
    designing, 11–13
    incapable of hosting dapps, 233–234
    as legal tender, 76–79
    and merkle root, 19–20
    and merkle trees, 21–22
    mining, 17–18
    overview of, 16
    scripting, 22
    and secure hashing, 20–21
    state transition, 16–17
Bitcoin Cash, 220
Bitfury, 28
Bitland initiative, 82
BitLicense, Ripple, 22
Bitmessage, 70
BitTorrent Sync, 70
block gas limit (BGL), 156–157, 235, 240, 242
blockchain
    business use cases. *See* business use cases
    Byzantine Generals Problem vs., 9
    categories of, 174–175
    challenges. *See* challenges, blockchain;
        technical challenges